KU-423-606
WITHDRAWN FROM
Thomas Rotherham
College
Learning Resources
Thomas Rotherham College
012516

Gifts to Make for Your Baby

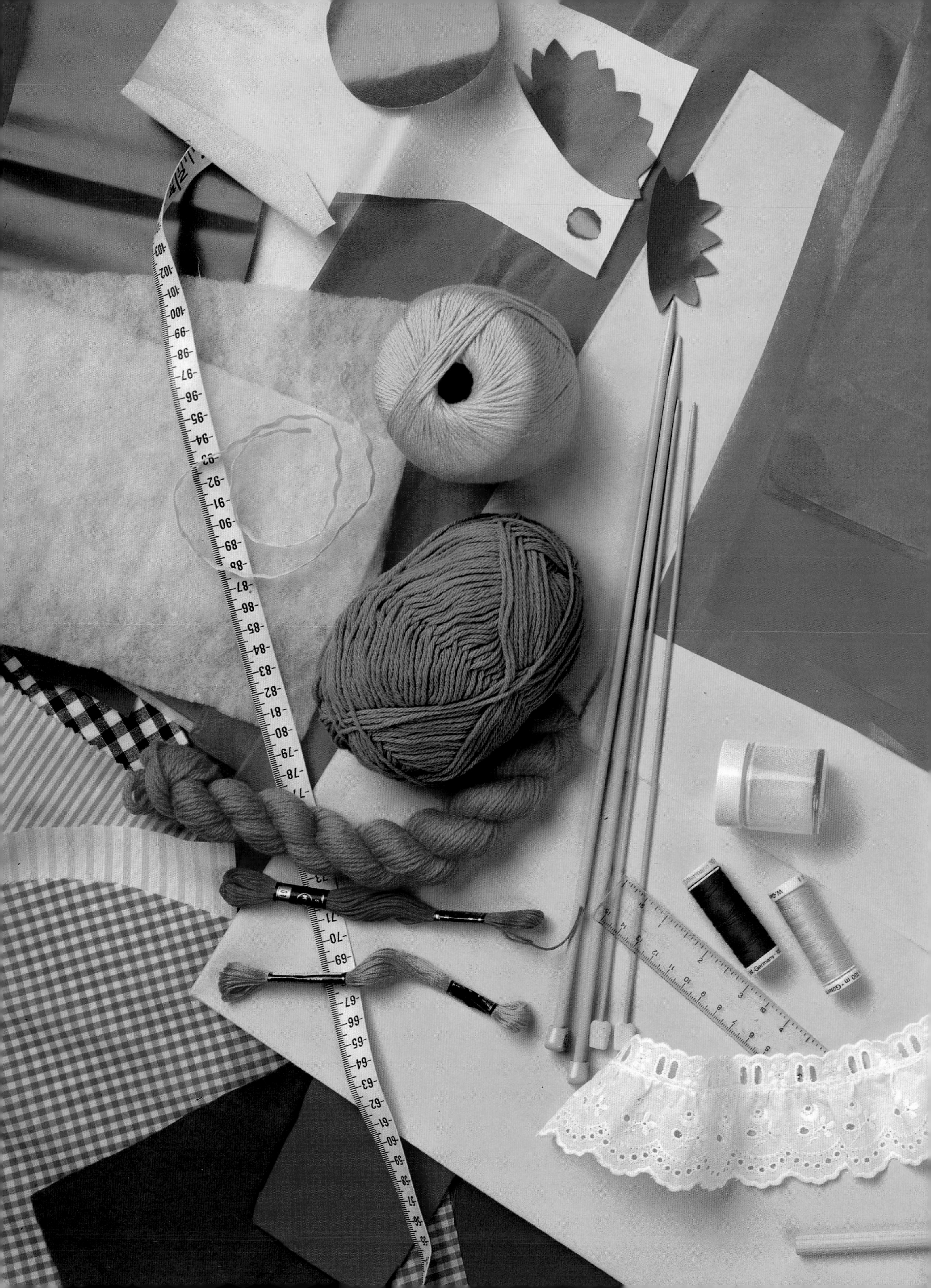

Gifts to Make for Your Baby

100 EASY-TO-MAKE TOYS, OUTFITS AND NURSERY ITEMS

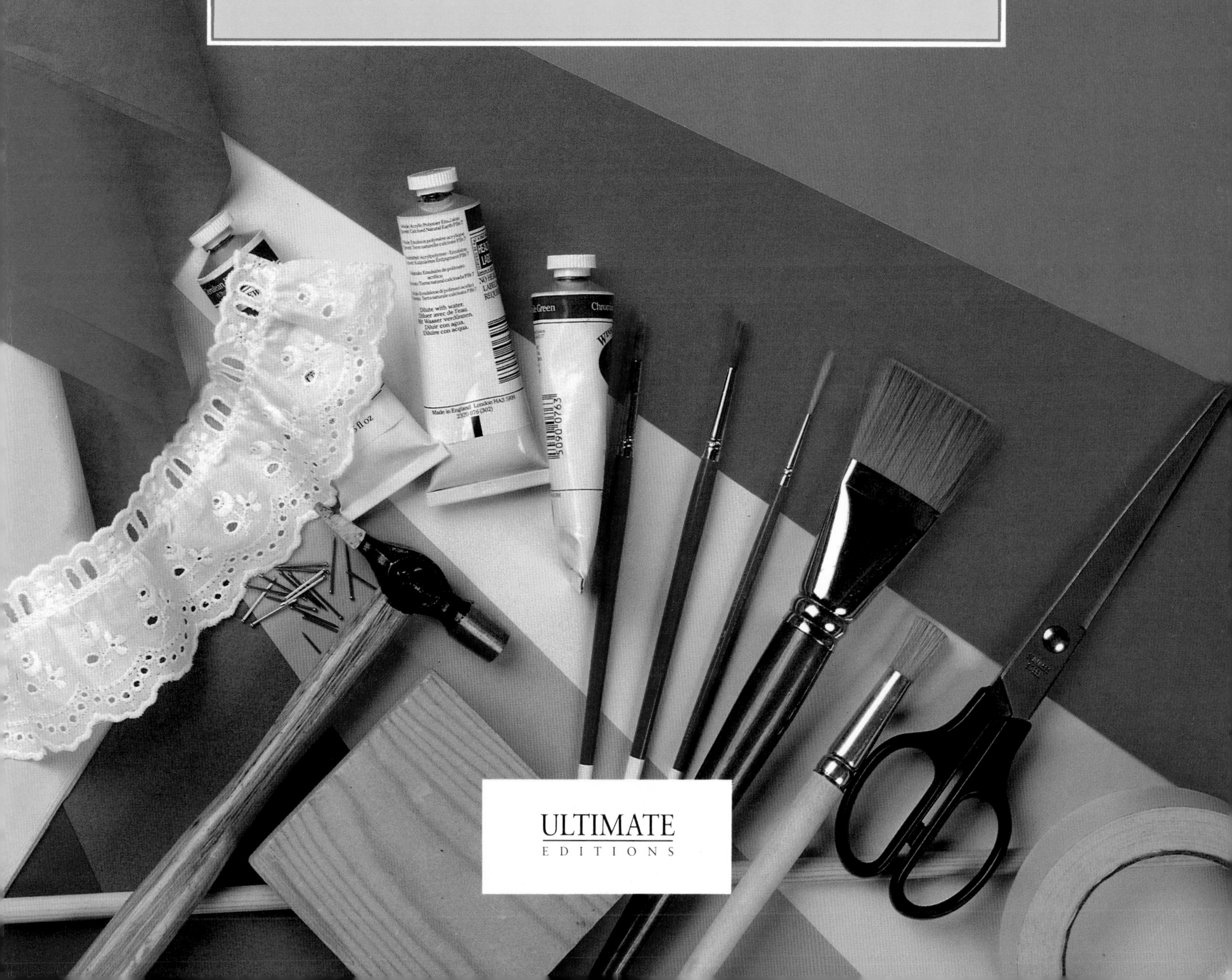

ULTIMATE
EDITIONS

First published in 1995 by Ultimate Editions

Ultimate Editions is an imprint of
Anness Publishing Limited
1 Boundary Row Studios
London SE1 8HP

Distributed in Australia by Reed Editions

This edition distributed in Canada by
Book Express, an imprint of
Raincoast Book Distribution Limited

Previously published as part of a larger compendium, *Baby Gifts*.

ISBN 1 86035 070 4

Editorial Director: Joanna Lorenz
Project Editor: Penelope Cream
Editor: Jane Royston
Designers: Kit and David Johnson
Photographer: Mark Gatehouse
Illustrators: John Hutchinson and Maggie Raynor

Printed in Singapore by
Star Standard Industries Pte. Ltd.
Typeset by MC Typeset Limited

HOW TO USE THE MEASUREMENTS

All craftspeople have their own way of working and feel most comfortable calculating in their preferred measurements. So, where applicable, the option of metric, imperial and cup measures are given. The golden rule is to choose only one set of measurements and to stick with it consistently throughout each project to ensure accurate results.

PUBLISHER'S NOTE

Crafts and hobbies are great fun to learn and can fill many hours of rewarding leisure time, but some special points should be remembered for safety, particularly when making gifts for babies and young children.

■ Always be aware of the materials you are using; use natural fabrics such as cotton and felt wherever possible, and make sure all sewing is strong and firm: double seam or stitch if in any doubt.

■ Always choose non-toxic materials, especially paints, glue and varnishes. Wood must always be smooth and free from splinters and sharp corners. Only use non-toxic flame retardant polyester stuffing or batting to fill soft toys.

■ Any gift with small pieces should not be given to young babies: they are experts at fitting even the most unlikely things into their mouths. Always pull with all your strength on buttons, safety eyes and other parts attached to a project: if an adult cannot remove them, a baby will not be able to either.

■ Secure small items such as bells or squeakers within soft toys inside a little fabric bag for extra safety.

■ Finally, make sure you do not leave your craft materials – such as craft knives, small saws, knitting needles, crochet hooks or adhesives – within the reach of young children.

SOME USEFUL TERMS

UK	US
Calico	Cotton fabric
Cast off	Bind off
Chipboard	Particle board
Cotton wool	Absorbent cotton
Double knitting yarn	Sport yarn
Drawing pins	Thumb tacks
Fretsaw	Scroll saw
Lawn	Fine cotton
Matt emulsion paint	Flat latex paint
Muslin	Cheesecloth
Panel pins	Finishing nails
Polystyrene	Styrofoam
PVC plastic	Vinyl plastic
Towelling	Terrycloth
Zip	Zipper

Contents

New Arrivals

Baby Announcement Card 6
Teddy Bear Card 7
Pop-up Card 8
Quilted Card 9
Rocking Cradle Card 10
Christening Shoes 11
Christening Robe 12
Crocheted Blanket 14
Crocheted Mittens 15
Matinee Jacket 16
Crocheted Bootees 17
Crocheted Bonnet 18
Crocheted Cardigan 19
Hooded Sweater 20
Knitted Bonnet 21
Knitted Collar 22
Knitted Cuff Bootees 23
Knitted Mittens 24
Baby's Gift Box 25
Keepsake Pin Cushion 26
Scented Sachets 27

All Dressed Up

Hooded Jacket 28
Appliqued Sleepsuit 30
Decorated Baby Shoes 31
Tie-dye Stretchsuit 32
Tall Bootees 33
Ric-rac Mitts 34
Leg Warmers 35
Busy Bee Slippers 36
Cutie Bootees 38
Padders 40
Hand Painted Stretchsuit 41
Sweetheart Shoes 42
Pompon Decorations 43
Child's Jacket 44
Bow-Tie T-Shirt 46
Poppy Hat 47
Party Pinafore 48
Decorated Hair Band 49
Reversible Dress 50
Smocked Dress 52
Toddler's Overall 54
Fairy Dress and Wand 56
Beetle Hat 58
T-Bar Shoes 60
Imp Hat 61
Fringed Bootees 62
Painted Shoes 63

Play and Learn

Feely Play Mat 64
Clutch Ball 66
Holding Ring 67
Bright-finned Fish 68
Appliqued Toys 70
Denim Bear 71
Bedtime Friends 72
Sun Toy 74
Surprise Play Cube 75
Sarah Sock Doll 76
Play Cube 78
Twirly Fish 79
Cuddly Duck 80
Smiley Toys 81
Crocheted Dolls 82
Hoppy Cushion 84
Pompon Mobile 85
Turtle Jigsaw 86
Ribbons and Bells 87
Clown Carousel 88
Tugboat 90
Rocking Parrot 91
Snake Mobile 92
Geometric Mobile 93
Tiger Stripes 94

In the Nursery

Pocketed Quilt 95
Height Chart 96
Stripy Toy Sack 97
Patchwork Quilt 98
Waist Hold-all 99
Bedroom Tidy 100
Changing Bag 102
Reversible Bumper 104
Nursery Basket 105
Baby Changing Bag 106
Tissue Box Cover 107
Bathtime Apron 108
Hooded Towel 109
Folded Hold-all 110
Practical Apron 112
Cylindrical Bag 113
Bathroom Pockets 114
Washbag 115
Decorated Towel 116
Lined Basket 117
Spiky Fabric Bib 118
Toy Bag 119
Beetle Drawer Freshener 120
Candy Cushion 121
Ribbon Motif Frame 122
Patchwork Frame 123
Tapestry Cushion 124
Spiky Cushion Cover 126

Index 127

Baby **A**nnouncement **C**ard

ANNOUNCE THE ARRIVAL OF YOUR BABY WITH THIS UNUSUAL PAPER COLLAGE CARD

YOU WILL NEED ■ Pieces of black and white card ■ White and lead pencils ■ Craft knife ■ Tracing paper ■ Coloured paper ■ Length of narrow lace ■ Scissors ■ Paper glue ■ Satin roses ■ Non-toxic acrylic paints ■ Small paintbrush

1 Fold the black and white pieces of card in half. Draw the oval shape, crescent moon and the star onto the front of the black card using a white pencil and cut them out with a craft knife.

2 Trace the outlines for the face, hat, hand and cuff onto the coloured paper and cut out using a craft knife. Cut the lace to the correct length to fit around the central frame.

3 Position the head, hands and other coloured cut-outs and glue them down. Glue a rose onto the baby's collar. Glue down the lace and position a rose bud at the base of the oval.

4 Finally, paint in the eyes, nose, ears and mouth.

Teddy Bear Card

THIS TECHNIQUE GIVES A PROFESSIONAL-LOOKING CARD

YOU WILL NEED ■ *Craft knife* ■ *Rectangle of coloured card* ■ *Metal ruler* ■ *Scissors* ■ *Motif cut from wrapping paper* ■ *Drawing paper* ■ *Spray adhesive* ■ *Adhesive foam strips*

1 Score the coloured card across the centre using a craft knife and metal ruler and fold it in half to form the card.

2 Roughly cut out your chosen motif, leaving a margin all around. Stick the motif to drawing paper using spray adhesive, working in a well-ventilated room. Cut out the backed motif carefully.

3 Stick the small strips of adhesive foam to the back of the motif.

4 Peel off the backing papers and carefully stick the picture to the front of the card.

Pop-up Card

A DELIGHTFUL SURPRISE CARD TO WELCOME A NEW BABY

YOU WILL NEED ■ *Craft knife* ■ *Thin card* ■ *Ruler* ■ *Pencil* ■ *Wax crayons* ■ *Felt-tip pens* ■ *Scissors* ■ *Strong clear glue*

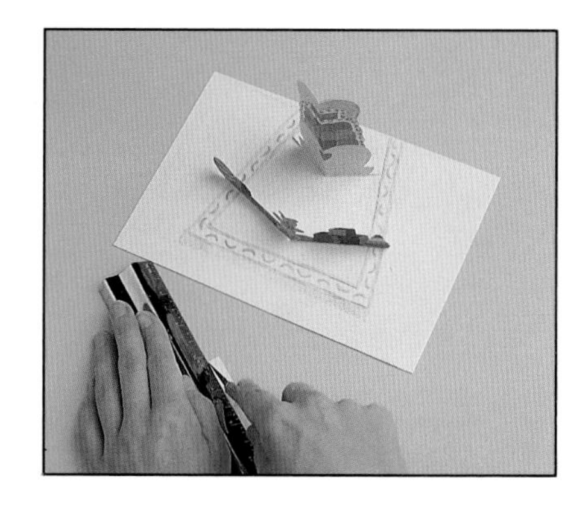

1 Cut a piece of card 22 × 15 cm (8¾ × 6 in), score lightly across the middle and fold in half along the score-line. Draw a rug in pencil and colour it in with wax crayons, picking out the details with pencil.

2 Draw the cradle and toy shapes carefully onto the thin card. Colour the cradle with wax crayons, outlining the detail of the lace pattern with a sharp pencil. Use felt-tip pens and wax crayons for the toy designs.

3 Carefully cut out the designs and score along the tabs on the front. Spread glue on the tabs, and stick into position on the rug.

4 Cut out, score and glue the remaining design in position. Check that the card closes properly.

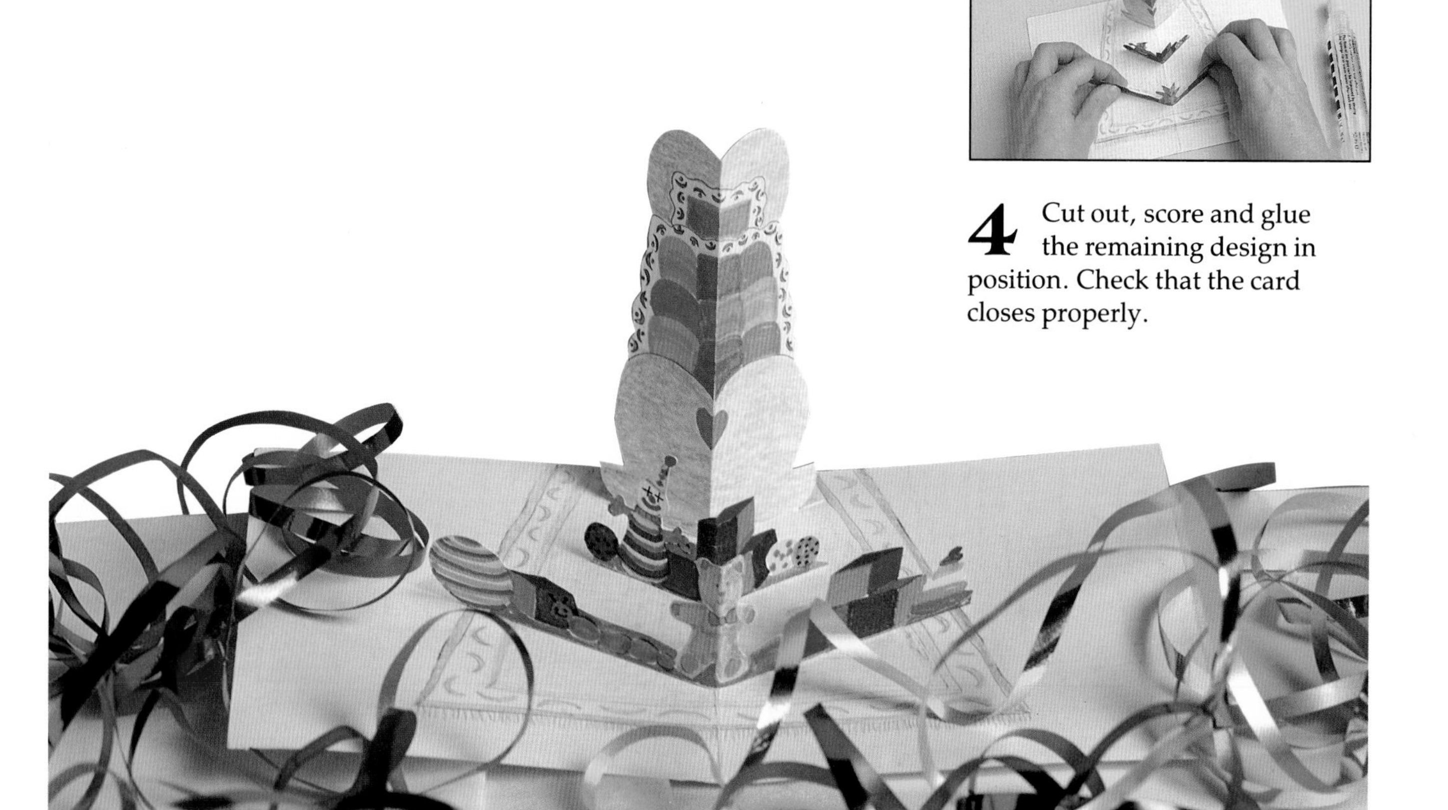

Quilted Card

THE TECHNIQUE USED FOR THIS CARD IS CALLED SHADOW QUILTING

YOU WILL NEED ■ Tracing paper ■ Pencil ■ Scissors ■ Pins ■ 13 × 13 cm (5¼ × 5¼ in) square of blue felt ■ Needle and embroidery thread ■ Cotton voile ■ Blue stranded cotton ■ Blank pre-cut window card ■ Blue wax crayon ■ Rubber-based glue

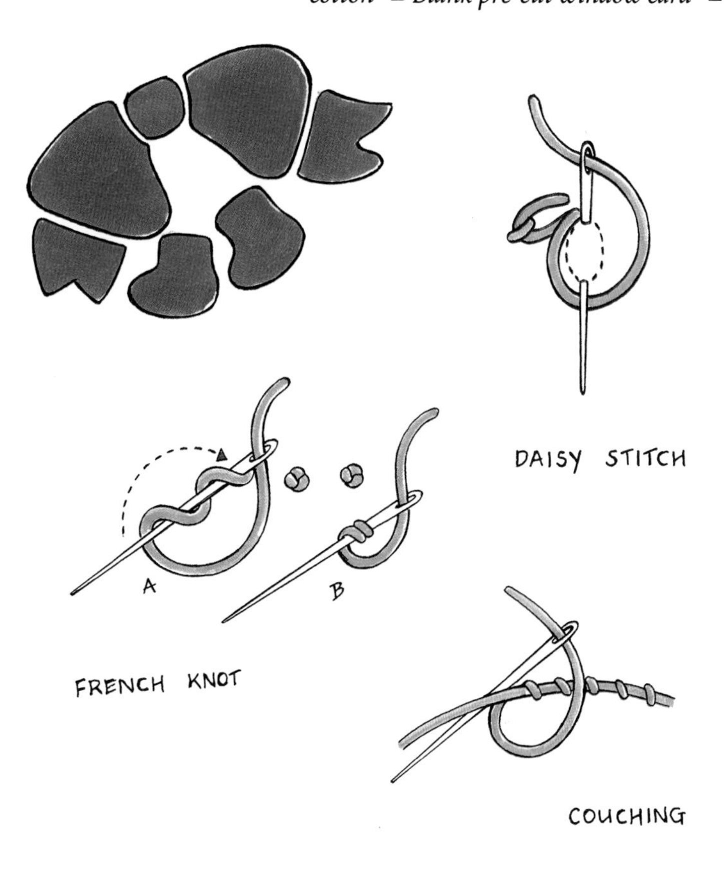

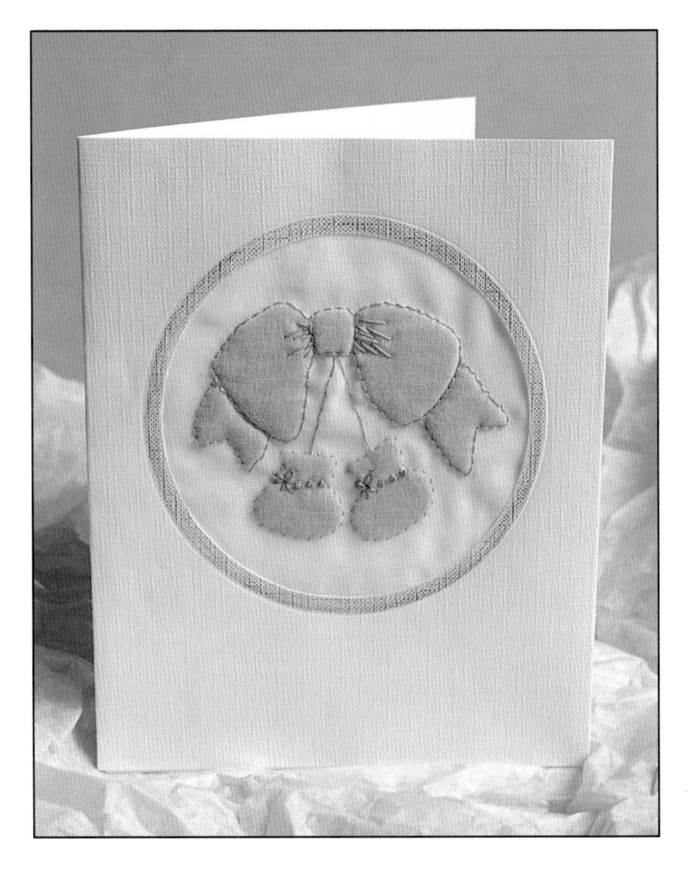

1 Trace around the template and cut out each section separately before pinning it onto the square of felt. Cut out all the pieces and pin then tack (baste) in position between 2 layers of voile.

2 Using 2 strands of embroidery thread in the needle, back stitch round the edge of the bow pieces and prick stitch round the bootees.

3 Decorate the bootees with lazy daisy stitch bows and French knots. Couch 2 lines from the bootees to the bows. Colour the edge of the card window with blue wax crayon before gluing the voile embroidery into place inside the front of the card.

Rocking **C**radle **C**ard

THIS IS A SIMPLE YET EFFECTIVE SPECIAL OCCASION CARD

YOU WILL NEED ■ *45 × 60 cm (18 × 24 in) pink card* ■ *Pencil* ■ *Paper* ■ *Metal ruler* ■ *Scissors* ■ *30 cm (12 in) lace, 12 mm (½ in) wide* ■ *Rubber-based glue* ■ *30 cm (12 in) white satin ribbon, 12 mm (½ in) wide*

1 Fold the card in half. Scale up the template onto paper and transfer it to the card. Cut out the shape through both layers. Return the template to the back of the card and mark the fold line. Carefully fold the card outwards along this line.

2 Ease the lace strip around the front edge of the card and glue it down. Fold over 6 mm (¼ in) of the lace and stick this to the back of the card.

3 Stick the top halves of card together down to the fold line. Make a ribbon bow and stick it to the front of the card.

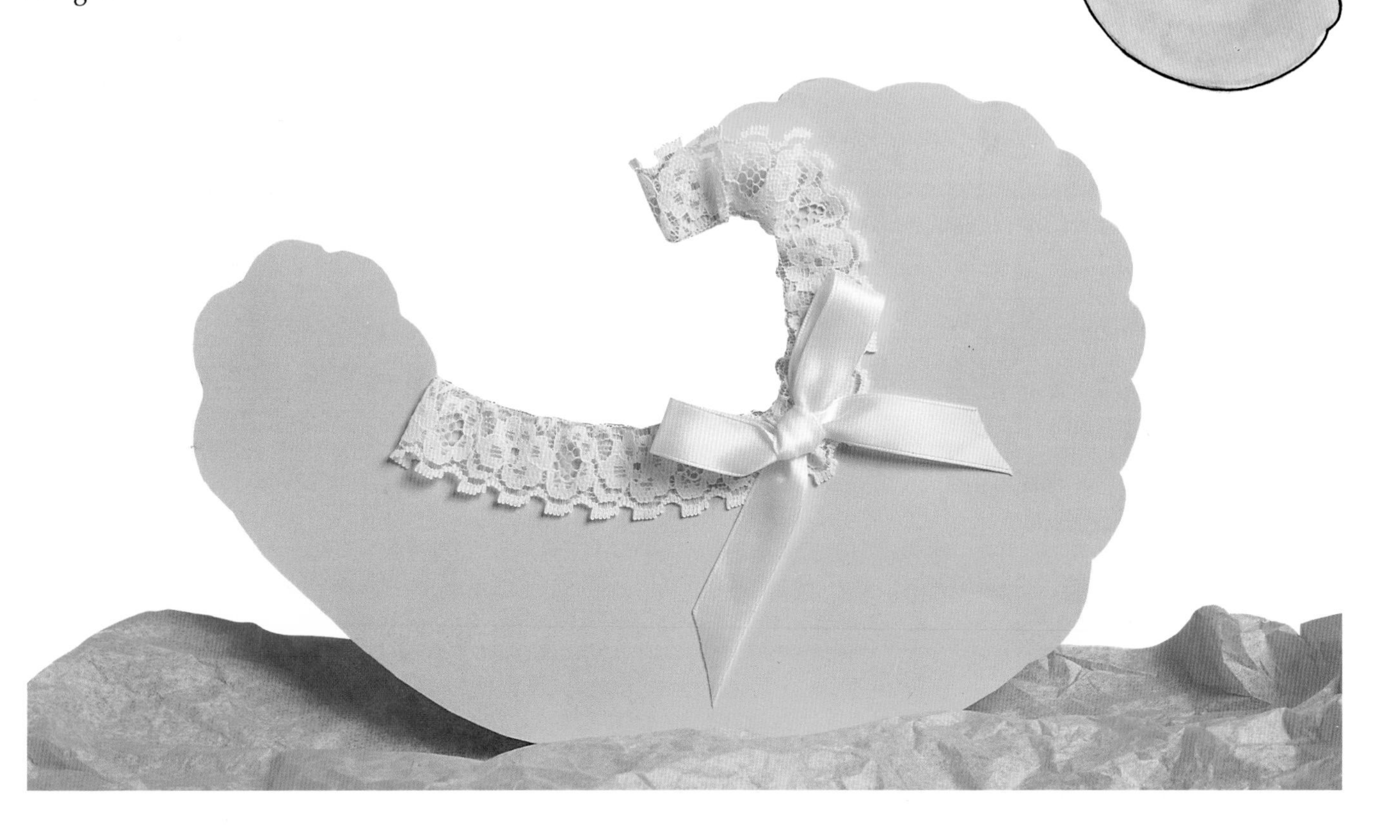

Christening Shoes

THESE PRETTY SHOES COMPLETE THE CHRISTENING OUTFIT

YOU WILL NEED ■ *50 g (2-ounce skein) white double knitting (sport) cotton* ■ *1 pair size 3 mm (US 3) knitting needles* ■ *Scissors* ■ *Large darning needle* ■ *2 small buttons or beads*

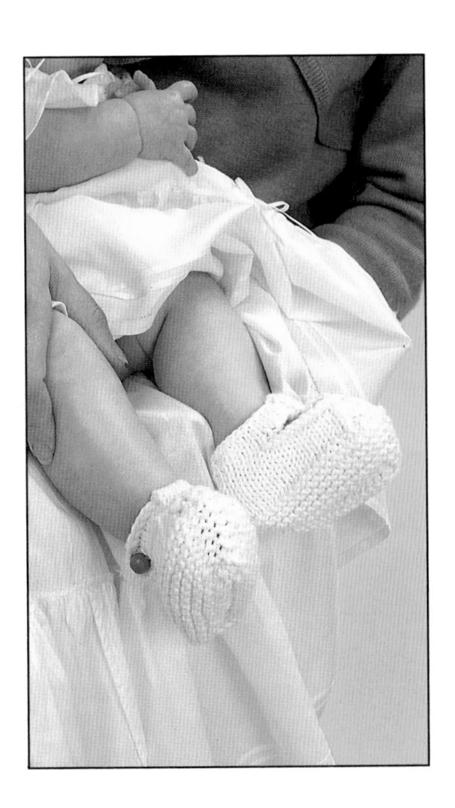

Tension (Gauge)
To knit this pattern, use 3 mm (US 3) needles, 21 sts and 30 rows to 10 cm (4 in) (st st).

MAIN SHOE
Beginning at the sole of the shoe, cast on 25 sts.
1st row: k 1, inc 1 (k into front and back of next st), k 9, inc 1, k 1, inc 1, k 9, inc 1, k 1.
2nd row and every alternate even numbered row: k to end.
3rd row: k 1, inc 1, k 11, inc 1, k 1, k 11, inc 1, k 1.
5th row: k 1, inc 1, k 13, inc 1, k 1, inc 1, k 13, inc 1, k 1.
7th row: k1, inc 1, k 15, inc 1, k 1, inc 1, k 15, inc 1, k 1.
9th row: k 1, inc 1, k 17, inc 1, k 1, inc 1, k17, inc 1, k 1.
11th row: k 1, inc 1, k 19, inc 1, k 1, inc 1, k 19, inc 1, k 1.
12th row: k to end (49 sts).

Start the lace pattern
13th row: k 17, sl 1, k 1, psso, k 3, k 2 tog, ynfwd, k 1, ynfwd, sl 1, k 1, psso, k 3, k 2 tog, k 17.
14th row and every alternate even numbered row: p to end.
15th row: k 17, sl 1, k 1, psso, k 2, ynfwd, sl 1, k 1, psso, k 1, k 2 tog, ynfwd, k 2, k 2 tog, k 17.
17th row: k 17, sl 1, k 1, psso, k 1, k 2 tog, ynfwd, k 1, ynfwd, sl 1, k 1, psso, k 1, k 2 tog, k 17.
19th row: k 17, sl 1, k 1, psso, ynfwd, sl 1, k 1, psso, k 1, k 2 tog, ynfwd, k 2 tog, k 17.
21st row: k 9, cast (bind) off 9, k 5, cast (bind) off 9, k 9.
Continue on these last 9 sts.
Work 4 rows st st. Cast (bind) off.
Return to 5 sts in centre for the front strap.
Beginning with a p row and with wrong side facing, work 15 rows st st. Cast (bind) off.

Ankle strap
Cast on 14 sts on same needle as remaining 9 sts (23 sts). Work 4 rows st st. Cast (bind) off.

Work the second shoe to match, this time reversing the position of the strap.

TO MAKE UP
Join the sole and heel seams. Fold the front strap under, making a loop wide enough to thread the ankle strap through. Hem the cast-off (bound-off) edge of the front strap to the inside of the work. Thread the ankle strap through the loop. Make a small buttonhole loop at the end of the ankle strap. Blanket stitch around the loop. Sew the buttons or beads firmly onto the shoes.

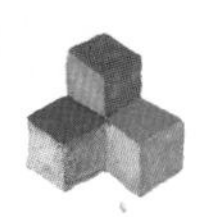

Christening Robe

THIS DELICATELY WORKED ROBE IS VERY SIMPLE TO MAKE

YOU WILL NEED ■ *Tracing paper* ■ *Pencil* ■ *Scissors* ■ *2.7 m (3 yd) white lawn (fine cotton)* ■ *Pins* ■ *Iron* ■ *Needle and fine medium white silk embroidery thread* ■ *Length of bias binding, 2 cm (¾ in) wide* ■ *4 × 7 mm (¼ in) buttons* ■ *2 m (80 in) narrow ribbon*

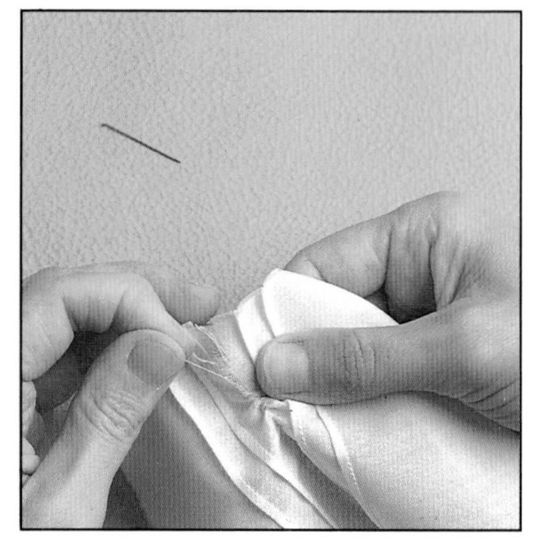

1 Scale up the pattern pieces onto tracing paper and cut them out, marking dots and fold lines for tucks onto the lawn (fine cotton). Press tucks on yoke and sleeve along fold lines and sew 3 mm (⅛ in) tucks. Press yoke tucks down and sleeve tucks outwards. Draw 17 threads from centre of pressed tucks.

2 Hemstitch with fine white silk embroidery thread along both edges of the area with drawn threads.

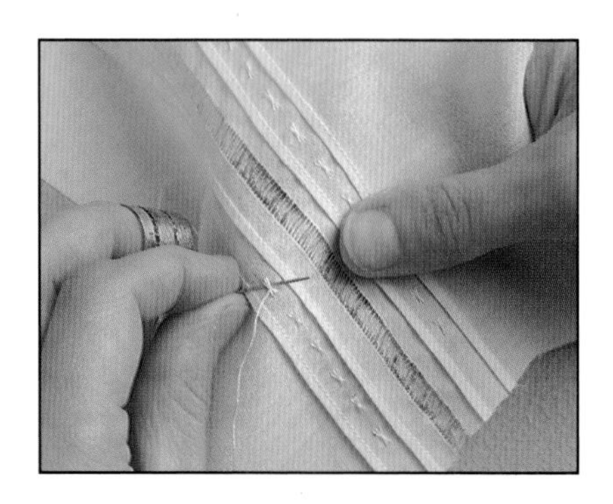

3 Embroider wheatsheafs in medium silk thread, spacing them at 10 mm (⅜ in) intervals between the tucks.

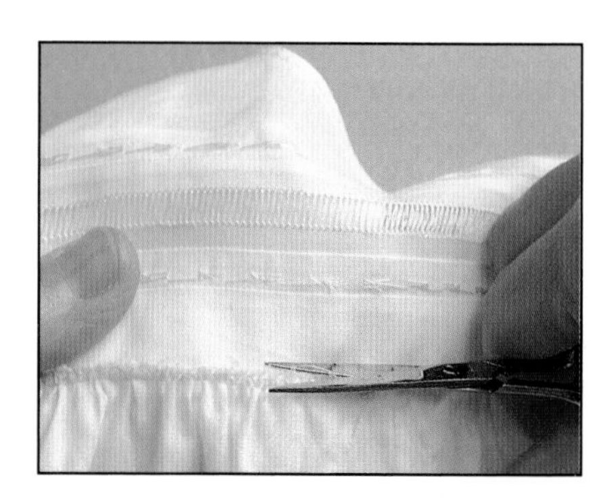

4 Stay-stitch along the neck edge and join yoke shoulder seams. Neaten all seams with zigzag stitch and trim to 10 mm (⅜ in). Gather the front and back skirts between the notches. Pin to yoke with right sides together. Adjust the gathers and stitch the skirts to the yoke.

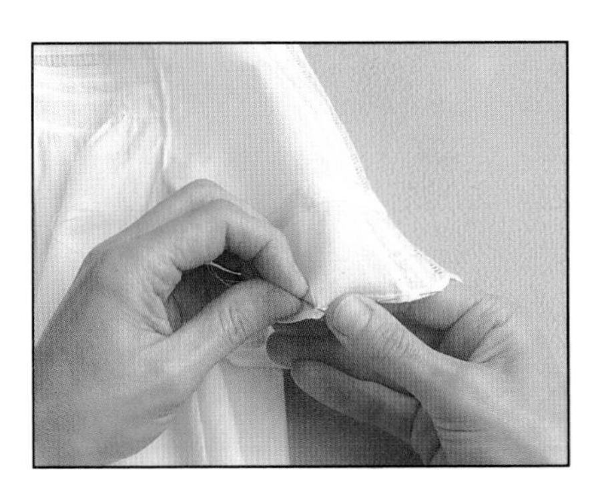

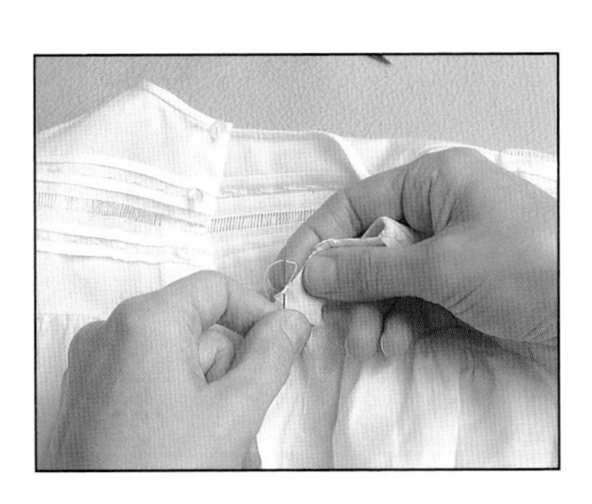

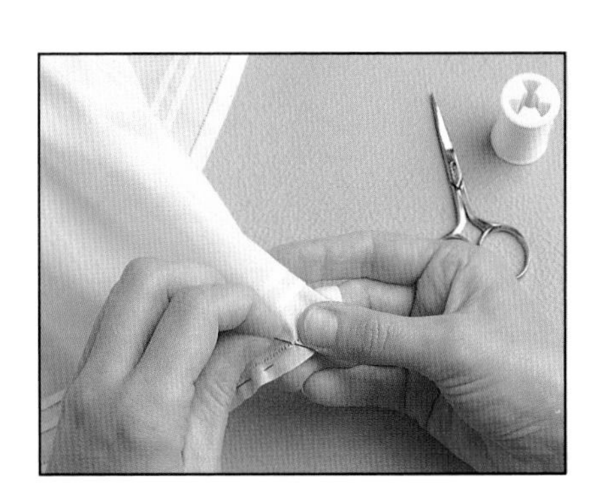

5 To make the sleeves, sew bias binding along the casing line close to the edge. Gather the head of each sleeve between the notches. Pin to armhole edges, adjust the gathers and stitch. Sew the side and back seams and finish the sleeves with a narrow hem.

6 Finish the neck edge neatly with a 2 cm (¾ in) bias strip. Add the buttons and sew thread hoops to fasten.

7 Sew the frill sections together. Sew tucks as before and press downwards. Gather the top edge before attaching it to the skirt, matching up the dots and seams. Narrow hem the frill or draw out several threads and hemstitch into position. Thread ribbon through the casing on the sleeves and secure at the seams. Sew a small bow in the centre of the yoke.

WHEATSHEAF STITCH

HEMSTITCH

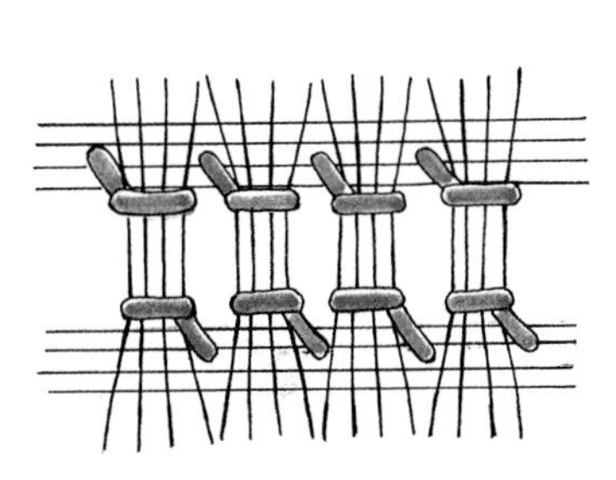

LADDER HEMSTITCH

FOLD LINE
BACK OPENING
SEW TO DOT
BACK
CUT 2

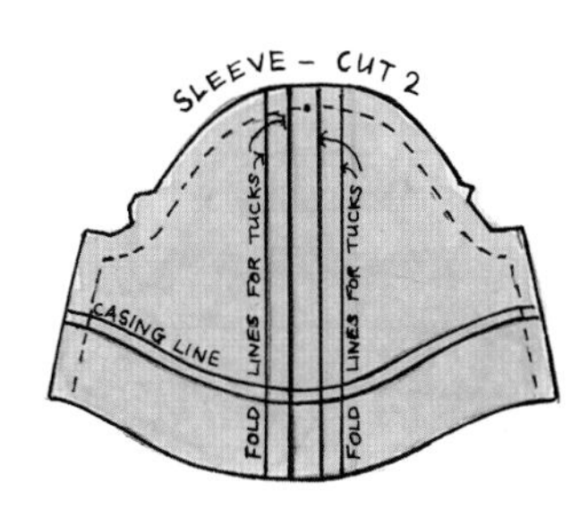

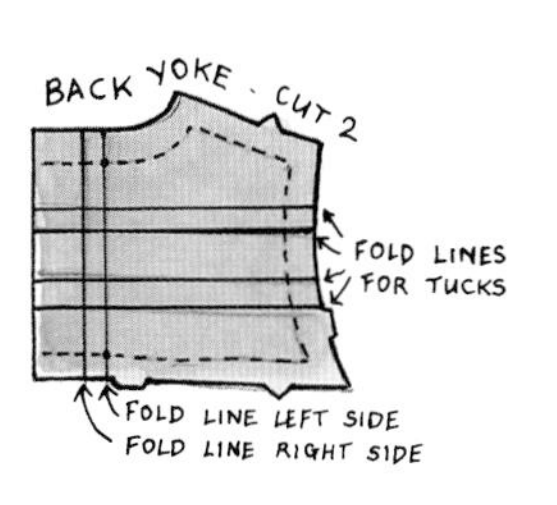

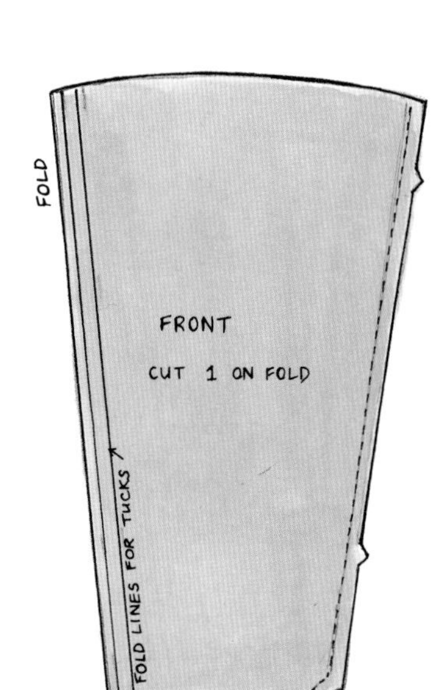

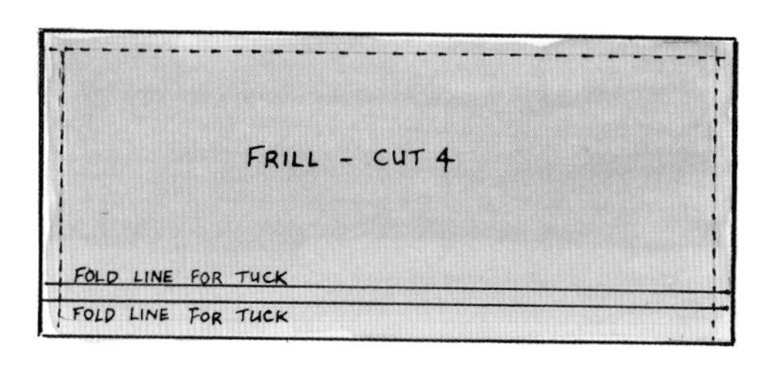

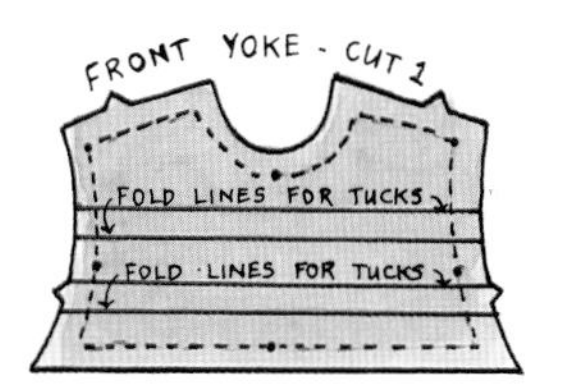

Crocheted **B**lanket

THIS DELICATE BLANKET HAS AN ATTRACTIVE SHAPED BORDER

YOU WILL NEED ■ *150 g (6 oz) 2-ply yarn* ■ *2 mm (B) crochet hook* ■ *Large darning needle*

MEASUREMENTS
85 cm (34 in) square.

Make 198 ch.
1st row: tr (dc) into 4th ch from hook, tr (dc) into each ch to end, turn with 3 ch.
2nd row: 3 tr (dc), miss 1 tr (dc), (1 tr (dc), 1 ch, 1 tr (dc)) into next st (1 V st made). Repeat 96 times, 4 tr (dc), turn with 3 ch.
3rd row: 3 tr (dc). V st in each ch 1, space 96 times, 4 tr (dc), turn with 3 ch.
Repeat 3rd row 7 times.
9th row: 4 tr (dc), 7 V st, 3 tr (dc) into each V st until 7 V st remain, 7 V st, 4 tr (dc), turn with 3 ch.
10th row: 7 V st, 4 tr (dc), 1 ch, (miss 1 tr (dc), 1 ch, 1 tr (dc) in next tr (dc)) repeat to last 4 tr (dc), 4 tr (dc), 7 V st, 4 tr (dc). Turn with 3 ch.
11th row: 4 tr (dc), 7 V st, 4 tr (dc), 1 ch, (1 tr (dc) over tr (dc), 1 ch, miss 1 ch) repeat to last 4 tr (dc), 4 tr (dc), 7 V st, 4 tr (dc), turn with 3 ch.
Continue keeping pattern until work measures 60 cm (24 in).
Next row: 4 tr (dc), 7 V st, 4 tr (dc) (1 tr (dc) in ch space, 1 tr (dc) over tr (dc)) to last 4 tr (dc), 4 tr (dc) over tr (dc), 7 V st, 4 tr (dc). Turn with 3 ch.
Next row: 4 tr (dc), V st to last 4 tr (dc), 4 tr (dc) over tr (dc).
Repeat last row 7 times.
Next row: 4 tr (dc) over 4 tr (dc), 3 tr (dc) into each V st to end of row. Fasten off.

Border
Make 10 ch.
1st row: 1 tr (dc) into 3rd ch from hook. 1 tr (dc), 2 ch, miss 1 ch, 1 dc (sc) into next ch, 2 ch, miss 1 ch (one lacet). 3 tr (dc), 2 ch, 1 dtr into base of last tr (dc), 5 ch. Turn.
2nd row: 2 tr (dc) into ch sp, 3 tr (dc), 3 ch, 2 tr (dc) into next 2 tr (dc), 1 tr (dc) into turning ch, 3 ch, turn.
3rd row: 2 tr (dc), 1 lc, 5 tr (dc), 2 tr (dc) into dtr sp, 2 ch, 1 dtr into sp, 5 ch, turn.
4th row: 2 tr (dc) into ch sp, 7 tr (dc), 3 ch, 2 tr (dc) into next 2 tr (dc), 1 tr (dc) into ch, 3 ch, turn.
5th row: 2 tr (dc), 1 lc, 9 tr (dc), 2 tr (dc) into dtr (dc) sp, 2 ch, 1 dtr into dtr sp, 5 ch, turn.
6th row: 2 tr (dc) into dtr sp, 11 tr (dc), 3 ch, 2 tr (dc) into next 2 tr (dc), 1 tr (dc) into turning ch, 3 ch, turn.
7th row: 2 tr (dc), 1 lc, 7 tr (dc), 3 ch, miss 1 tr (dc), 5 tr (dc), 2 tr (dc) into dtr, sp 2 ch, 1 dtr (dc), into dtr sp, 5 ch, turn.
8th row: 2 tr (dc) into ch sp, 5 tr (dc), 3 ch, miss 2 tr (dc), 5 tr (dc), 3 ch, miss 2 tr (dc), 1 dc (sc) into ch sp, 3 ch, miss 2 tr (dc), 5 tr (dc), 3 ch, 2 tr (dc) into next 2 tr (dc), 1 tr (dc) into turning ch, 3 ch, turn.
9th row: 2 tr (dc), 1 ch, 1 lc, 3 tr (dc), miss 2 tr (dc), 3 ch, 1 dc into ch sp, 1 dc (sc) into dc (sc) of previous row, 1 dc (sc) into ch sp, 3 ch, miss 2 tr (dc), 5 tr (dc), 2 tr (dc) into ch sp, 1 quad tr (dc) into sp, 3 ch, turn.
10th row: miss 2 tr (dc), 5 tr (dc), 2 tr (dc) into ch sp, 3 ch, miss 1 dc (sc), dc (sc) into next dc (sc), 3 ch, 2 tr (dc) into ch sp, 3 tr (dc), 3 ch, 2 tr (dc) into next 2 tr (dc), 1 tr (dc) into turning ch, 3 ch, turn.
11th row: 2 tr (dc), 1 lc, 5 tr (dc), 2 tr (dc) into ch sp, 1 ch, 2 tr (dc) into next ch sp, 5 tr (dc), miss 2 tr (dc), 1 dtr into ch sp, turn.
12th row: 3 ch, miss 2 tr (dc), 5 tr (dc), 1 tr (dc) into ch sp, 7 tr (dc), 3 ch, 2 tr (dc) into next 2 tr (dc), 1 tr (dc) into turning ch, 3 ch, turn.
13th row: 2 tr (dc), 1 lc, 11 tr (dc), miss 2 tr (dc), 1 dtr into sp, 3 ch, turn.
14th row: miss 2 tr (dc), 9 tr (dc), 3 ch, 2 tr (dc) into next 2 tr (dc), 1 tr (dc) into turning ch, 3 ch, turn.
15th row: 2 tr (dc), 1 lc, 7 tr (dc), 1 dtr into sp turn.
16th row: miss 2 tr (dc), 5 tr (dc), 3 ch, 2 tr (dc) into next 2 tr (dc), 1 tr (dc) into turning ch, 3 ch.
17th row: 2 tr (dc), 1 lc, 3 tr (dc), 2 ch, 1 dtr into sp, 5 ch, turn.
Repeat from 2nd row to 17th row until the border is long enough, allowing for a slight gathering. Sew on the border.

Crocheted **M**ittens

A PRETTY AND PRACTICAL PAIR OF MITTENS FOR BABIES UP TO 3 MONTHS OLD

YOU WILL NEED ■ *50 g (2-ounce skein) 4-ply yarn* ■ *2.5 mm (C) crochet hook*

Make 33 ch.
1 dc (sc) in 4th ch from hook, 1 dc (sc) in each ch to end of row. Turn with 3 ch. (29 dc (sc).)
1st row: 3 tr (dc) in alternate dcs (scs) to end of row. Turn with 3 ch. (15 3tr (dc) groups.)
2nd row: 3 tr (dc) in each space to end of row. Turn with 3 ch.
3rd row: repeat row 2 twice more. Turn with 2 ch on row 4.
5th row: 1 dc (sc) in each tr (dc) to end of row. Turn with 2 ch.
6th row: To make picot: * 3 dc (sc) over next 3 dc (sc), 3 ch, ss into first of 3 ch. Repeat from * to end. Fasten off. Rejoin yarn to one end of beginning ch.
Next row: 4 ch (miss 1 ch, 1 ch, 2 tr (dc)), to end of row. Turn with 3 ch. (Row in which to insert the draw threads.)
2nd row: 1 tr (dc) into tr (dc), (tr (dc) into space, 2 tr (dc)), to end of row. Turn with 3 ch.
3rd row: tr (dc) into each tr (dc). (29 trs (dcs).) Turn with 3 ch. Repeat 3rd row 5 times.
8th row: 1 tr (dc), dec 1 in next 2 tr (dc), 8 tr (dc), dec 1 in next 2 tr (dc), 1 tr (dc), dec 1 in next 2 tr (dc), 8 tr (dc), dec 1 in next 2 tr (dc), 2 tr (dc), turn with 3 ch.
9th row: 1 tr (dc) in each tr (dc), to end. Turn with 3 ch.
10th row: 1 tr (dc), dec 1 in next 2 tr (dc), 6 tr (dc), dec 1 in next 2 tr (dc), 1 tr (dc), dec 1 in next 2 tr (dc), 6 tr (dc), dec 1 in next 2 tr (dc), 2 tr (dc), turn with 3 ch.
11th row: 20 tr (dc). Fasten off.

Draw threads
(Make 2 alike)
5 ch, ss into first ch, 105 ch, ss into 5th ch from hook. Fasten off.
Sew sides and top of mitten.
Thread drawstring through eyelet holes and tie in a bow. Repeat for second mitten.

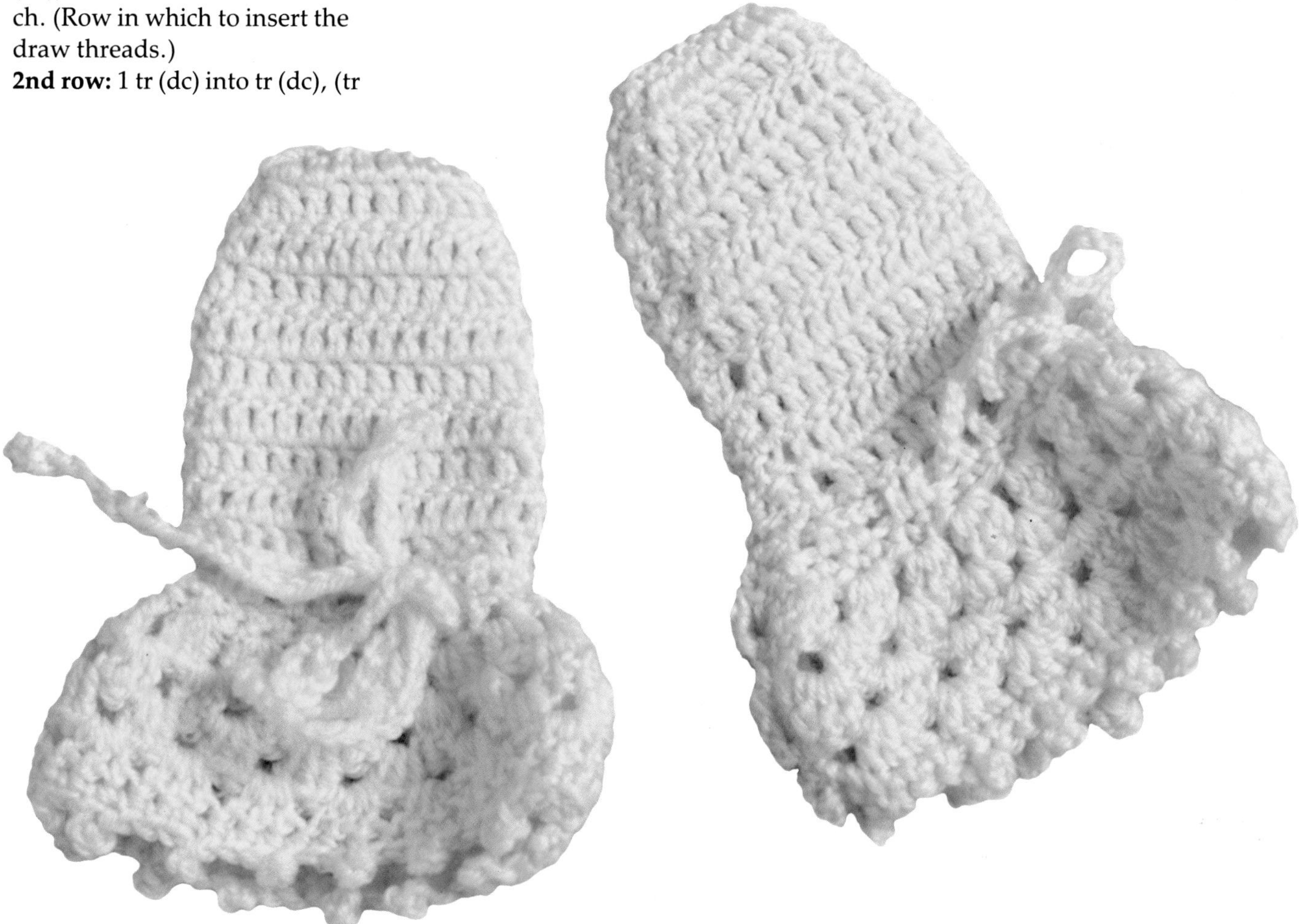

Matinée Jacket

THIS COSY JACKET WILL FIT UP TO A 50 CM (20 IN) CHEST

YOU WILL NEED ■ *400 g (2 × 8-ounce skeins) 4-ply yarn* ■ *3.5 (E) crochet hook* ■ *Tape measure* ■ *Large darning needle* ■ *3 small buttons*

BACK
Make 62 ch.
3 tr (dc) into 4th ch from hook.
*Miss 2 ch, 3 tr (dc) into next st.
Repeat from * to last 2 sts, 1 tr (dc) in last st, turn with 3 ch.
2nd row: 1 tr (dc) into 1st sp, 3 tr (dc) into each sp to end of row, turn with 3 ch.
3rd row: 3 tr (dc) in each sp, 1 tr (dc) into end st, turn with 3 ch.
Work for 5 rows. Turn with 3 ch.
9th row: *1 tr (dc) in sp. 1 tr (dc) over each tr (dc) to end of row. (58 tr (dc).) Turn with 3 ch.
Work in trs (dcs) on these 58 sts for 16.5 cm (6½ in).
Next row: ss over 7 sts, tr (dc) to last 7 sts, turn with 3 ch. Work on these remaining sts until armhole measures 7.5 cm (3 in). Fasten off.

RIGHT FRONT
Make 32 ch.
Tr (dc) into 4th ch from hook, 2 tr (dc) into same st. *Miss 2 ch, 3 tr (dc) into next st. Repeat from * to end of ch, turn with 3 ch.
Next row: 3 tr (dc) into each sp to end of row, 1 tr (dc), turn with 3 ch.
Continue for 6 more rows.
9th row: 3 tr (dc) in 1st sp, 3 trs (dcs) in each of next 3 sps, 1 tr (dc) in each tr (dc). Tr (dc) to end of row. (19 trs (dcs).) Turn with 3 ch.
Next row: 18 tr (dc), 3 groups of tr (dc) in sps, 2 tr (dc) in last 2 trs (dcs). Return with 3 ch.
Continue in pattern and tr (dc) until work matches back to armhole.
Next row: ss over 6 tr (dc) at armhole edge.
Continue on remaining sts until work is 3 rows less than back.
Next row: ss over 8 sts at neck edge, complete row.
Next rows: dec 1 st at neck edge on next 2 rows. Fasten off.

LEFT FRONT
As above; reverse shapings.

SLEEVES
Make 33 ch. Work in tr (dc) group pattern for 3 rows.
4th row: tr (dc) into each tr (dc). (29 tr (dc).)
Repeat this row until sleeve measures 20 cm (8 in).

TO MAKE UP
Sew shoulder seams and sleeves. Sew sleeve and side seams. 5 ch, miss 1 st, 1 dc (sc) into next st, and repeat round neck to next edge. Sew on buttons. Use sps in pattern as buttonholes.

Crocheted **B**ootees

THESE WARM BOOTÉES MATCH THE MATINÉE JACKET

YOU WILL NEED ■ *50 g (2-ounce skein) 4-ply yarn* ■ *3.5 mm (E) crochet hook*
Scissors ■ *Large darning needle*

Make 30 ch. 1 dc (sc) into 3rd ch from hook. 1 dc (sc) into each ch to end of row. Turn with 3 ch.
1st row: 2 tr (dc), *miss 1 dc (sc), 1 ch, 3 tr (dc) into next 3 dc (sc). Repeat from * to end of row. Turn with 3 ch.
2nd row: 3 tr (dc) into each space (7 groups).
Turn with 3 ch.
Repeat 2nd row 3 times turning with 3 ch on 5th row.
6th row: *Miss 1 tr (dc), 2 tr (dc), 1 ch. Repeat from * to end of row. Turn with 2 ch.
7th row: 1 dc (sc) into next tr (dc), *1 dc (sc) in space, 2 dc (sc) in next 2 tr (dc). Repeat from * to end of row. Turn with 2 ch.
8th row: dc (sc) in each dc (sc) to end of row. (26 dc (sc).). Turn with 2 ch. Repeat twice more.
11th row: dec over next 2 dc (sc). 8 dc (sc), dec once in next 2 dc (sc), 2 ch, turn.
(Mark 7th st in remaining sts for centre of heel.)
12th row: dc (sc) into each dc (sc) to end of row, turn with 2 ch.
Repeat 12th row 3 times.
16th row: dec 1 st each end of next and following 4th row then each end of next row.
21st row: dc (sc) in each st to end of row. Fasten off. Rejoin yarn to first dec row on edge furthest away from 13 unworked sts. 2 ch. 1 dc (sc) into same row end, 1 dc (sc) into each following row end, 6 dc (sc) across toe, 1 dc (sc) into each row end, 1 dc (sc) into each of 13 unworked sts.
Work 4 rows of dc (sc) on these sts, turning with 2 ch. Fasten off.

Make second bootee, reversing instructions after eyelet hole row.

Draw threads
5 ch, ss into 1st ch, 105 ch, ss into 4th ch from hook.

TO MAKE UP
Sew sides of cuff and foot seam. Thread through draw threads.

Crocheted **B**onnet

A COMFORTABLE CROCHETED BONNET FOR CHILLY DAYS OUT

YOU WILL NEED ■ *50 g (2-ounce skein) 4-ply yarn* ■ *3.5 mm (E) crochet hook* ■ *Tape measure*

Make 5 ch, ss into 1st ch to form a ring.
1st row: 3 ch for 1st tr (dc), 11 tr (dc) into ch ring, ss into 3rd ch.
2nd row: 3 ch, tr (dc) into same st, 2 tr (dc) into each tr (dc) to end of row, join with ss.
3rd row: 3 ch, * 2 tr (dc) into next tr (dc), 1 tr (dc). Repeat from * to end of round. Join with ss.
4th row: 3 ch, * 2 tr (dc) into next tr (dc), 2 tr (dc). Repeat from * to end of round. Join with ss.
5th row: 3 ch, * 2 tr (dc) into next tr (dc), 3 ch. Repeat from * to end.
6th row: 3 ch, * 2 tr (dc) into next tr (dc), 4 tr (dc). Repeat from * to end. 1 tr (dc) into 3 ch base, join with ss. 3 ch, * 2 tr (dc) into next tr (dc), 5 ch. Repeat from * to end. 1 tr (dc) into base of 3 tr (dc).
7th row: 3 ch, * 2 tr (dc) into next tr (dc), 5 ch. Repeat from * to end of round. 5 tr (dc) into base of 7 ch.
8th row: 3 ch, * 2 tr (dc) into next tr (dc), 6 tr (dc). Repeat from * to last 3 sts of round, 2 tr (dc) into next tr (dc), 2 tr (dc), 1 tr (dc) into base of 3 ch. Join with ss.
9th row: 3 ch, tr (dc) to last 20 sts, turn with 4 ch.
10th row: * Miss 1 tr (dc), tr (dc) in tr (dc) to end. Turn with 3 ch.
Repeat rows 9–10 six times. Fasten off. Join yarn at other end of row. Repeat rows 9–10 three times then row 9 once more.
Work one row crab st (dc (sc) worked from left to right).
Turn back 6 rows (inc crab st) to right side for the brim.
Join yarn to right side bottom edge. Edge tog 2 ch, 2 dc (sc) into each end st up to crown. (30 dc (sc).)
* 1 dc (sc) into tr (dc), miss 1 tr (dc). Repeat from * 10 times. 2 dc (sc) into each end st to end of row. Turn with 2 ch.
Next row: 1 dc (sc) in each dc (sc) to crown, 1 dc (sc) in alternate dcs (scs) over crown, dc (sc) in each dc (sc) to end of row. Turn with 2 ch.
Next row: 1 dc (sc) in each dc (sc) to end of row, turn with 3 ch.
Next row: 1 tr (dc) in alternate dcs to end of row. Turn with 2 ch.
Next row: * 1 dc (sc) in ch sp, dc (sc) in tr (dc). Repeat from * to end of row. Fasten off.

Braid

2 ch, 1 dc (sc) into 2nd ch, 1 ch, turn. Repeat until 68 cm (27 in) long. Thread through bonnet.

Crocheted Cardigan

A BUTTON-THROUGH CARDIGAN THAT FITS UP TO A 45 CM (18 IN) CHEST

YOU WILL NEED ■ *100 g (4-ounce skein) 4-ply yarn* ■ *3 mm (D) crochet hook* ■ *Tape measure* ■ *Large darning needle* ■ *5 small buttons*

BACK

Make foundation ch of 63 sts.
1 tr (dc) in 4th ch from hook. 1 tr (dc) in each ch to end of row. Turn with one ch.
1st row: 1 dc (sc) into ch sp, * 3 ch, 1 dc (sc) into ch sp. Repeat from * to end. Dc (sc) into turning ch.
2nd row: 3 ch, * 2 tr (dc) into ch loop, 1 ch. Repeat from * to end. 1 tr (dc). Repeat these 2 rows until work measures 16.5 cm (6½ in).
Next row: ss 9 sts. Work pattern to last 9 sts. Turn with 1 tr (dc).
Work in pattern over 41 sts until armhole measures 10 cm (4 in). Finish with 2nd row.

RIGHT FRONT

Make 28 ch. 1 tr (dc) into 4th ch from hook, tr (dc) into each ch to end of row, turn with 1 ch.
1 dc (sc) into tr (dc), * 3 ch, miss 2 tr (dc). Repeat from * to end of row. Turn with 3 ch.
Next row: * 2 tr (dc) into ch sp, 1 ch. Repeat from * to end of row. Turn with 1 ch.
Continue in pattern until work measures 16.5 cm (6½ in).
Next row: ss over 9 sts, pattern to end of row, turn with 1 ch.
Next row: 1 tr (dc) into next ch loop, 1 ch, continue in pattern to last 2 sts, 1 ch, 2 dc (sc) into ch sp, turn with 3 ch.
Continue in pattern dec 1 st at neck edge each row until 3 groups left. Continue in pattern until armhole matches back. Fasten off.

LEFT FRONT

Work as right front but reverse shapings.

SLEEVES

Make 37 ch. Tr (dc) into 4th ch from hook. Tr (dc) into each ch to end of row. Pattern as for back increasing 1 st every alternate row until there are 55 sts. Continue until work measures 18 cm (7 in).
Next row: 2 ch, * 2 tr (dc) into ch loop, 1 tr (dc) into dc (sc). Repeat from * to end of row. Fasten off.

Front border

Make 9 ch.
1st row: 1 dc (sc) into 3rd ch from hook, dc (sc) in each ch to end. Turn with 2 ch.
2nd row: 7 dc (sc), 2 ch.
3rd row: 3 dc (sc), 2 ch, miss 2 ch, 3 dc (sc), turn with 2 ch.
4th row: 2 dc (sc), 2 dc (sc) into ch sp, 3 dc (sc). (1 buttonhole made.) Turn with 2 ch.
Repeat 2nd row 8 times.
13th row: As 3rd row.
Repeat last 10 rows until 5 buttonholes have been made.
Continue 8 dc (sc) border until long enough to reach round neck and front. Fasten off.

TO MAKE UP

Join shoulders. Sew in sleeves. Join sleeve and underarm sections. Sew border to cardigan with buttonholes on the right side for a girl or the left side for a boy. Finally, sew on buttons to line up with buttonholes.

Hooded **S**weater

THIS COSY SWEATER IS GIVEN IN TWO SIZES, 3 AND 6 MONTHS

YOU WILL NEED ■ 200 g (8-ounce skein) ecru double knitting (sport) yarn ■ 100 g (4-ounce skein) yellow double knitting (sport) yarn ■ 1 pair size 3 mm (US 3) knitting needles ■ 1 pair size 3.5 mm (US 4) knitting needles ■ Tape measure ■ Scissors ■ Iron ■ Large darning needle

Tension (Gauge)
Using 3.5 mm (US 4) needles, 21 sts and 30 rows to 10 cm (4 in) (st st).

BACK AND FRONT
Start at lower front edge. With 3 mm (US 3) needles and yellow yarn cast on 58(62) sts.
Work 4 rows in k 1, p 1 rib.
Change to 3½ mm (US 4) needles and the ecru yarn. Continue in st st (1 row k, 1 row p) and increase 1 st at both ends of every alternate row 13 times (84(88) sts). Continue in st st until work measures 34(39.5) cm (13¼ (15½) in).

Shape neck
K 37(38), cast (bind) off 10(12) sts, k 37(38) sts. Work each side of neck separately. Cast (bind) off at neck edge on alternate rows, 3 sts once, 2 sts twice and 1 st 3 times. Continue straight until work measures 39(45) cm (15¼(18) in) ending on neck edge, at the centre of the work.

Inc row: cast on 10 sts for back neck, k to end.
Next row: p to end.
Leave remaining 37(38) sts on a spare needle.
Rejoin yarn at neck edge and complete other side of neck to match reversing shaping and ending at straight edge.
Inc row: k 37(38), cast on 10(12) sts, k 37(38) from spare needle (84(88) sts). Continue straight until work measures 69(81) cm (27½(32½) in) ending with a wrong side row.
Dec row: dec 1st each end of next and following alternate row 12 times more (58(62) sts). Change to 3 mm (US 3) needles and yellow yarn. Work 4 rows k 1, p 1 rib. Cast (bind) off.

HOOD
With 3.5 mm (US 4) needles and yellow yarn cast on 42(44) sts. Continue in st st, keeping front edge straight throughout and inc 1 st at beginning of every 10th row 1(2) times, then every following 8th row 5(4) times (48(50) sts). Continue straight until work measures 19(20) cm (7½(8) in) ending with a right side row. Cast (bind) off 1 st at beginning of next and following alternate rows 3 times more. Cast (bind) off 2 sts at beginning of alternate rows twice. Work 1 row ending at back edge (centre of work) (40(42) sts).

Cast on at beginning of next and following alternate rows 2 sts twice and 1 st 4 times (48(50) sts. Dec 1 st at back edge on next and every following 8th row 5(4) times more and then every following 10th row 0(1) time (42(44) sts).

Continue straight until work measures 46(49) cm (18¼(19¼) in ending with a wrong side row. Cast (bind) off.

Hood edging
Using 3 mm (US 3) needles and ecru yarn, pick up 99(103) sts along front edge of hood. Work 4 rows k1, p1 rib. Cast (bind) off.

SLEEVES
(Knit 2 alike)
Using 3 mm (US 3) needles and ecru yarn, cast on 32(34) sts. Work 6 rows k 1, p 1 rib. Change to 3½ mm (US 4) and yellow yarn. Inc 1 st each end of next and every alternate row 13 times (60(62) sts). Then every following 3rd row 5(6) times (70(74) sts). Cast (bind) off.

TO MAKE UP
Press all the pieces. Join back hood seam. Sew hood to neck. Place markers 15(16) cm (6(6¼) in) below shoulder on front and back for sleeve position. Sew sleeve between markers using backstitch. Join sleeve and side seams.

Knitted Bonnet

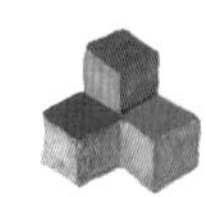

THIS COSY BONNET WILL FIT BABIES UP TO 6 MONTHS

YOU WILL NEED ■ *1 pair size 3 mm (US 3) knitting needles* ■ *100 g (4-ounce skein) white double knitting (sport) cotton* ■ *Iron* ■ *Length of narrow white ribbon* ■ *Length of wider white ribbon*

Tension (Gauge)
Using a pair of 3 mm (US 3) needles, 21 sts and 30 rows to 10 cm (4 in) (st st).

Beginning at the front row edge, cast on 76 sts.
1st row: k to end.
2nd row and every even numbered row from this point: k 6, p 64, k 6.
3rd row: k to end.
5th row: picot edge k 6 (ynfwd, k 2 tog) to last 6 sts, k6.
7th row: k to end.
9th row: k to end.
11th row: eyelets for ribbon k 6 *k 2, ynfwd, k 2 tog. Repeat from * to last 6 sts, k 6 sts.
13th row: k to end.

Begin lace pattern as follows
15th row: k 9, *ynfwd, sl 1, k 1, psso, k 6. Repeat from * to last 9 sts, k 9.
16th row and every even numbered row: k 6, p 64, k 6.
17th row: k 7, *k 2 tog, ynfwd, k 1, ynfwd, sl 1, k 1, psso, k 3. Repeat from * to last 8 sts, k 8.
19th row: as row 15.
21st row: k to end.
23rd row: k 13, *ynfwd, sl 1, k 1, psso, k 6. Repeat from * to last 13 sts, k 13.
25th row: k 11, *k 2 tog, ynfwd, k 1, ynfwd, sl 1, k 1, psso, k 3. Repeat from * to last 9 sts, k 9.
27th row: as row 23.
29th row: k to end.
31st row: k 9, *ynfwd, sl 1, k 1, psso, k 6. Repeat from * to last 9 sts, k 9.
33rd row: k 7, *k 2 tog, ynfwd, k 1 ynfwd, sl 1, k 1, psso, k 3. Repeat from * to last 8 sts, k 8.
35th row: as row 31.

Shape head as follows
Rows 37 and 38: cast (bind) off 27 sts at beginning of next 2 rows. Continue shaping for back of head on remaining 22 sts working in garter stitch (knit every row) for 24 rows then dec 1 st at each end of every 4th row a total of 4 times, 14 sts. Cast (bind) off.

TO MAKE UP
Press bonnet well from wrong side. Fold under front edge of bonnet on picot and hem cast-on edge to wrong side of work. Join back of head seams. Thread narrow ribbon through eyelets and sew ends to inside of work. Cut 2 lengths of wide ribbon. Make 2 loops, 2.5 cm (1 in) long, at one end of ribbon and sew to each corner of bonnet.

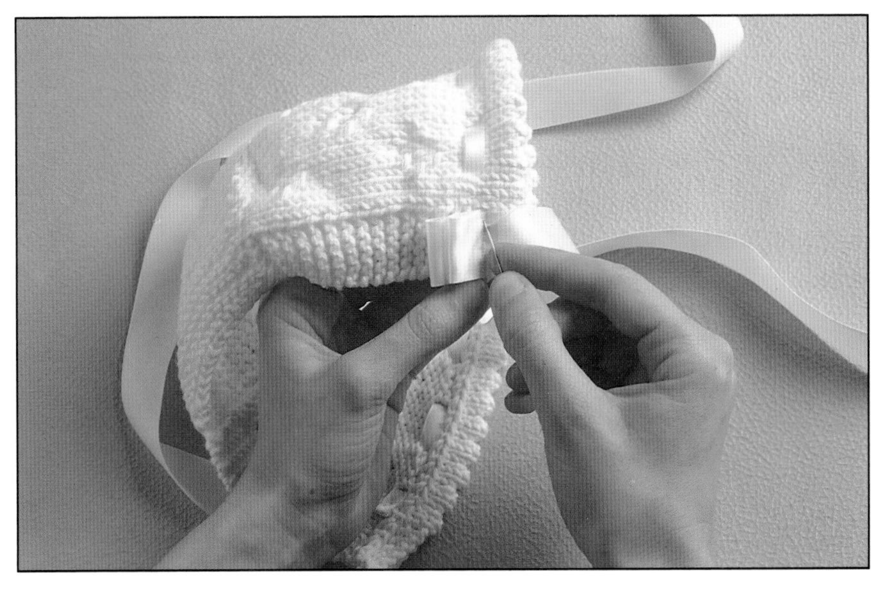

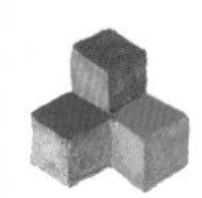

Knitted **C**ollar

THIS DELICATE COLLAR IS EASY TO KNIT

YOU WILL NEED ■ *50 g (2-ounce skein) white double knitting (sport) cotton* ■ *1 pair size 4 mm (US 5) knitting needles* ■ *Iron* ■ *Length of narrow white ribbon*

Tension (Gauge)
One repeat (8 rows of pattern) measures 3.75 cm (1½ in) long by 3.75 cm (1½ in) wide.

Cast on 5 sts.
1st row: k 1, ynfwd, k 2 tog, ynfwd, k 2 (6 sts).
2nd row: k 2, (ynfwd, k 1) twice, ynfwd, k 2 tog (8 sts).
3rd row: sl 1, ynfwd, k 2 tog, ynfwd, k 3, ynfwd, k 2 (10 sts).
4th row: k 2, ynfwd, k 5, ynfwd, k 1, ynfwd, k 2 tog (12 sts).
5th row: sl 1, ynfwd, k 5, ynfwd, k 1, ynfwd, sl 1, k 1, psso, k 3 tog, ynfwd, k 2 (12 sts).
6th row: k 3, ynfwd, sl 1, k 1, psso, k 1, k 2 tog, ynfwd, k 2, ynfwd, k 2 tog (12 sts).
7th row: sl 1, ynfwd, k 2 tog, k 2, ynfwd, sl 1, k 2 tog, psso, ynfwd, k 4 (12 sts).
8th row: Cast (bind) off 7 sts, k 2, ynfwd, k 2 tog (5 sts).

Repeat 8 rows 10 times more, ending on 7th row. Cast (bind) off.

TO MAKE UP
Attach ribbon to inside corners.

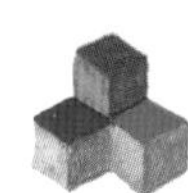

Knitted Cuff Bootees

THESE STRIPY BOOTEES WILL FIT BABIES UP TO 3 MONTHS OLD

YOU WILL NEED ■ *1 pair of 3.5 mm (US 4) knitting needles* ■ *Small quantity of double knitting (sport) yarn in ecru and yellow* ■ *Large darning needle*

Tension (Gauge)
Using 3.5 mm (US 4) needles, 21 sts and 30 rows to 10 cm (4 in) (st st).

Starting at the cuff and using ecru yarn, cast on 29 sts. Work 16 rows garter st (every row knit). Change to yellow yarn and work 10 rows garter st.

Instep
Slip 10 sts from each side of work onto a thread and leave. Continue on 9 sts in the centre. Work 14 rows garter st.
Next row: change to yellow yarn, and with right side facing k 10 sts from thread, pick up and k 12 sts along side of instep, k 9 sts in centre, pick up and k 12 sts along other side of instep, k 10 sts from thread (53 sts).
Work 7 rows garter st. Change to ecru yarn.

Shape sole
Next row: k 30, k 2 tog, turn.
Next row: k 8, k 2 tog, turn.
Next row: k 8, k 2 tog, turn.
Rep last 2 rows until 6 sts remain each side of centre 9 sts.
Next row: turn, k to end. Cast (bind) off.
Work second bootee to match.

TO MAKE UP
Join the heel and back seams, reversing the seam on the last 6 rows to turn over for the cuff.

Knitted **M**ittens

THESE COSY MITTENS WILL FIT BABIES UP TO 6 MONTHS

YOU WILL NEED ■ *1 pair 3 mm (US 3) knitting needles* ■ *Small amount of yarn and acrylic mix double knitting (sport) yarn in ecru and yellow* ■ *1 pair 3.5 mm (US 4) knitting needles* ■ *Large darning needle* ■ *Scissors*

Tension (Gauge)
Using 3.5 mm (US 4) needles, 21 sts and 30 rows to 10 cm (4 in) (st st).

CUFF
Using 3 mm (US 3) needles and ecru yarn cast on 32 sts. Work 10 rows k 1 p 1 rib. Break yarn. Change to 3½ mm (US 4) needles and yellow yarn.

To make eyelets:
(k 2 ynfwd, k 2 tog) to end.
Starting with a p row work 18 rows st st.
Dec row: (k 2 tog) to end.
Next row: p to end.
Dec row: (k 2 tog) to end.
Next row: p to end.
Dec row: (k 2 tog) to end.
Break yarn and thread through remaining sts. Pull up and secure.

To make the braided cords
Cut 6 × 70 cm (28 in) strands of yarn, 3 of ecru and 3 of yellow. Knot strands together at one end leaving 2 cm (¾ in) of yarn at end for the tassel. Pin the knot to a fixed object. Braid the yarn then knot, leaving spare yarn at one end. Brush and trim the ends.

TO MAKE UP
Join seams lengthwise, right sides together. Thread cords through eyelets of mittens.

Baby's Gift Box

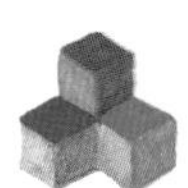

THE PERFECT PRESENT FOR A NEW MOTHER

YOU WILL NEED ■ *Scissors* ■ *Piece of striped fabric to cover base* ■ *Square wooden box with clear lid* ■ *Tape measure* ■ *Sticky tape* ■ *Rubber-based glue* ■ *Length of pre-gathered lace* ■ *White yarn* ■ *Large darning needle* ■ *2 small white pompons* ■ *About 30 cotton buds (swabs)* ■ *Rubber band* ■ *3 pieces of ribbon* ■ *Needle and thread* ■ *3 satin roses* ■ *1 face cloth* ■ *Small bunch artificial flowers* ■ *Piece of lace fabric* ■ *Small round soap* ■ *Duck motif or any other motif* ■ *1 natural sponge* ■ *Baby brush* ■ *Baby bear or other small ornament* ■ *4–6 absorbent cotton balls*

1 Cut the fabric to the size of the box base, plus 6 cm (2⅜ in) all round. Place the base on the wrong side of the fabric and fold the edges over, securing them with pieces of sticky tape.

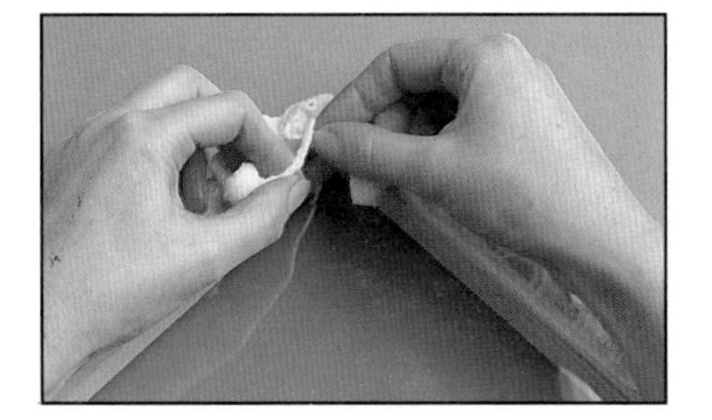

2 Glue the lace around the box. To make the corner bow, take 3 lengths of yarn and, using a darning needle, pass each strand through a pompon. Tie the strands at one end and trim. Braid the yarn until you reach 5 cm (2 in) from the end. Pass the yarn through the other pompon and pull until the braid meets the pompon. Finish off in the same way. Sew a bow to one corner.

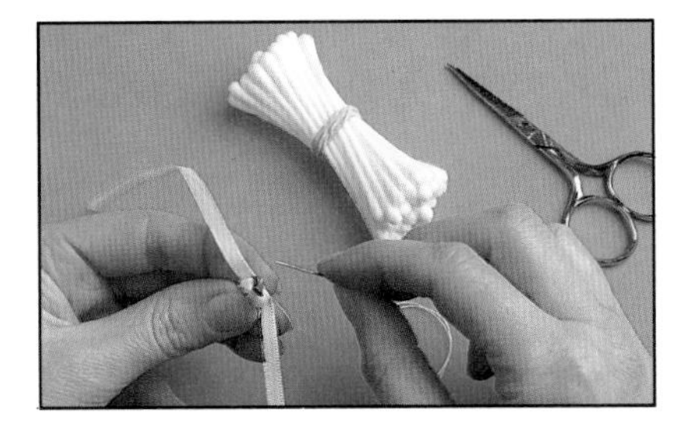

3 Take the cotton buds (swabs) and secure together with a rubber band. Fold a 3 cm (1¼ in) length of ribbon in half to find the centre, and sew a small satin rose in place. Sew the other roses on either side. Wrap the ribbon around the bunch of cotton buds (swabs), ensuring that the rubber band is completely covered and the roses centred. Tie at the back and trim the ends.

4 Fold the face cloth to fit the box and tie a ribbon into a bow around it. Tuck a small bunch of artificial flowers under the bow. Wrap the lace fabric around the soap and gather the edges at one side. Tie a ribbon to hold in place. Trim the top and glue the motif to the front. Arrange the decorated objects attractively in the box together with the sponge, baby brush and the ornament, filling in any gaps with absorbent cotton balls. Replace the lid.

Keepsake Pin Cushion

THIS ORNAMENTAL PIN CUSHION MAKES AN ATTRACTIVE MEMENTO

YOU WILL NEED ■ *Needle and thread* ■ *1 m (40 in) lace, 2 cm (¾ in) wide* ■ *Pins* ■ *2 pieces of quilted raw silk fabric, 18 × 13 cm (7 × 5¼ in)* ■ *2 pieces of cotton fabric, 18 × 13 cm (7 × 5¼ in)* ■ *Tape measure* ■ *Decorative motifs* ■ *Bran or sawdust* ■ *Heart-shaped pearl motif* ■ *Funnel*

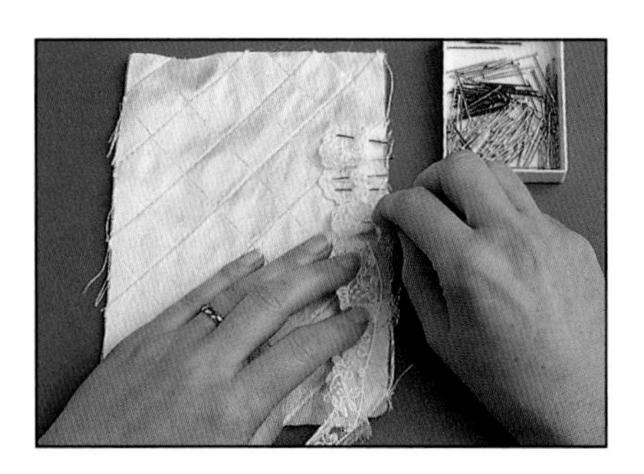

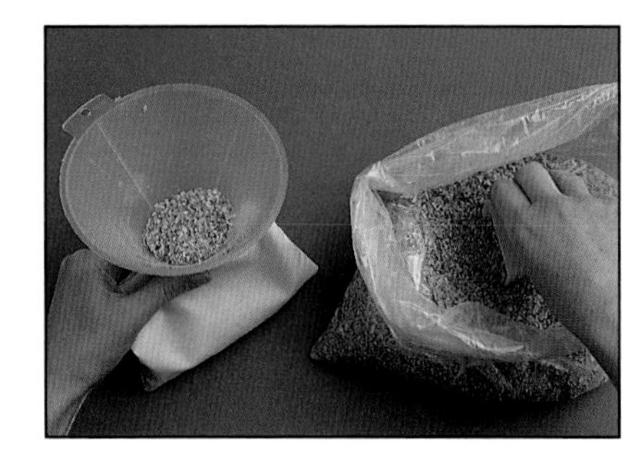

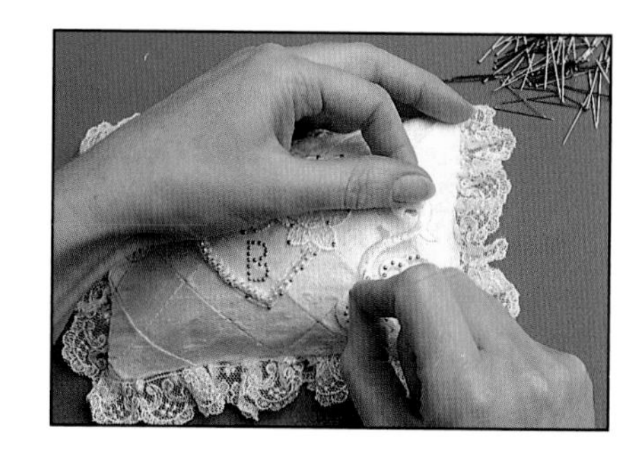

1 Sew a running stitch along the lace and gather. Pin the lace to the right side of 1 piece of silk, 1.5 cm (⅝ in) from the edge and tack (baste). Lay the other piece of silk on top so that right sides are together. Pin and tack (baste) leaving one short end open. Remove the pins and stitch. Turn through.

2 Pin the 2 pieces of cotton fabric with right sides together, and tack (baste). Remove the pins and stitch all round a 6 cm (2¼ in) opening. Turn the bag through and pour the bran or sawdust through the opening using a funnel until you have a firm, plump cushion. Slip stitch the opening to close.

3 Place the bag inside the silk cover. Hand stitch the opening together behind the lace. Position the motifs and use the pins to hold them in place. You could also include the baby's initials in your design.

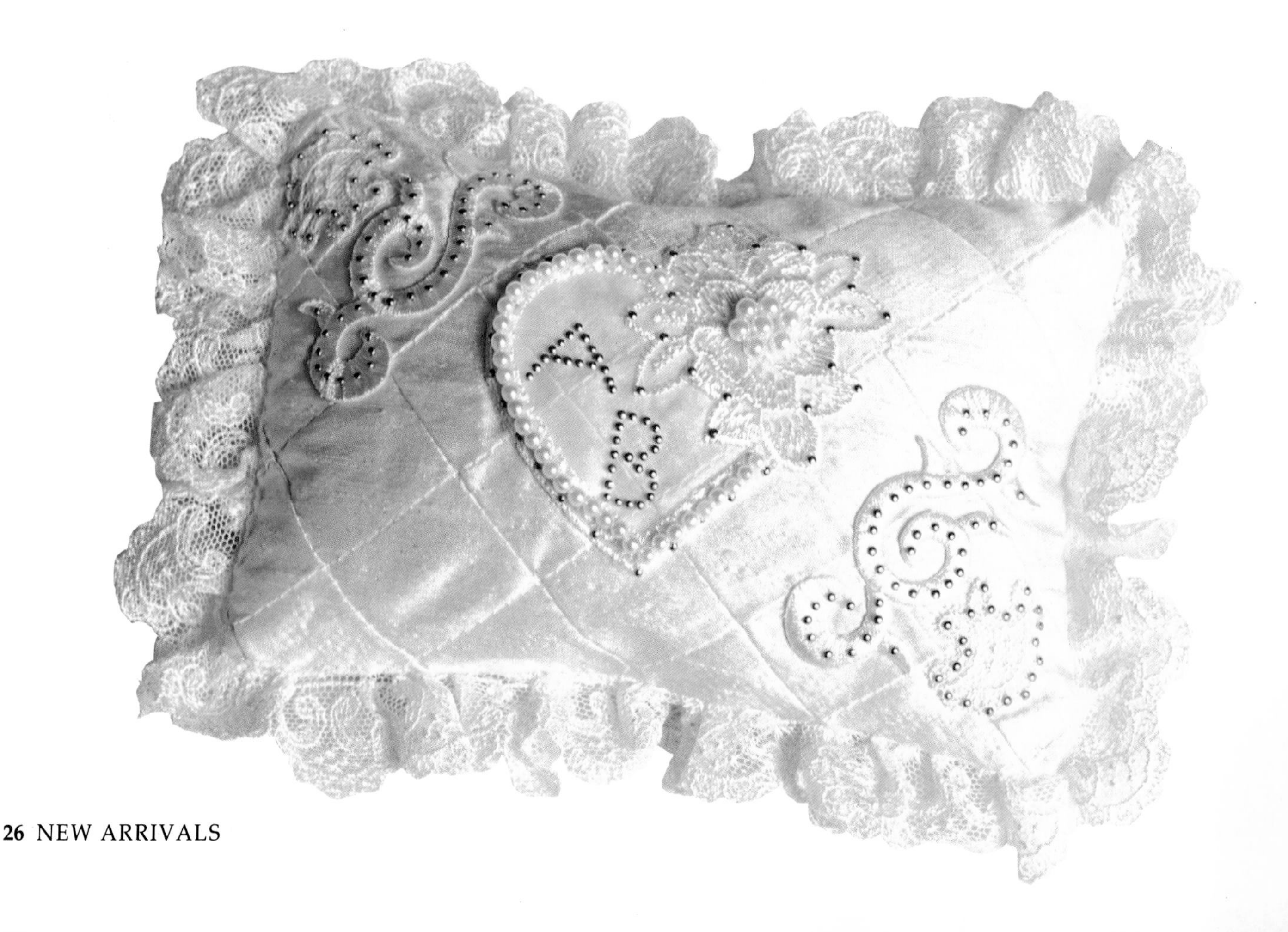

Scented Sachets

THESE CRIB-SHAPED SACHETS ARE PERFECT FOR FRESHENING DRAWERS

YOU WILL NEED For each sachet: ■ *9 × 7.5 cm (3½ × 3 in) piece of wadding (batting)* ■ *20 × 18 cm (8 × 7 in) white cotton fabric* ■ *Pins* ■ *Needle and thread* ■ *Dried lavender* ■ *Scissors* ■ *36 cm (14 in) broderie anglaise ribbon, 7.5 cm (3 in) wide* ■ *Tape measure* ■ *36 cm (14 in) double-sided satin ribbon, 6 mm (¼ in) wide*

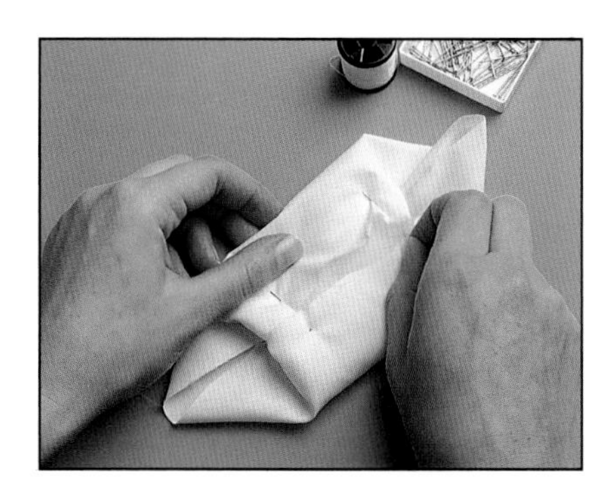

1 Place the wadding (batting) in the centre of the white fabric, pin down the fabric over the wadding (batting) and tack (baste). Fold the ends to form triangles as if wrapping a parcel. Place a spoonful of dried lavender in the centre.

2 Carefully fold in half lengthwise so that the sides meet, and slip stitch together. At end of the seam, fold down the triangle and sew to the centre seam. Oversew back along the seam, and catch in the other triangle to finish the inner bedding of the crib.

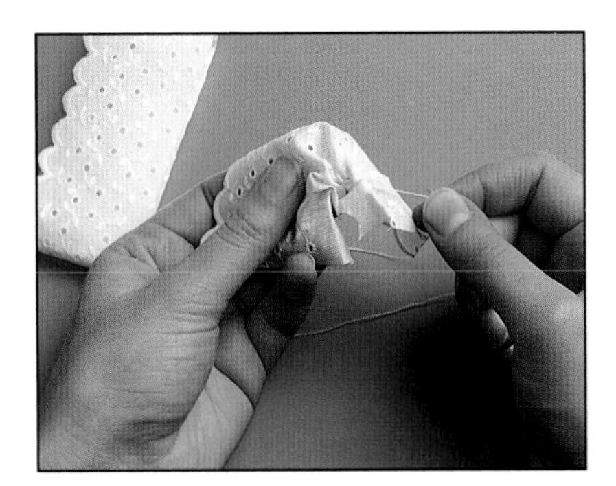

3 Cut a 23 cm (9 in) length of broderie anglaise and fold in half, right sides together. Fold in 2.5 cm (1 in) of the selvage edge, sew the end and then turn right side out. Use the remaining broderie anglaise ribbon to make the crib hood by gather stitching 12 mm (½ in) from the selvage edge. Pull the thread while tucking in the seam, and fasten to form the hood.

4 Tuck the hood into the crib, pin into position and then oversew to secure. Position the lavender 'bedding' in the crib. Tie a bow in the satin ribbon. Sew the bow onto the crib, passing the needle through to secure the bedding. Pass the ribbon over the crib and sew to the outside. Leave the end of the ribbon hanging if you are going to hang the sachet inside a wardrobe.

Hooded Jacket

THESE DIMENSIONS FIT A 6-MONTH BABY BUT CAN BE ADJUSTED FOR ANY AGE

YOU WILL NEED ■ *Paper and pencil if you need to re-scale dimensions* ■ *Tape measure* ■ *Scissors* ■ *Ready-quilted cotton fabric* ■ *Plain fabric in a co-ordinating colour* ■ *Pins* ■ *Needle and thread* ■ *Iron* ■ *2 or 3 toggles*

1 Scale up the templates according to your calculated size, measuring from neck to hem, and cut out the 2 'T' shapes in quilted fabric for the back and front. Cut one of the shapes in half down the centre front. Cut 4 strips of plain fabric for the shoulder stripes to the depth of the sleeve from shoulder to underarm and, for the size given here, 5 cm (2 in) wide. Turn the long raw edges under 6 mm (¼ in), tack (baste) and press. Pin and tack (baste) them to the sleeves on the 2 front pieces and back so that the raw edge of the side seam and inside edge of the strip form a straight line. Appliqué the 4 strips in place and remove the tacking (basting).

2 Assemble the jacket fronts and back with right sides together. Pin, tack (baste) and stitch each underarm and side seam, rounding off the seam under each arm. Trim the seam allowance to 6 mm (¼ in) and carefully clip the curve under the arm to allow it to turn well. Oversew the raw edges together.

3 With wrong sides together, fold the hood in half along one longer side. Pin and tack (baste) the seam and sew it 6 mm (¼ in) from the edge on the right side. Turn it to the wrong side, press the seam and sew a second line of stitching, 6 mm (¼ in) from the first. Mark the centre bottom of the hood (the edge at the opposite end to the hood seam).

Temporarily position the hood centre to match the centre back and front. Fold the hood sides in so they meet in the centre of the hood. Mark where the folds on the hood sides meet the jacket top with a pin on each side. Pin and tack (baste) the shoulders and sleeves together from the pins outwards. Stitch the seams and neaten the raw edges.

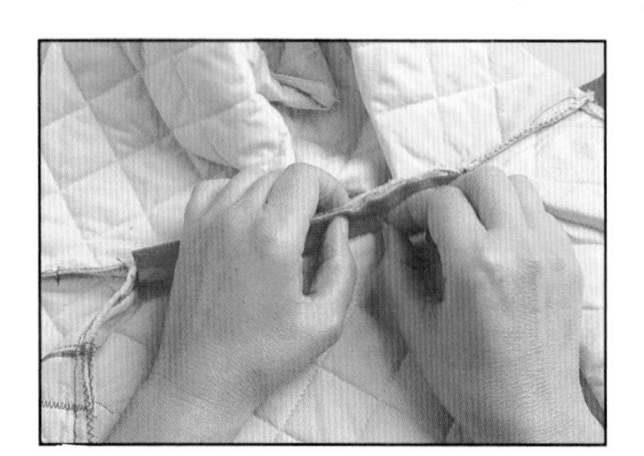

4 Folding the hood as before, match the centre back of the hood with the jacket centre back, with right sides together and the jacket inside out. Pin the hood to the back, then to the fronts when you reach the shoulder stitching, making 2 sets of seams that meet in a 'Y' shape. Stitch the seams. Trim the seams on the jacket fronts only and oversew. Bind the back hood seam.

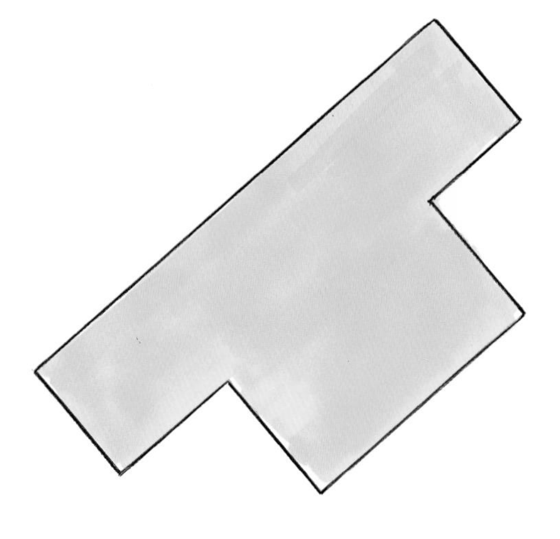

HOOD

5 Cut sufficient bias binding from the plain fabric to go around the entire garment. Make some loops for the toggles, folding and pressing them into shape. Pin, tack (baste) and sew the binding to the jacket edge, right sides together, beginning on the hem. Enclose the toggle loops on the side of one front.

Enclose the binding ends neatly when you return to the beginning. Press the stitching line firmly from the right side to give a crisp edge before you turn the binding to the inside and hem it to the inside of the jacket. Hem the sleeves and sew on the toggles.

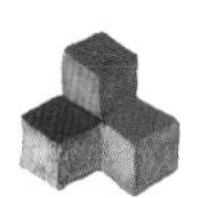

Appliquéd Sleepsuit

LIVEN UP A PLAIN SLEEPSUIT BY ADDING A FRIENDLY ANIMAL MOTIF

YOU WILL NEED ■ *Fabric with pretty motif* ■ *Scissors* ■ *Fusible iron-on bonding paper* ■ *Iron* ■ *Plain sleepsuit* ■ *Needle and embroidery thread*

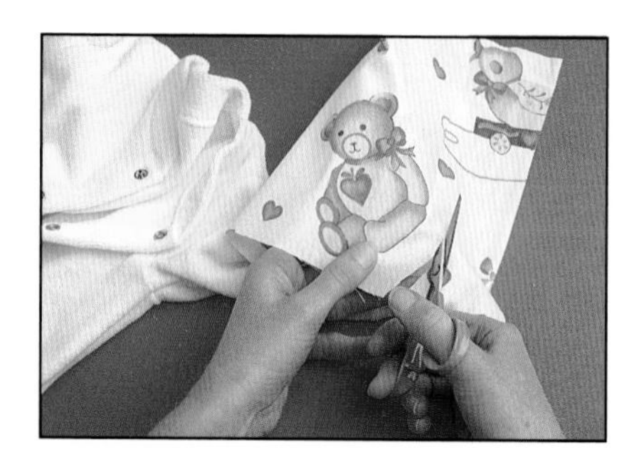

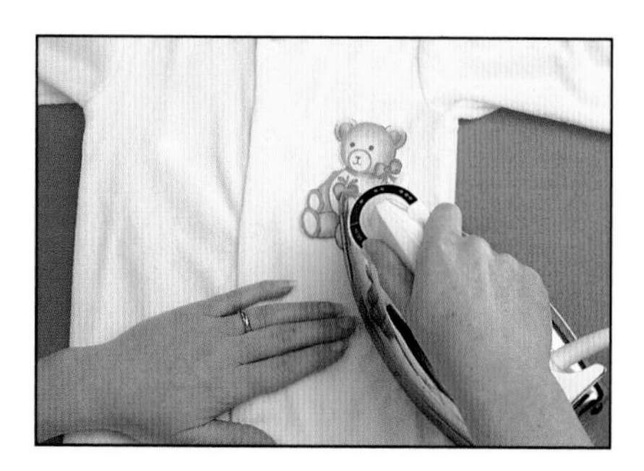

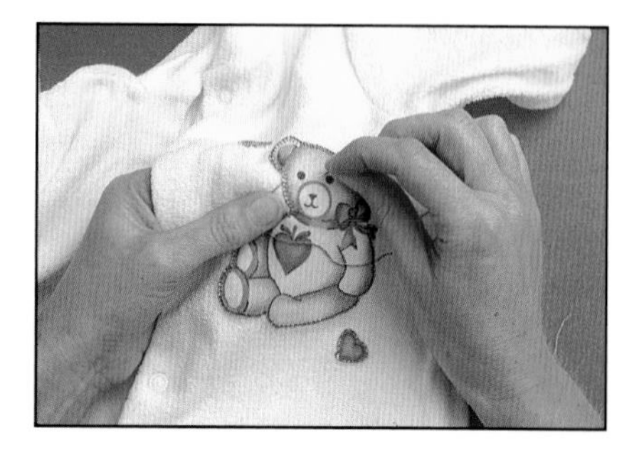

1 Decide on the motif to be used and cut out of the fabric, leaving a wide margin all around the motif.

2 Cut a piece of fusible bonding paper to the same size and iron on according to the manufacturer's instructions. Cut out the paper-backed motif and iron into place on the sleepsuit.

3 Using two strands of embroidery thread, neatly blanket stitch around the motif. Press well with the iron.

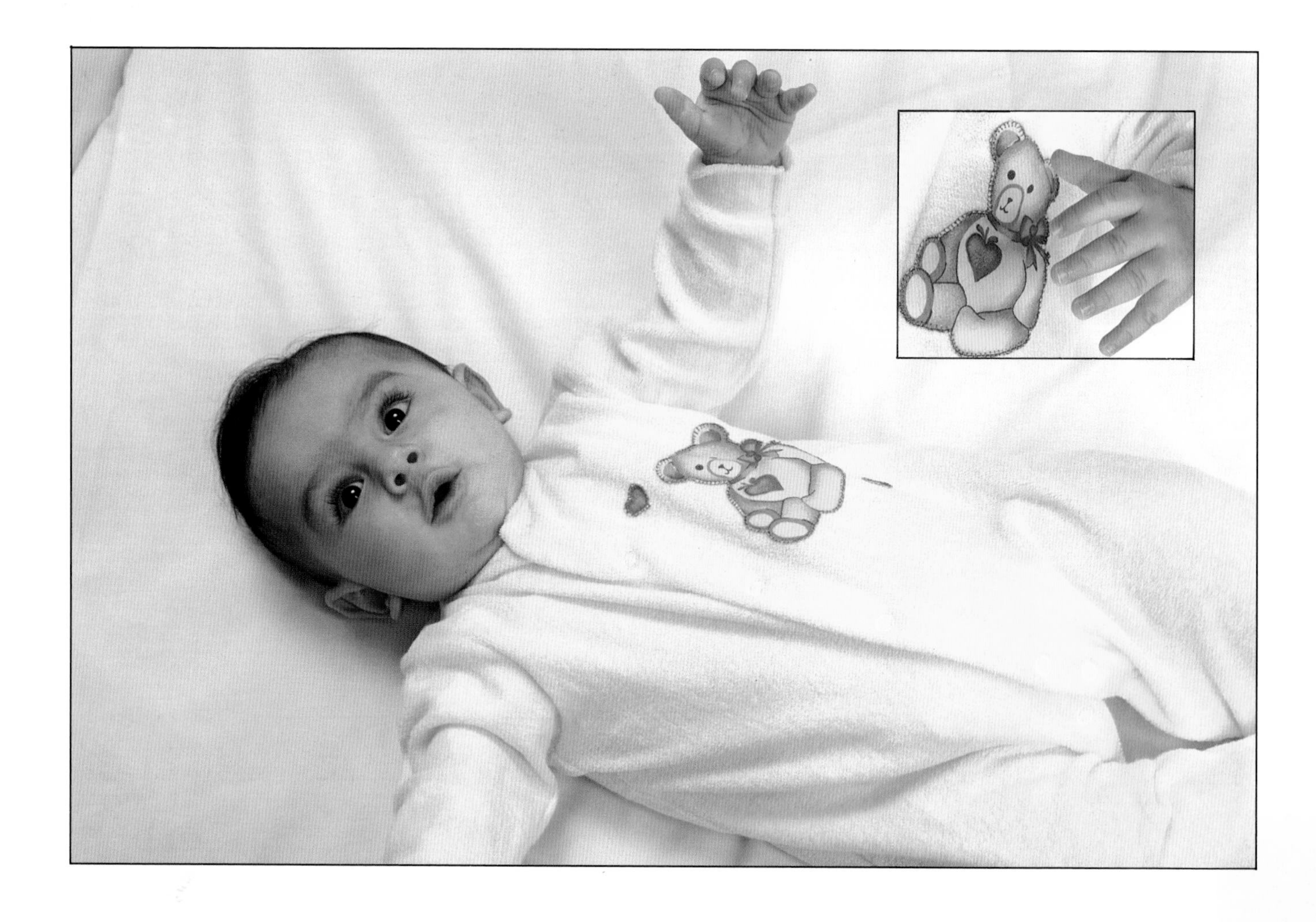

Decorated Baby Shoes

TRANSFORM PLAIN SHOES INTO A PRETTY PARTY PAIR

YOU WILL NEED ■ *Pink embroidery silk* ■ *Scissors* ■ *Needle* ■ *Plain fabric baby shoes* ■ *Pink gingham ribbon*

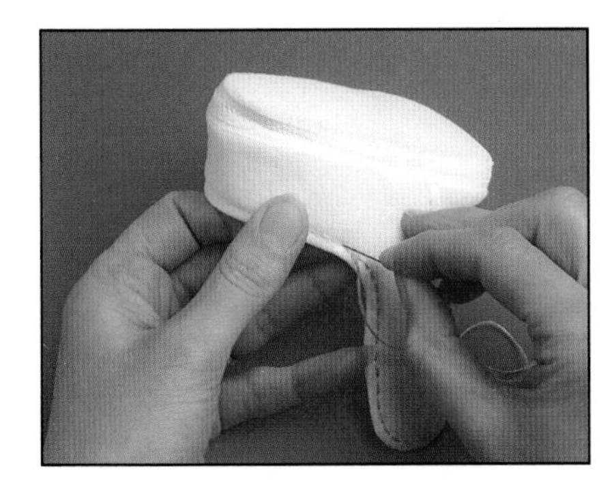

1 Take a length of the pink embroidery silk and pull out 3 strands with which to work. Thread a needle and sew a small running stitch around the edges of each of the shoes.

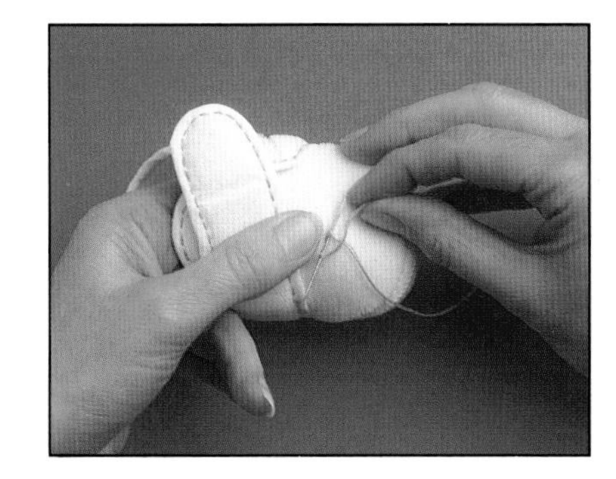

2 Still using 3 strands of the pink embroidery silk, sew 3 small French knots at intervals down the front of each shoe. Finish off the thread neatly on the underside.

3 Make 2 small bows from the gingham ribbon, clipping a 'V' shape into each of the ends as shown. Sew the bows into position on the front of each of the shoes to complete.

Tie-dye **S**tretchsuit

A STRETCHSUIT IS ONE OF THE MOST USEFUL AND POPULAR BABYWEAR ITEMS

YOU WILL NEED ■ *Scissors* ■ *Ball of string* ■ *Tape measure* ■ *Plain white stretchsuit* ■ *Dye* ■ *Large saucepan or bucket* ■ *Rubber gloves* ■ *Iron*

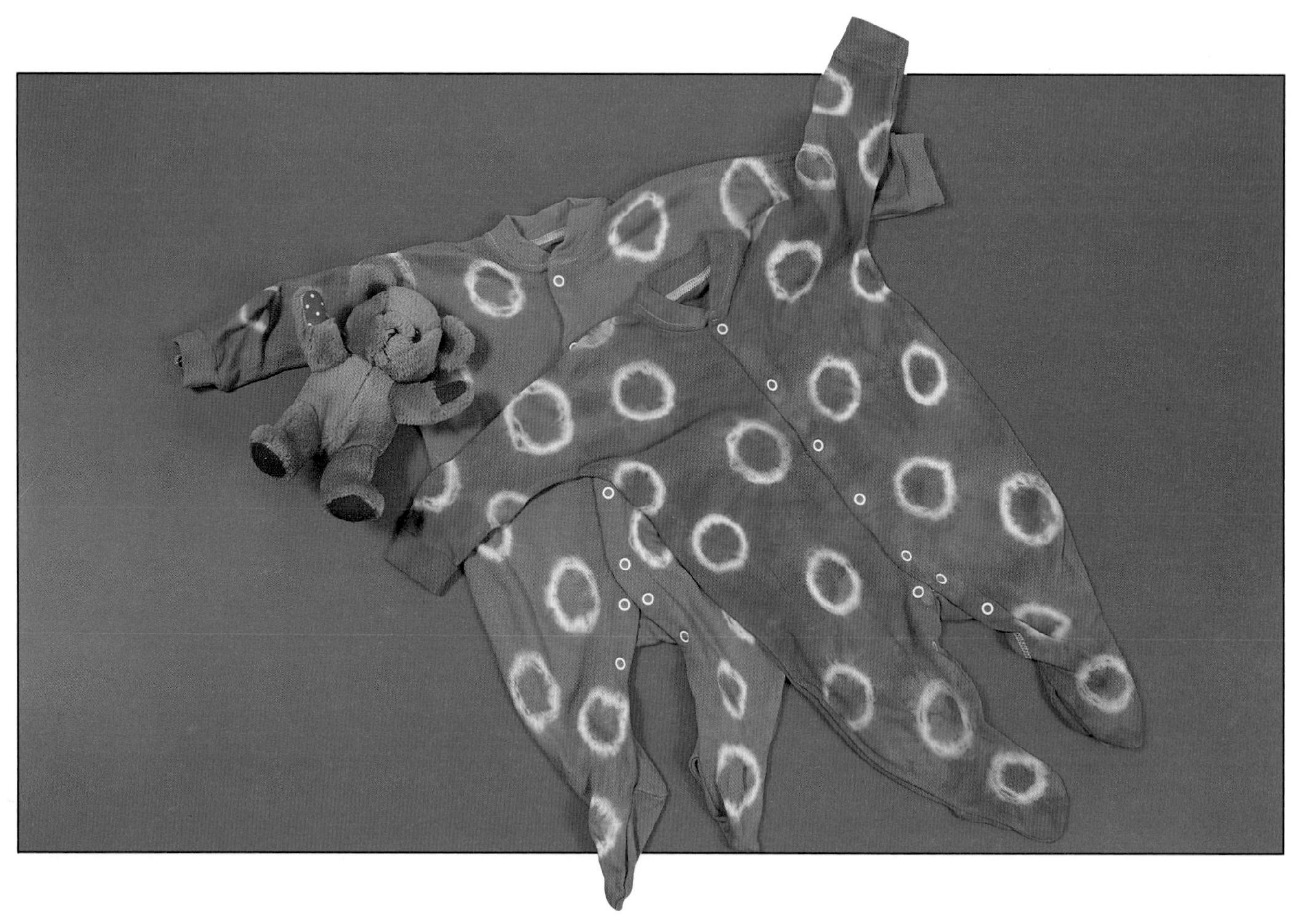

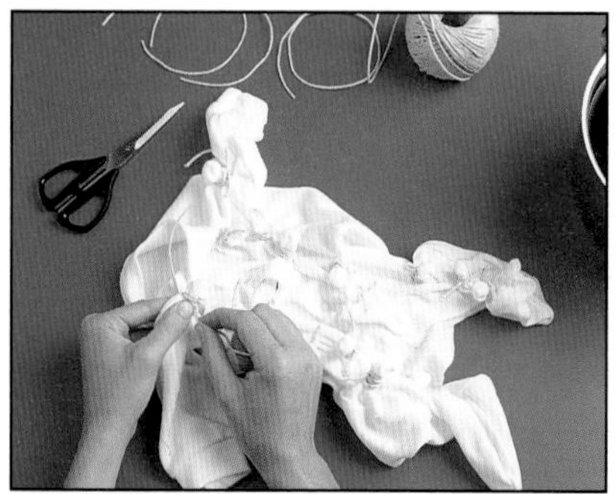

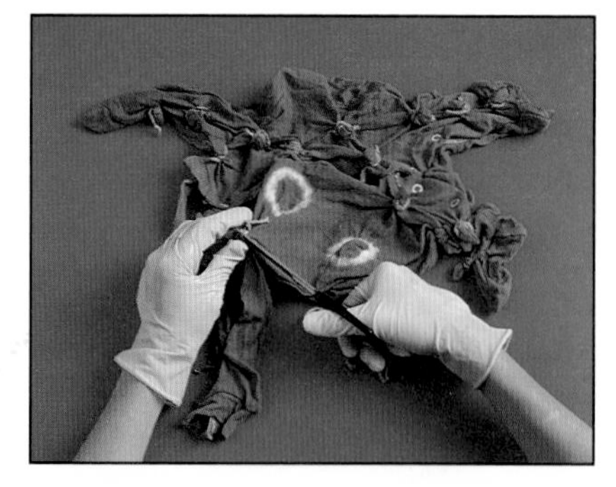

1 Cut several pieces of string about 18 cm (7 in) long. Pinch an area of the stretchsuit and tie string tightly around it, making a 'peak'. Repeat at intervals all over the front and back of the stretchsuit until all the spaces are used up.

2 Prepare the dye in a large saucepan or bucket, according to the manufacturer's instructions. Wearing rubber gloves if you wish, immerse the stretchsuit in the dye, making sure that it is completely covered, then leave for the recommended time.

3 Still wearing gloves (if used), rinse out the stretchsuit under cold running water until the colour stops running. Cut the strings, open out the stretchsuit and leave it to dry naturally. Wash the suit and press it with a cool iron before use.

Tall Bootees

THESE LONG, STRIPED BOOTEES WILL FIT BABIES UP TO 4 MONTHS

YOU WILL NEED ■ *1 pair 3.5 mm (US 4) knitting needles* ■ *Oddments of double knitting (sport) cotton in red, pink, yellow, orange, turquoise and purple* ■ *Large darning needle*

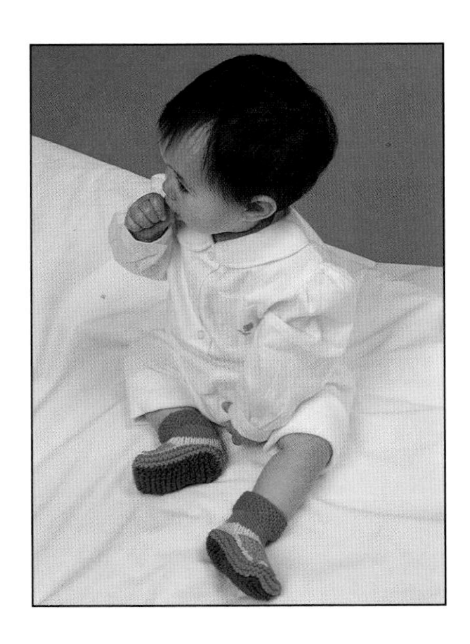

Tension (Gauge)
Using 3.5 mm (US 4) needles, 21 sts and 30 rows to 10 cm (4 in) (st st).

Top
Using red cotton, cast on 27 sts and work 8 rows in garter st (every row knit). Change to pink and work 6 rows in st st. Change to yellow and work a further 4 rows st st.

To shape the instep
Slip 9 sts either side onto a thread and leave. Continue on 9 sts in centre. Using orange work 14 rows garter st.
Next row: with right side facing and yellow yarn k 9 sts from thread, pick up and k 12 sts along side of instep, k 9, pick up and k 12 sts along other side of instep, k 9 st from thread (51 sts).
P 1 row yellow.
Change to turquoise and work 6 rows garter st.

To shape the side
Change to purple and continue in garter st.
Next row: k 29, k 2 tog, turn.
Next row: k 8, k 2 tog, turn.
Next row: k 8, k 2 tog, turn.
Repeat last 2 rows until 6 sts remain each side of centre 9 sts, turn, k to end, cast (bind) off.

TO MAKE UP
Join heel and back seam.

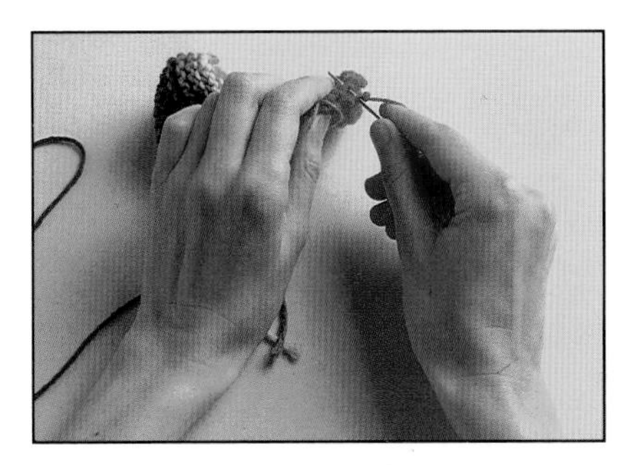

Ric-rac Mitts

THESE SNUG MITTS WILL PREVENT A YOUNG BABY FROM SCRATCHING ITSELF

YOU WILL NEED ■ *Marker pen* ■ *White paper* ■ *Piece of cotton jersey fabric* ■ *Pinking shears* ■ *Needle and thread* ■ *Elastic* ■ *Scissors* ■ *32 cm (12 in) ric-rac braid*

1 Using the template as a guide, cut out the mitt shape from a piece of white paper. Draw around this 4 times on the cotton jersey fabric and cut out the pieces with pinking shears.

2 Fold over the straight edge of each mitt piece and sew it down. Sew the pieces together in pairs, right sides together, leaving the straight edges open.

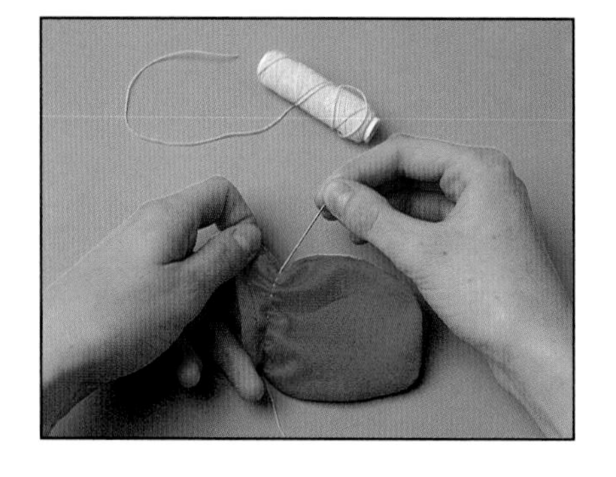

3 Turn the mitts right side out and sew a line of elastic about 2.5 cm (1 in) from each of the mitt openings.

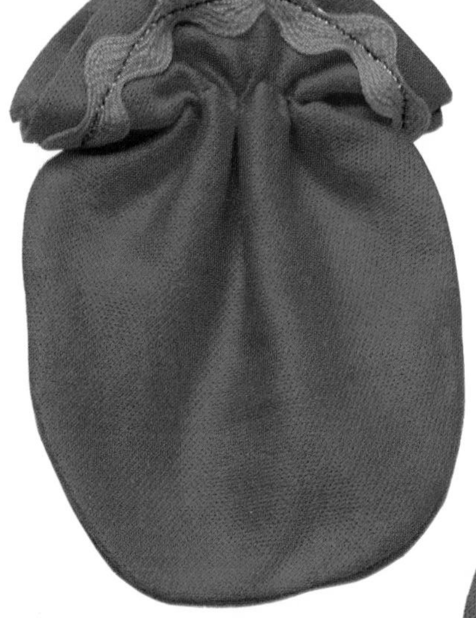

4 Cut the ric-rac in 2 and sew a length around the opening edge of each mitt.

Leg Warmers

THESE COSY LEG WARMERS ARE GIVEN IN TWO SIZES, 0–2 YEARS AND 3–4 YEARS

YOU WILL NEED ■ Small quantity of double knitting (sport) yarn in each colour: Pink – A, Yellow – B, Turquoise – C, Purple – D, Red – E, Natural – F, Orange – G ■ 1 pair of 3.5 mm (US 4) knitting needles ■ 1 pair of 4 mm (US 5) knitting needles ■ Large darning needle

Tension (Gauge)
Using 4 mm (US 5) needles, 20 sts and 26 rows to 10 cm (4 in) (st st).

Using 3.5 mm (US 4) needles and yarn A, cast on 40 (46) sts. Work 10 (12) rows k 1, p 1, rib. Change to 4 mm (US 5) needles and yarn B. Work 2 (4) rows st st.

Stripes
Work 2 rows in yarn C, 2 rows in yarn D, 2 rows in yarn C, 2 rows in yarn D.
Change to yarn B and work 2 (4) rows st st.

Square pattern
K 4 in yarn E, k 4 in yarn F to end of row.
Next row: p 4 in yarn F, p 4 in yarn E to end.
Repeat last 2 rows 1 more time.

Stripes
Work 2 rows in yarn A, 2 rows in yarn G, 2 rows in yarn A.

Square pattern
K 4 in yarn F, k 4 in yarn E to end.
Next row: p 4 in yarn E, p 4 in yarn F to end.
Repeat last 2 rows 1 more time.
Change to yarn B and work 2 (4) rows st st.

Stripes
Work 2 rows in yarn C, 2 rows in yarn D, 2 rows in yarn C, 2 rows in yarn D.
Change to yarn B and work 2 (4) rows st st.
Change to 3.5 mm (US 4) needles and yarn G. Work 10 (12) rows k 1, p 1, rib.
Cast (bind) off.

TO MAKE UP
With right sides together, sew up the seams using backstitch. Turn right side out.

Busy Bee Slippers

THESE FUN SLIPPERS FIT CHILDREN AGED 18–24 MONTHS

YOU WILL NEED ■ *3.5 mm (E) crochet hook* ■ *40 (1½ oz) black double knitting (sport) cotton* ■ *Scissors* ■ *40 g (1½ oz) yellow double knitting (sport) cotton* ■ *Tape measure* ■ *Large darning needle* ■ *10 g (1½ oz) white double knitting (sport) cotton* ■ *10 g (½ oz) light blue double knitting (sport) cotton*

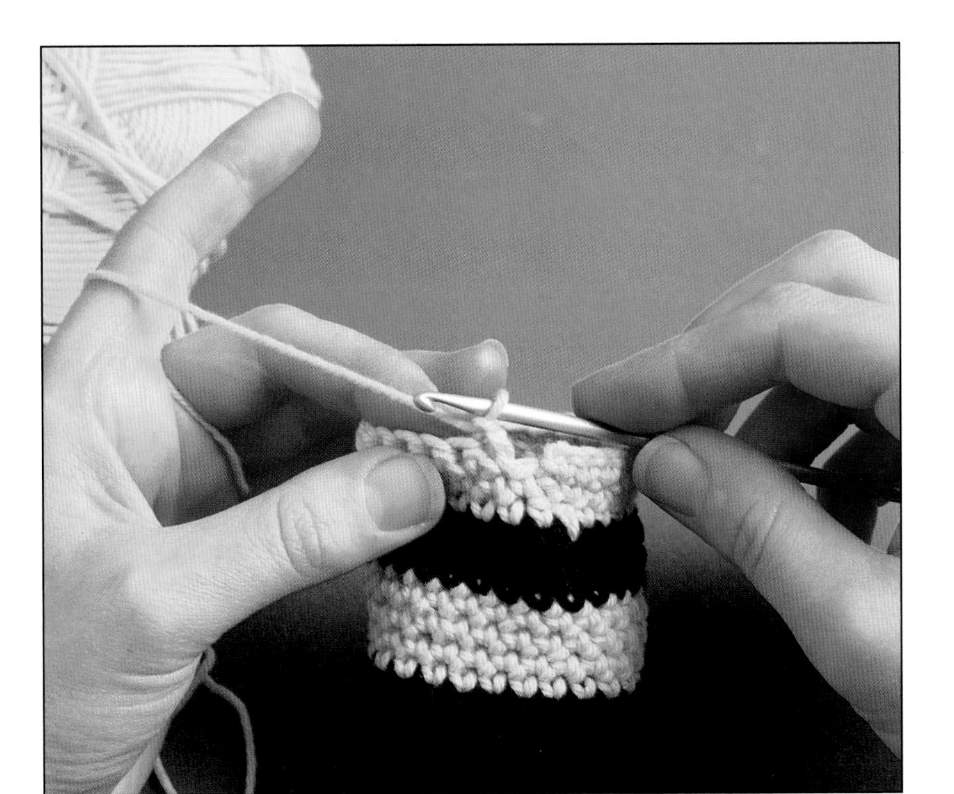

MAIN SLIPPER

Starting at the toe end of the slipper, use black cotton to work the bee's head as follows:

1st row: 3 ch, join into a ring with 1 ss in 1st chain, 1 ch, 6 dc (sc) into ring. Close with 1 ss in first st.
2nd row: 2 ch, 2 dc (sc) in each of next 6 sts, ss in first st.
3rd row: 2 ch, 2 dc (sc) in each of next 12 sts, ss in first st.
4th row: 2 ch, 1 dc (sc) in each of next 24 sts, ss in first st.
Repeat 4th row five more times.
10th row: Cut black cotton and join yellow cotton to work bee's body as follows:
Repeat 4th row four times.
14th row: Cut yellow cotton and join black cotton; using black cotton work as follows:
Repeat 4th row three times.
17th row: Cut black cotton and cast (bind) off last st. Rejoin yellow cotton 12 sts away from last black stitch. This is the centre front of the slipper. Using yellow cotton, work 2 ch, 1 dc (sc) in each of next 24 sts, 1 ch, turn. Now work back along this row as follows:
18th row: 1 dc (sc) in each of next 24 sts, 1 ch, turn. Repeat 18th row twice more.
21st row: Cut yellow cotton and join black cotton; using black cotton work 1 dc (sc) in each of next 24 sts, 1 ch, turn. Repeat 21st row twice more.
24th row: Cut black cotton and join yellow cotton; using yellow cotton work 1 dc (sc) in each of next 24 sts, 1 ch, turn. Repeat 24th row three more times.
28th row: Cut yellow cotton and join black cotton; using black cotton work 1 dc (sc) in each of next 24 sts, 1 ch, turn.
29th row: 1 dc (sc) in each of next 8 sts, miss 1 st, 1 dc (sc) in each of next 6 sts, miss 1 st, 1 dc (sc) in each of next 8 sts, 1 ch, turn.
30th row: 1 dc (sc) in each of next 7 sts, miss 1 st, 1 dc (sc) in next st, miss 1 st, 1 dc (sc) in next 2 sts, miss 1 st, 1 dc (sc) in next st, miss 1 st, 1 dc (sc) in last 7 sts. Cast (bind) off leaving a 20 cm (8 in) end.
Turn slipper inside out and stitch in all ends. Repeat rows 1–30 for 2nd slipper.

EYES

(Make 4 alike)
Using black cotton, work bee's eyes as follows:
1st step: 3 ch, ss in first chain to form ring, 1 ch, 5 dc (sc) into ring, ss in first st.

2nd step: Cut black cotton and join white cotton. Work 1 ss in each of next 6 sts. Cast (bind) off last st leaving a 20 cm (8 in) end of cotton to stitch eye to head.

WINGS

(Make 4 alike)
Using light blue cotton, work bee's wings as follows:
1st step: 3 ch, join into a ring with 1 ss in first ch. 1 ch, 5 dc (sc) into ring, ss in first st.
2nd step: 1 ch, 2 dc (sc) in first st, 1 dtr and 1 tr (dc) in next st, 1 tr (dc), 2 dtrs, 1 tr (dc) in next st, 1 dtr and 1 tr (dc) in next st, 2 dc (sc) in last st, ss in first st, 2 ch, cast (bind) off, leaving a 15 cm (6 in) end.

TO MAKE UP

Stitch eyes to bee's head using the 20 cm (8 in) ends of cotton still attached to each eye. Stitch wings to bee's body using the 15 cm (6 in) ends of cotton still attached to each wing. Position wings at beginning of the first black stripe up from bee's head and about 1.5 cm (5/8 in) either side of the centre front.

Lastly, using the 20 cm (8 in) end of cotton still attached to the back end of the slipper, stitch up the back opening.

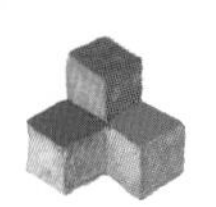

Cutie Bootees

MAKE THESE SOFT BOOTEES FOR AN 8 TO 14-MONTH-OLD BABY

YOU WILL NEED ■ *Tracing paper* ■ *Ruler* ■ *Pencil* ■ *White paper* ■ *18 × 115 cm (7 × 45 in) main fabric* ■ *Pins* ■ *Scissors* ■ *10 × 32 cm (4 × 12½ in) velvet fabric* ■ *10 × 32 cm (4 × 12½ in) foam, 1 cm (3/8 in) thick* ■ *Felt-tip pen* ■ *Needle and thread* ■ *2.72 m (3 yd) of 1.5 cm (5/8 in) wide reversible ribbon* ■ *Tape measure* ■ *Coloured pencil* ■ *Iron*

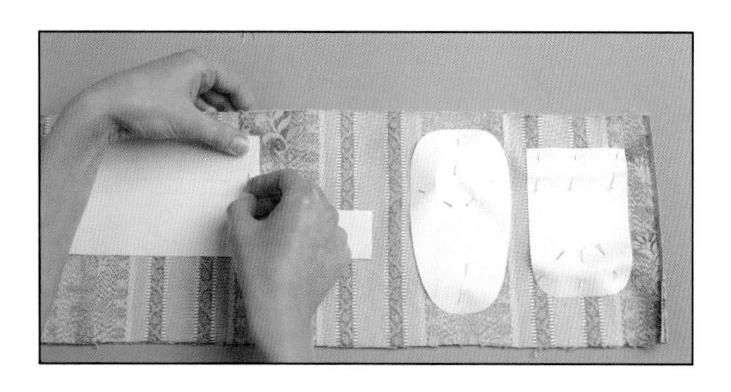

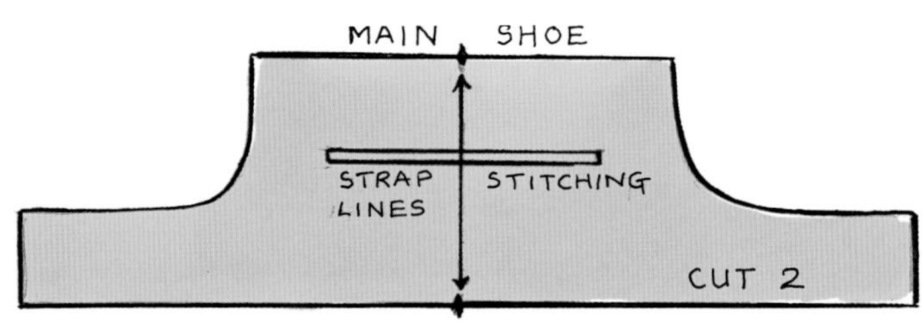

1 Scale up the templates using tracing paper. Seam allowances are included. Transfer to white paper, marking the grain lines and notch positions. Fold the main fabric in half by placing selvages together. Lay all pattern pieces on the fabric, making sure grain lines run parallel to the selvages. Pin and cut out pieces.

Mark the notch positions with a snip in the fabric. Fold the velvet fabric in half and pin sole pattern on. Cut out and notch. Place sole pattern on foam. Using a felt-tip pen, draw around pattern twice. Cut out, just inside the pen line.

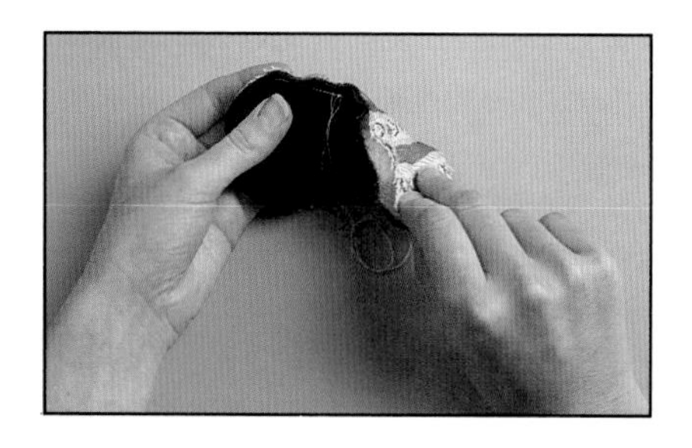

2 Lay the main fabric sole wrong side up. Place foam sole onto it and top with the velvet fabric sole, right side up. Pin and tack (baste) all 3 pieces together. Sew all the way around, 5 mm (3/16 in) from the edge.

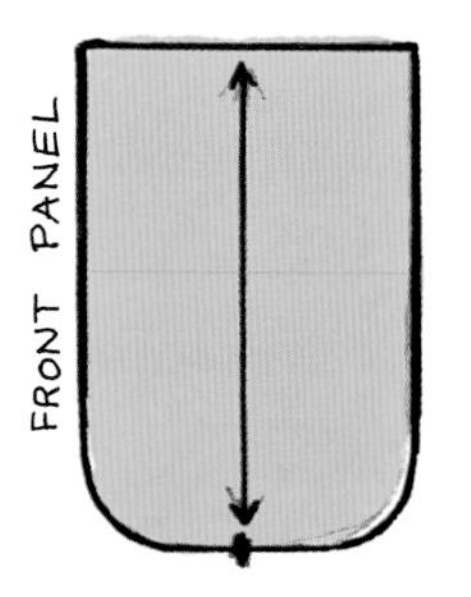

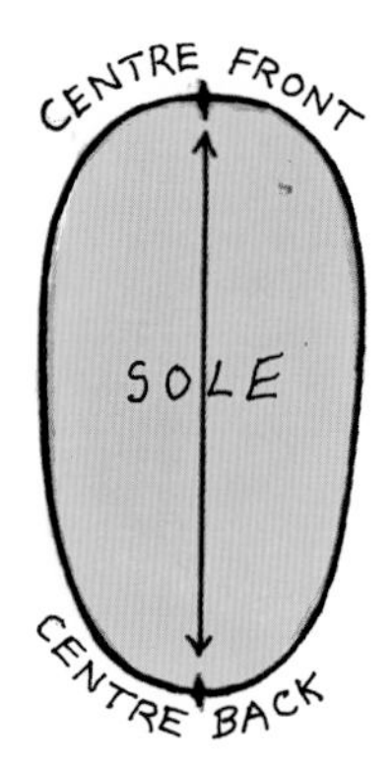

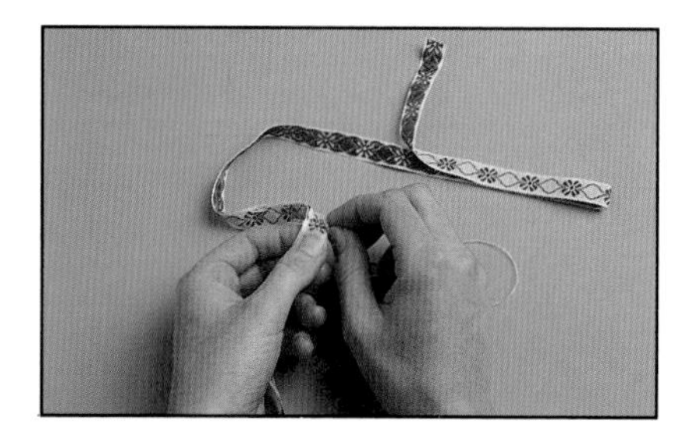

3 For each bootee, cut a piece of ribbon to 112 cm (42 in). Turn each end back 26 cm (10¼ in) (wrong sides together). Tack (baste) and sew along both edges.

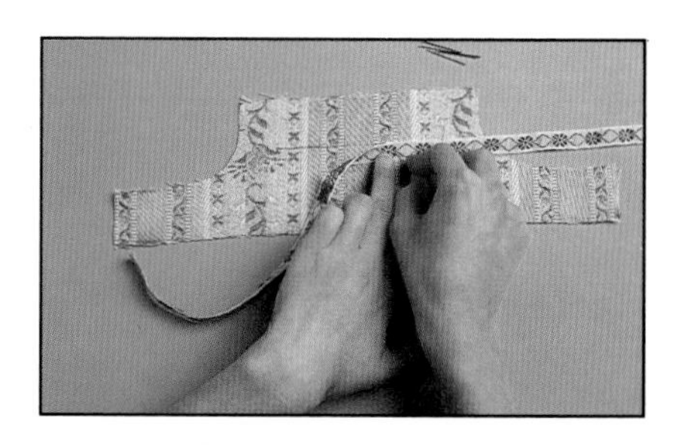

4 On main shoe piece mark a line with coloured pencil to indicate where bootee strap is to be stitched (see template). Fold strap in half to find the centre. Match this point with the centre back line of main shoe piece. Pin strap along pencil line, with both pieces having right sides up. Sew strap in place along the top and bottom edges. Remove the pins.

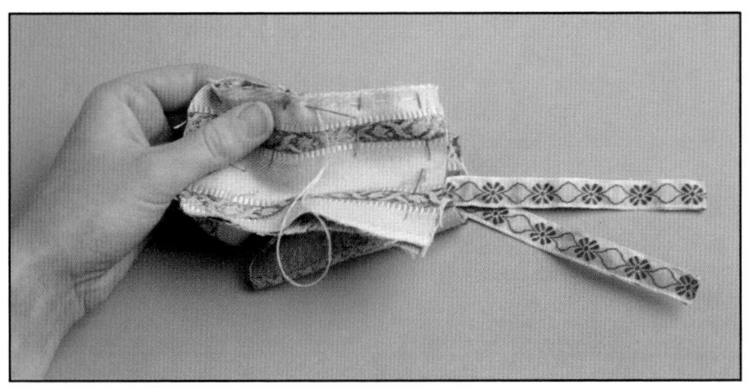

5 On the main shoe piece, neaten the centre front edges with zigzag stitch. Fold the main shoe piece in half, right sides together. Sew the centre front seams together, 1 cm (3/8 in) from the edge. Press the seam open.

Pin the front panel to the main shoe piece. Match the centre front positions. Tack (baste) and sew 6 mm (1/4 in) from edge. Neaten the edge with zigzag stitch.

6 Turn the upper shoe's unfinished edge in 1 cm (3/8 in) to wrong side. Tack (baste) into position. Neaten with a length of ribbon measuring 24 cm (9½ in). Tack (baste) ribbon into place. Sew along top and bottom edges of the ribbon. Remove all the tacking (basting) threads.

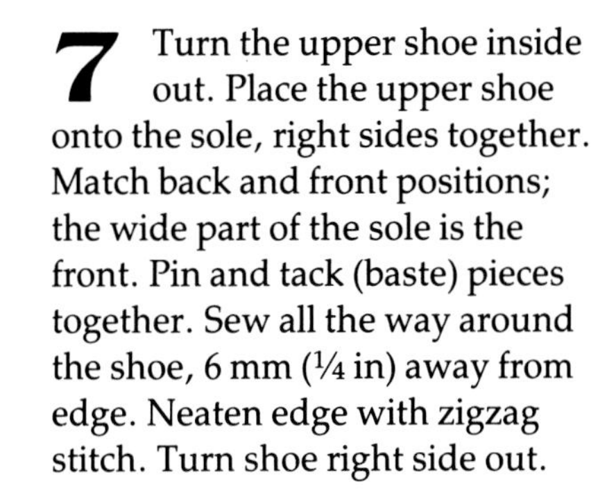

7 Turn the upper shoe inside out. Place the upper shoe onto the sole, right sides together. Match back and front positions; the wide part of the sole is the front. Pin and tack (baste) pieces together. Sew all the way around the shoe, 6 mm (1/4 in) away from edge. Neaten edge with zigzag stitch. Turn shoe right side out.

Padders

SOFT AND COMFORTABLE, THESE PADDERS ARE MORE DURABLE THAN BOOTEES

YOU WILL NEED ■ *Pencil* ■ *White paper* ■ *Tape measure* ■ *Scissors* ■ *0.5 m (½ yd) of fabric for the padders* ■ *0.5 m (½ yd) of contrasting fabric for the lining* ■ *Pins* ■ *Needle and thread* ■ *Iron* ■ *Narrow elastic* ■ *1 m (40 in) ribbon, 1 cm (⅜ in) wide*

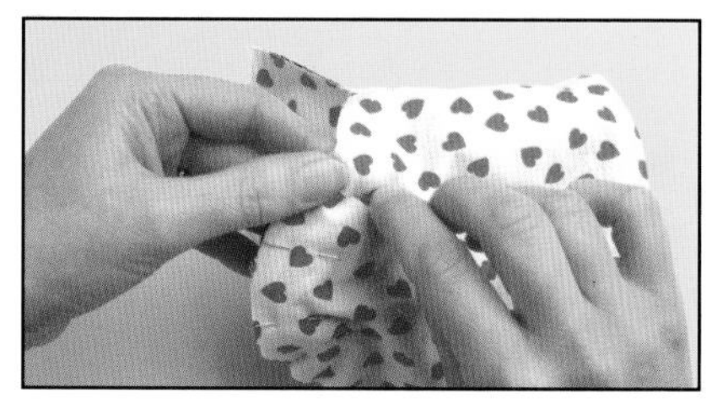

3 Place the wrong sides of the outer and lining bases together and tack (baste). Find the centre of the padder and base and pin together. Continue to pin around the base. Tack (baste) and sew leaving a 1.5 cm (⅝ in) seam allowance.

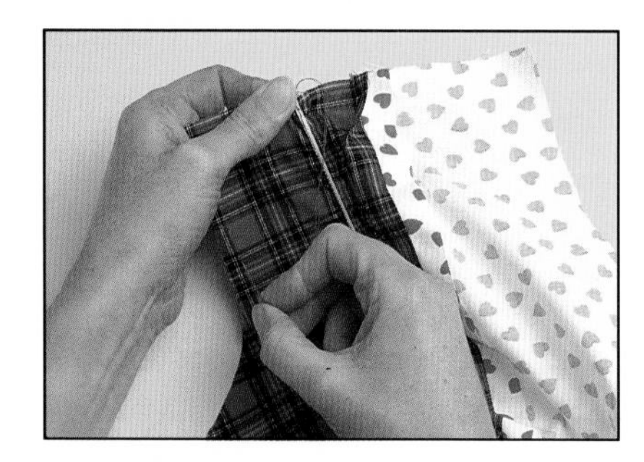

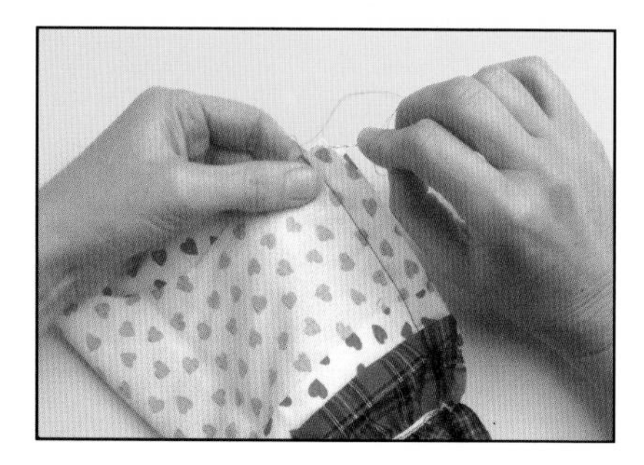

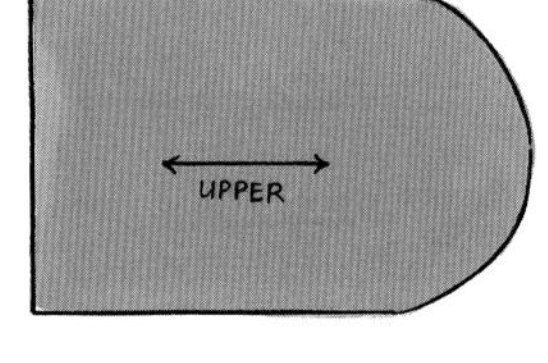

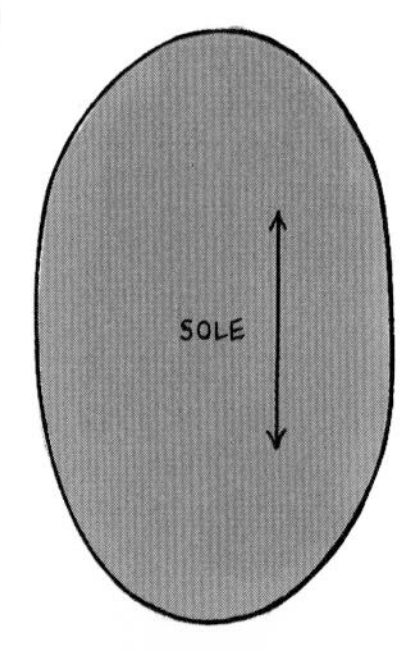

1 Using the templates, cut out a pattern in paper, adjusting the height of the curve and the length of the base to fit the baby's foot. Using this pattern, cut out 2 tops and 2 bases from each of the fabrics (8 pieces).

With right sides together, pin and tack (baste) the lining to the outer fabric along the long edge. Sew leaving a 1.5 cm (⅝ in) seam allowance. Press open. Place the elastic 3.5 cm (1¼ in) from the seam on the wrong side of the outer fabric. Sew the elastic in place, stretching it as it is sewn.

2 Pin and tack (baste) the side seams together. Sew together leaving a 1.5 cm (⅝ in) seam allowance. Fold the padder with wrong sides together and pin the two raw edges together. Tack (baste) the edges.

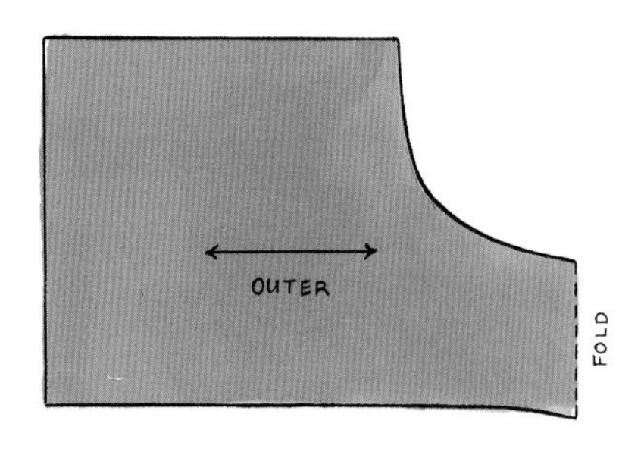

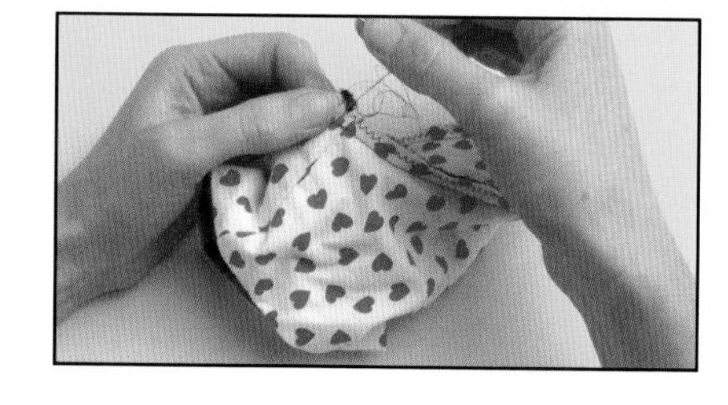

4 Using zigzag stitch, sew around the base and trim the seam. Turn out. Sew the ribbon at the back of the padder on the elastic line. Bring it to the front and tie into a bow.

Hand **P**ainted **S**tretchsuit

PUT A LITTLE LIFE AND COLOUR INTO YOUR NEWBORN CHILD'S STRETCHSUIT

YOU WILL NEED ■ *Paper* ■ *Plain stretchsuit* ■ *Paintbrushes* ■ *Fabric paints in several colours* ■ *Iron*

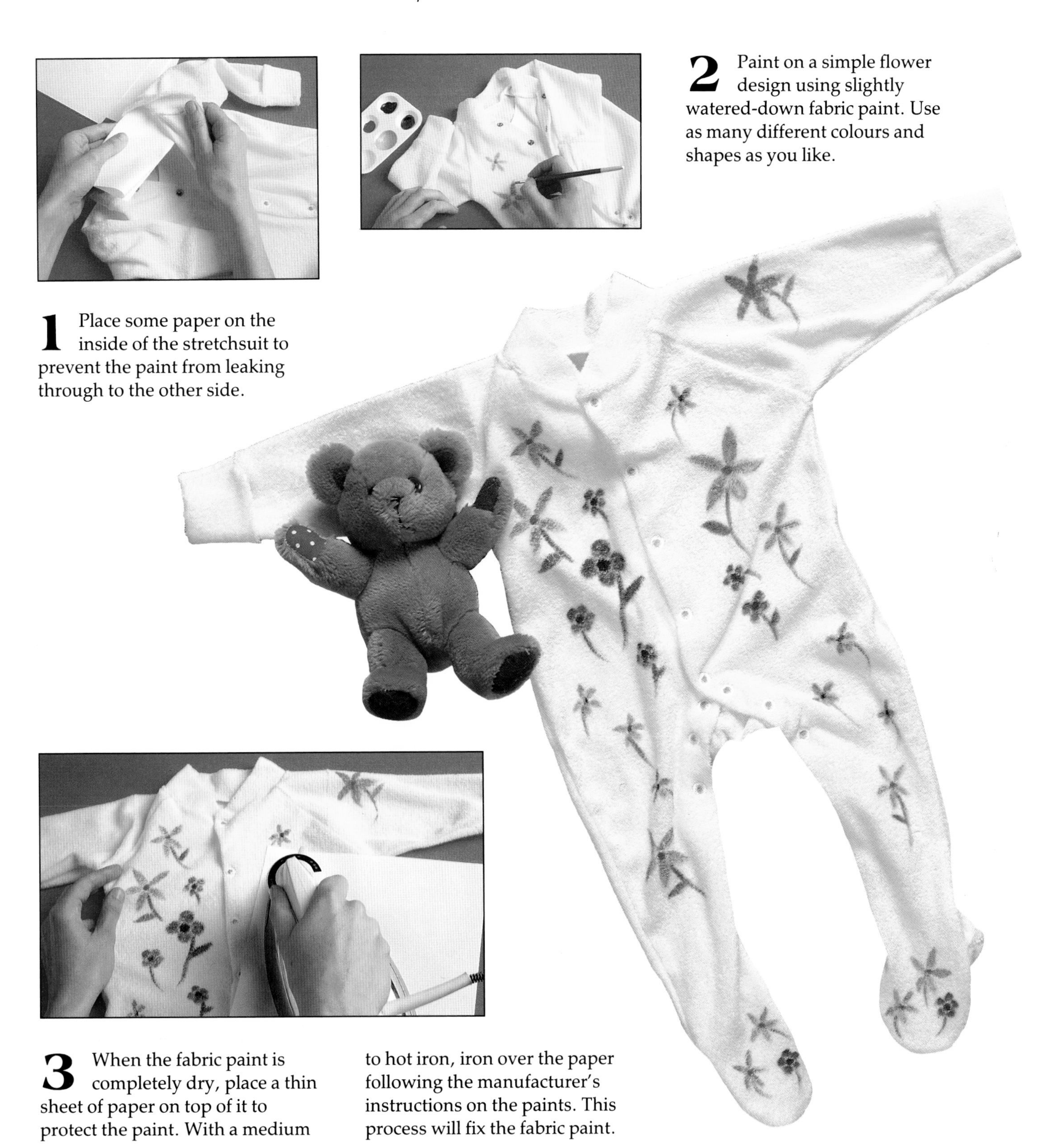

2 Paint on a simple flower design using slightly watered-down fabric paint. Use as many different colours and shapes as you like.

1 Place some paper on the inside of the stretchsuit to prevent the paint from leaking through to the other side.

3 When the fabric paint is completely dry, place a thin sheet of paper on top of it to protect the paint. With a medium to hot iron, iron over the paper following the manufacturer's instructions on the paints. This process will fix the fabric paint.

Sweetheart **S**hoes

THESE IRRESISTIBLE SHOES ARE VERY EASY TO MAKE

YOU WILL NEED ■ *2 squares of 23 × 23 cm (9 × 9 in) blue felt* ■ *Pins* ■ *Pencil* ■ *Pinking shears* ■ *Square of 23 × 23 cm (9 × 9 in) lilac felt* ■ *Needle and thread* ■ *Iron* ■ *Red stranded embroidery thread* ■ *Small sharp scissors* ■ *45 cm (18 in) red ribbon, 3 mm (1/8 in) wide* ■ *Scrap of red felt*

1 Fold the blue felt squares diagonally in half and pin together. Using the template as a guide, draw the shoe upper on 1 half of each piece and cut out with pinking shears. Cut out 2 shoe soles from lilac felt. Pin the uppers together in pairs and then stitch along the centre front and centre back edges, taking a 1 cm (3/8 in) seam allowance.

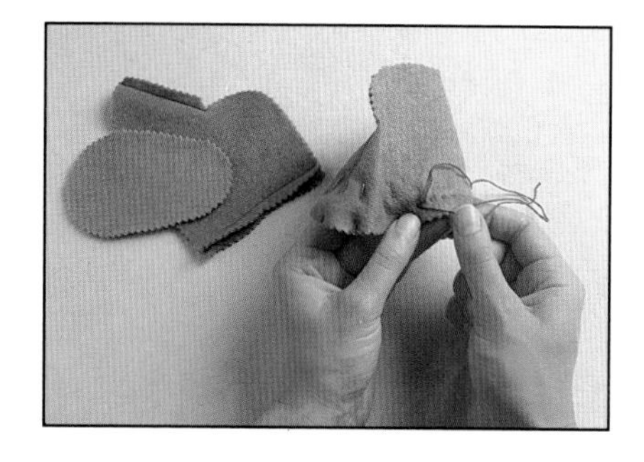

2 Press the seams open. Turn the shoe uppers right side out. Pin the uppers to the soles matching the seams to the dots. Sew together taking a 1 cm (3/8 in) seam allowance using stranded embroidery thread.

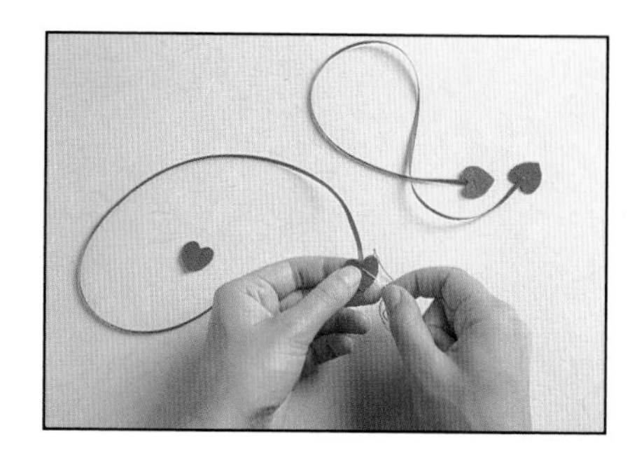

3 Cut the ribbon in half. Cut 4 hearts from red felt and sew each heart securely to the ends using 2 strands of red stranded embroidery thread. Sew the centre of each ribbon to the back seam 3.5 cm (1½ in) below the upper edge. Turn down this edge as a cuff. Tie the ribbon in a bow at the front. Sew the bow to the shoe.

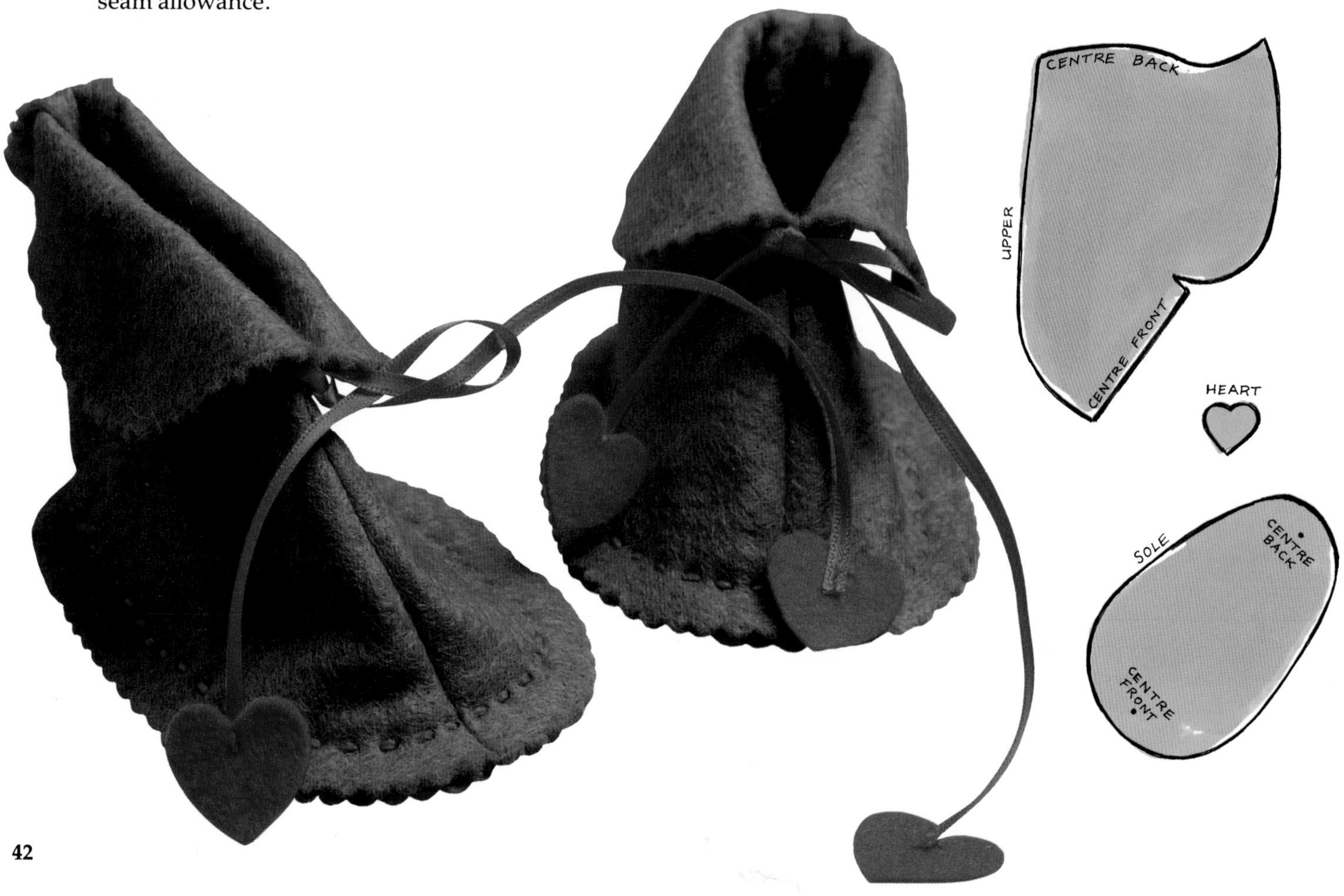

Pompon Decorations

POMPONS CAN BE USED TO LIVEN UP ALMOST ANYTHING!

YOU WILL NEED ■ *Pencil* ■ *Something circular to draw round, e.g. spice jar, small glass* ■ *Stiff card* ■ *Scissors* ■ *Oddments of yarn* ■ *Ruler* ■ *Large darning needle*

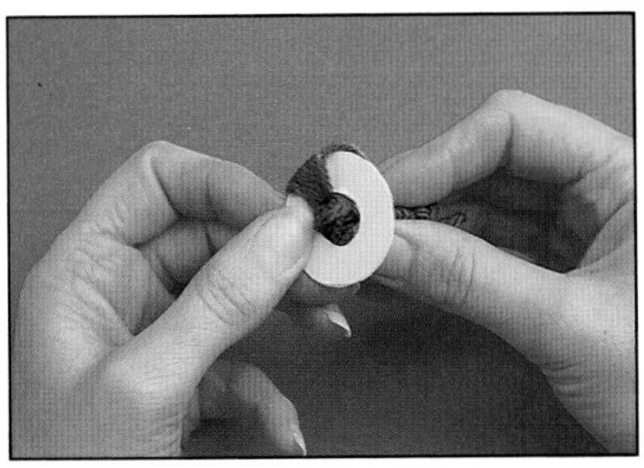

1 Draw around your circular object onto the stiff card. The circle will define the final size of the pompon. Cut out 2 identical circles, then cut a slightly smaller circle out of the centre of each so that you are left with 2 rings. Place them on top of each other. Wind a long piece of yarn into a ball, small enough to go through the hole in the middle. Start winding the yarn around the 2 rings, threading it through the middle. Keep winding until the hole has been completely filled.

2 Carefully push one blade of the scissors between the 2 pieces of card and cut the yarn all the way around the outer edge of the ring.

3 Once this is done, carefully separate the two cards, tie some yarn tightly around the middle of the pompon and knot. Remove the card.

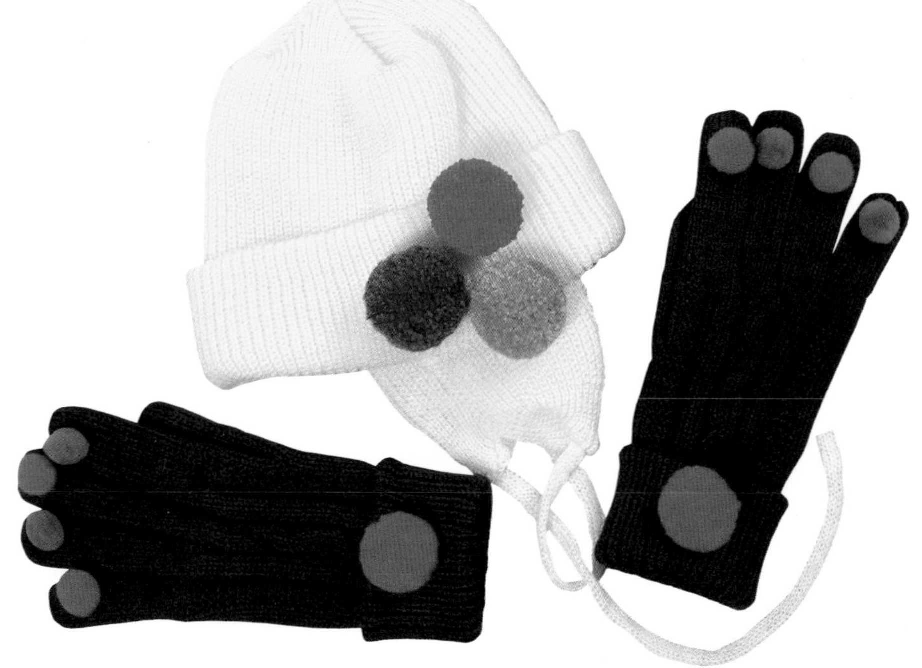

4 To decorate the hat, cut 6 rings of card 4 cm (1½ in) in diameter. Following the instructions given above, make 3 pompons in different colours. When tying the middle of each pompon, leave one long end of the yarn. Use this to sew into the hat. Position the pompons on the side of the hat and sew into place.

5 To decorate the gloves, cut 20 rounds of card 1.5 cm (⅝ in) in diameter. Following the instructions above, make 5 pompons in one colour and 5 in a contrasting colour. Sew each pompon onto the end of each finger, alternating the colours. It is helpful to push something into the fingers of the gloves to help prevent sewing into the back. Make 2 further pompons using a 3 cm (1¼ in) diameter card. Sew onto the cuff of each glove.

Child's Jacket

ANY 1 OR 2-YEAR-OLD WOULD LOOK GREAT IN THIS CHINESE-STYLE JACKET

YOU WILL NEED ■ Tracing paper ■ Tape measure ■ Pencil ■ Scissors ■ 75 × 115 cm (30 × 45 in) fabric ■ Pins ■ Needle and thread ■ Iron ■ 2.37 m (2 2/3 yd) of 2 cm (3/4 in) wide satin bias binding ■ 3 × 22 mm (7/8 in) button moulds (optional)

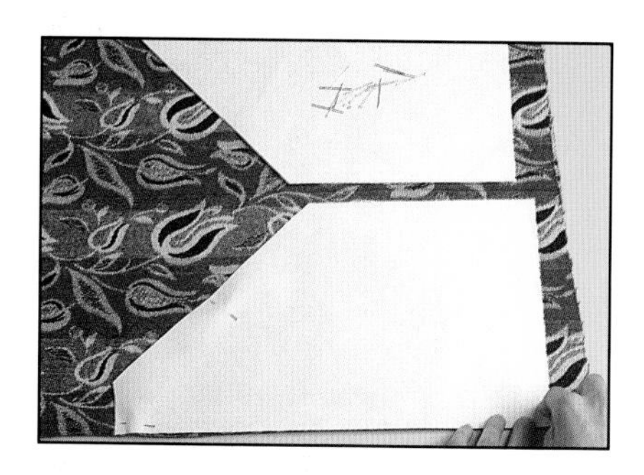

1 Trace the templates and scale them up to the size required. To find this, measure your baby from the back of the neck to the waist and scale up the template accordingly. A 1 cm (3/8 in) seam allowance is included on all template edges.

Fold the fabric in half with the selvages together. Place the centre back edge of the back jacket pattern piece onto the fold. Place the sleeve and front jacket pattern pieces on the fabric, ensuring that grain lines (the double arrowed lines marked on templates) run parallel to the selvages. Pin and cut out all the pieces. Snip the fabric to mark notch positions.

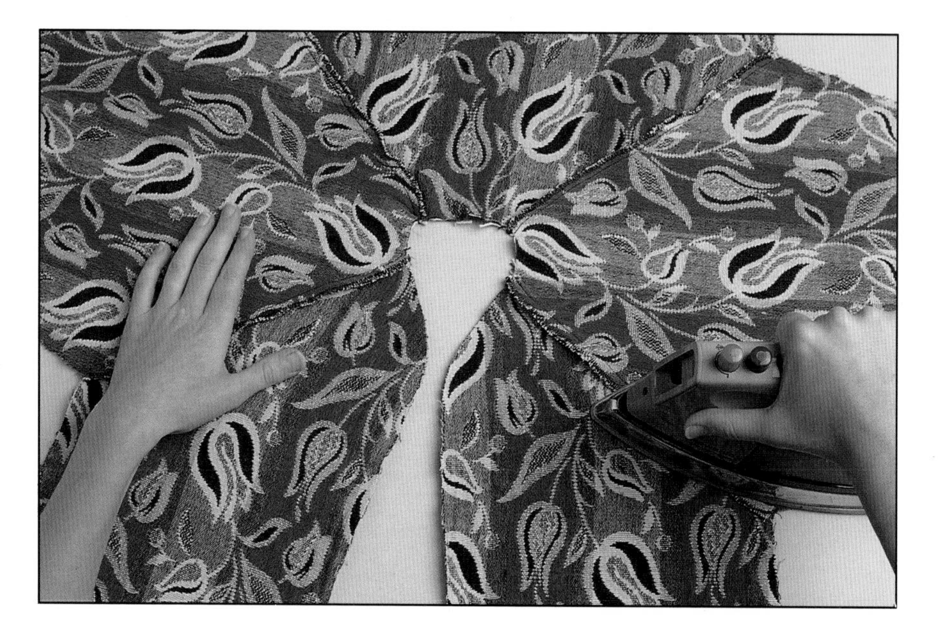

2 Pin sleeve to back, right sides together, along raglan style line, matching notches. Sew along this line. Neaten edge with zigzag stitch. Press seam towards back jacket. Repeat for the other sleeve. Pin front to sleeve, right sides together, along raglan style line. Sew along this line. Neaten edge with zigzag stitch. Press seam towards front jacket. Repeat with remaining front piece.

FRONT
CUT 2

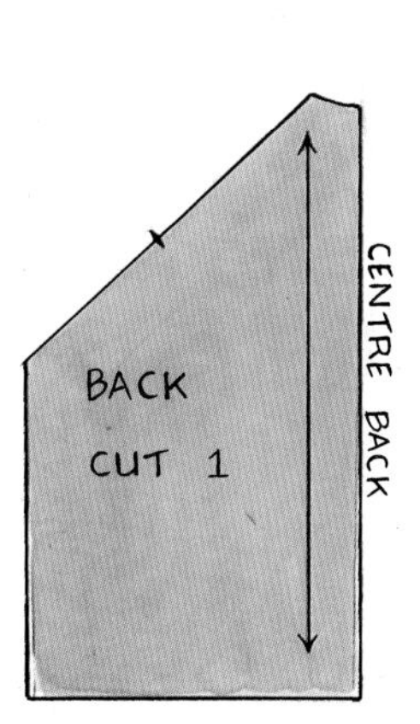

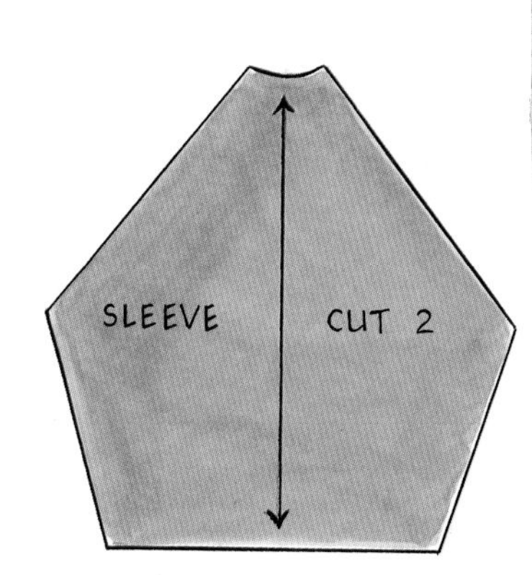

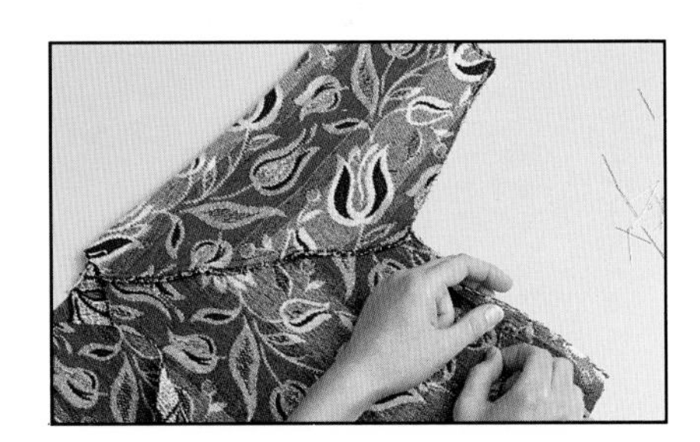

3 Pin front and back jacket pieces, right sides together, along sleeve and side seams. Starting at end of sleeve and working towards the underarm seam, sew together. Continue down side seam to end of jacket. Snip at underarm point. Neaten edge with zigzag stitch. Repeat with other side of jacket.

4 To finish the jacket edges, cut a length of satin bias binding measuring 185 cm (74 in). Open out one of the folded edges of the binding. Starting at the centre back of jacket hem, pin and tack (baste) binding to jacket, right sides together, all the way around the edge until you reach where you started. Take care not to stretch the fabric, especially around the corners. Sew in place 1 cm (3/8 in) from the edge.

5 Turn the bias binding over to the wrong side of the work. Pin and tack (baste) binding down, all the way around the jacket. Top stitch into place. Remove all tacking (basting) threads. To finish the sleeve edges, cut a length of satin bias binding measuring 26 cm (10½ in). Work as for the jacket edges and repeat for remaining sleeve.

6 Cover the 3 button moulds with matching fabric, following the manufacturer's instructions. Make 3 buttonholes (on the right side for girls or the left side for boys), each measuring 2.5 cm (1 in). Sew on the buttons.

Bow-Tie T-Shirt

IT'S EASY TO SMARTEN UP A PLAIN T-SHIRT USING FABRIC PAINTS

YOU WILL NEED ■ *Scissors* ■ *Large piece of card* ■ *Cotton T-shirt* ■ *Tracing paper* ■ *Pencil* ■ *Fine black fabric pen* ■ *Green, orange and pink fabric paints* ■ *Paintbrushes* ■ *Iron*

1 Cut a piece of card to the size of the T-shirt and slip it inside in order to give a firm base and to prevent the paint from bleeding through to the back.

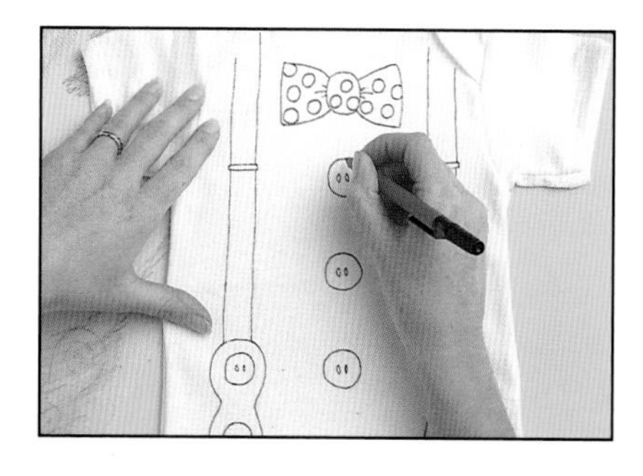

2 Using the templates as a guide, lay the tracing paper over the T-shirt and draw on the design to fit the shirt. Transfer the design to the T-shirt by reversing the tracing paper and scribbling over the lines. Draw over the outline in black fabric pen.

3 Fill in the design with the brightly coloured fabric paints. Do not take too much paint onto the brush each time, especially when painting details.

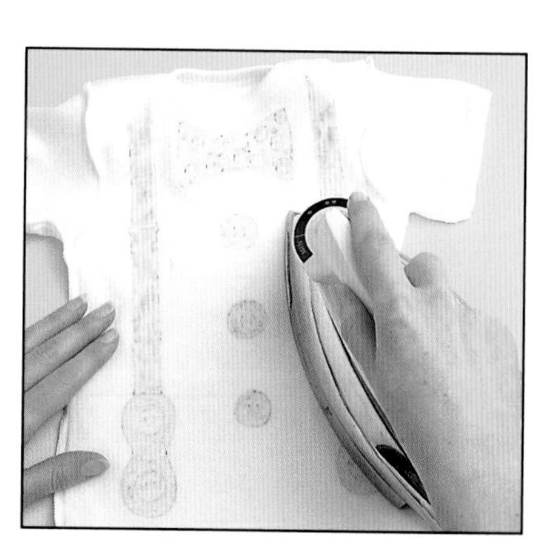

4 Once the paints are dry, turn the T-shirt inside out and press on the inside to fix the paint, as specified in the manufacturer's instructions.

Poppy Hat

THIS FLOWERY HAT IS PERFECT FOR LONG SUMMER DAYS

YOU WILL NEED ■ *Pencil* ■ *White paper* ■ *Scissors* ■ *Ruler* ■ *Pieces of brown, red and green felt* ■ *Absorbent cotton balls* ■ *Needle and thread* ■ *Straw hat*

1 To make the petals, draw a shape 6 × 4 cm (2¼ × 1½ in) at the widest point and cut out of the paper. Using this pattern, cut out 6 petals in the red felt. Cut 2 leaf shapes from green felt. To create the centre of the poppy, cut a 6 cm (2¼ in) square of brown felt and another length of brown felt 2 × 5 cm (¾ × 2 in) with a small fringe cut down one length. Lay a small absorbent cotton ball in the centre of the brown felt square and draw the felt up around it. Stitch neatly in place.

2 Wrap the fringed piece of brown felt around the centre piece, with the fringe side up. Sew in place and carefully cut off any excess.

3 Sew a small tuck in the narrow part of each of the red petals. Lay each petal against the poppy centre and sew in place. Continue round using all the petals, overlapping each one. Repeat the same process to make the second poppy.

4 Finish by sewing the completed poppies onto one side of the hat. Place a leaf shape on either side of the poppies and sew in place.

Party Pinafore

THIS PRETTY PINAFORE DRESS FITS 1 TO 2-YEAR-OLDS

YOU WILL NEED ■ *Scissors* ■ *Tape measure* ■ *0.5 m (½ yd) of cotton fabric, 115 cm (45 in) wide* ■ *Needle and thread* ■ *Iron* ■ *Pins* ■ *Tailor's chalk*

1 First make the shoulder straps. Cut a 9 cm (3½ in) strip across the width of the fabric. Cut this into 4 equal lengths of 26 cm (10¼ in).

2 Sew the straps together in pairs, with right sides together, leaving 3 cm (1¼ in) open at each end for turning. Press and turn right side out.

3 Cut the remaining fabric in half lengthwise. Mark a 10 cm (4 in) gap in the centre of the top edges of both pieces of fabric.

Gather up the fabric evenly on either side of the central section on both the back and front of the pinafore until it fits the shoulder straps exactly. Pin the straps in position and then sew them in place securely. Sew up the side seams and trim to neaten.

4 Turn up the hem to the length required. Pin and stitch all round. Remove the pins and press the pinafore.

Decorated Hair Band

THIS PRETTY HAIR BAND WILL APPEAL TO CHILDREN OF ALL AGES

YOU WILL NEED ■ *Pencil* ■ *Plain coloured hair band* ■ *6 different coloured yarns* ■ *Scissors* ■ *Large darning needle*

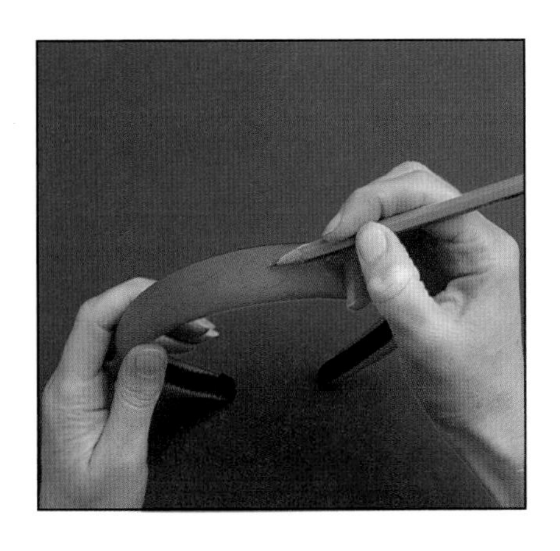

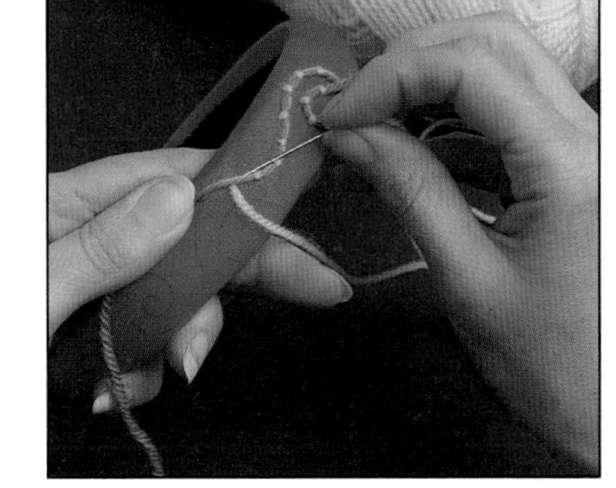

2 To start the embroidery, lay a length of yarn along a pattern line, leaving a long thread at each end. Thread the needle with a contrasting coloured length of yarn and secure the first length of yarn at even intervals with a small stitch into the fabric. Finish by sewing the end into the hair band. Rethread the original yarn and sew each end into the hair band to secure.

1 Using a pencil, draw your design onto the hair band.

3 Following the pattern, use 2 different coloured yarns in the same way, remembering to secure all the ends by sewing them into the hair band. Finish by sewing French knots and small crosses using the last 2 colours.

To sew a French knot, stitch into the fabric at the required position. Hold the thread down with the left thumb and encircle it 2 or 3 times with the threaded needle. Still holding the thread firmly, twist the needle back to the starting point and insert it close to where the original thread emerged. Pull the thread through and secure.

Reversible Dress

CHOOSE CONTRASTING FABRICS TO MAKE TWO DRESSES IN ONE!

YOU WILL NEED ■ *Tape measure* ■ *Pencil* ■ *Paper* ■ *90 × 115 cm (1 yd × 45 in) plain fabric* ■ *122 × 115 cm (48 × 45 in) patterned fabric* ■ *Scissors* ■ *Iron-on interfacing* ■ *Iron* ■ *Needle and thread* ■ *Pins* ■ *Velcro*

1 Scale up the templates to the size required. Find this by measuring from the base of the child's neck to the desired hemline, and add a small seam allowance. Make paper patterns and cut out the pieces from the plain and patterned fabric, shortening the pattern at the dotted line for the plain dress. Also cut out 2 pieces of patterned fabric measuring 18 × 100 cm (6 × 39 in) to make the ruffle.

Iron the interfacing to the wrong side of the pocket. Doublestitch the straight edge and pin and tack (baste) 1.5 cm (⅝ in) around the edge. Stitch to the plain dress front and trim.

2 With right sides together, adjust and pin the ruffle to the lower edge of the patterned dress and stitch 1.5 cm (⅝ in) from edge, stitch again 6 mm (¼ in) from edge, press towards the top.

3 Double stitch the 2 ruffle pieces together along the side seam, trim, fold over and stitch to the hem. Gather stitch 6 mm (¼ in) from top of ruffle.

4 Pin both garments right sides together. Stitch the back edges. Double stitch the neck edges and armholes. Trim.

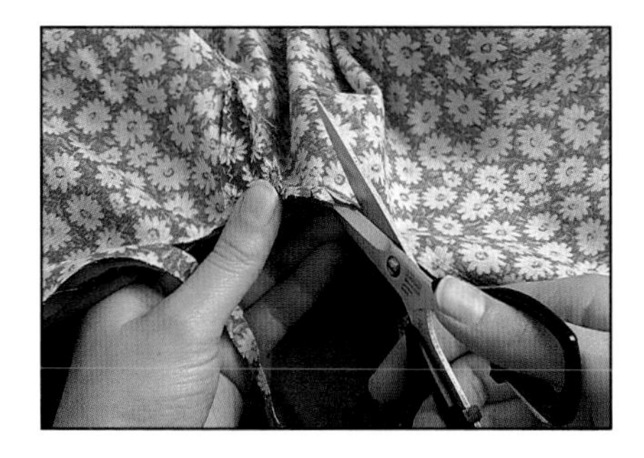

5 Trim and nick the edges to ease the curves. Turn right side out and press the garment.

6 With the patterned dress facing, pull through the plain shoulder edges, pin together and double stitch a 1.5 cm (⅝ in) seam. Press open. Fold the patterned front shoulder seam over the back and neatly hand stitch. Press the dress and sew Velcro to the back edges. Adjust and stitch the hems to finish.

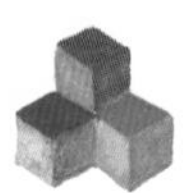

Smocked Dress

SMOCKING BECOMES SIMPLE WHEN WORKED ON A FRESH COTTON GINGHAM

YOU WILL NEED ■ *Tape measure* ■ *Scissors* ■ *Gingham fabric in a 6 mm (1/4 in) check* ■ *Iron* ■ *Needle and thread* ■ *Pins* ■ *Embroidery thread in toning colours*

1 This design can be adapted in order to fit any age or size. Calculating the fabric width you require is best done by working a small, measured practice section and opening it out once you have smocked it. The smocked fabric should cling gently.

Cut out the fabric for the dress, allowing for the smocking, a seam in the back, a generous hem, and a 4 cm (1½ in) allowance at the top. Turn down the top raw edge 4 cm (1½ in) to the wrong side, and press it down along the grain.

2 Starting 4 cm (1½ in) in from the right-hand side and 2 cm (¾ in) down from the folded top, knot a long thread on the upper corner of a light square. Take the needle behind the square and then out at the top left-hand corner.

Continue all the way along until you are 4 cm (1½ in) away from the opposite end. Leave the thread end loose, winding it around a pin to secure it. You will be working through the folded top for a few rows. Work as many rows of gathers as you are going to need for the size of your dress.

3 Draw up the gathers evenly until the tubes of fabric at the front and back are quite firm and lie tightly together. Secure all the thread ends on pins at the left-hand edge, wound in a figure of eight to ensure they cannot come undone.

4 Select your first embroidery colour and use 3 strands of thread. Your first line of smocking should start about 3 squares down and is worked on the front. Working from left to right, start at the top right-hand corner of the first square immediately to the left of the first tube. Knot the end of the thread, and bring the needle through to start working a line of cable stitches. Work a second line, inverting the stitches. Smocking stitches are worked on the surface of and directly behind the tubes. Use honeycomb stitch for the main depth of the work, using the gingham square as the depth of each stitch, and finish with 2 further close lines of cable stitches. The gingham will make it easy to keep straight lines. Vary the colours of your embroidery threads as you work. Oversew the thread securely at the end of each row. If you run out of thread mid-row, secure the thread end lightly on the inside and re-start with a knot behind the tube at which you finished.

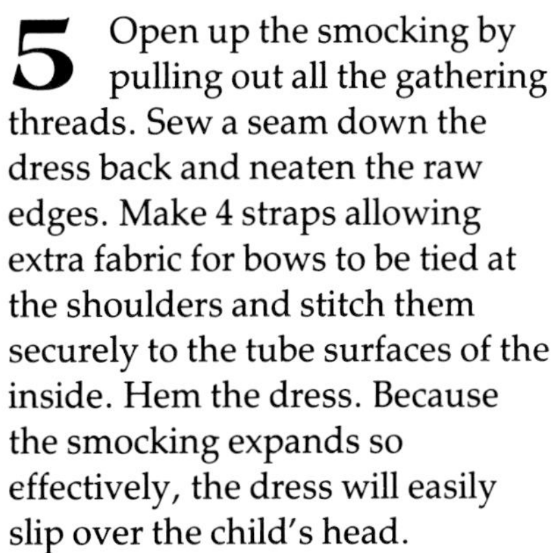

5 Open up the smocking by pulling out all the gathering threads. Sew a seam down the dress back and neaten the raw edges. Make 4 straps allowing extra fabric for bows to be tied at the shoulders and stitch them securely to the tube surfaces of the inside. Hem the dress. Because the smocking expands so effectively, the dress will easily slip over the child's head.

CABLE STITCH

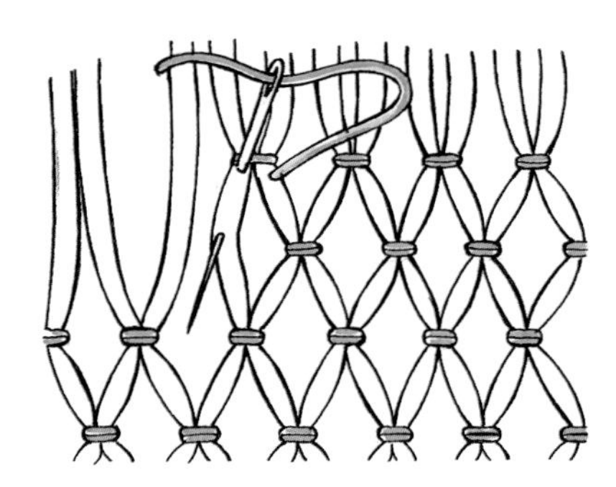

HONEYCOMB STITCH

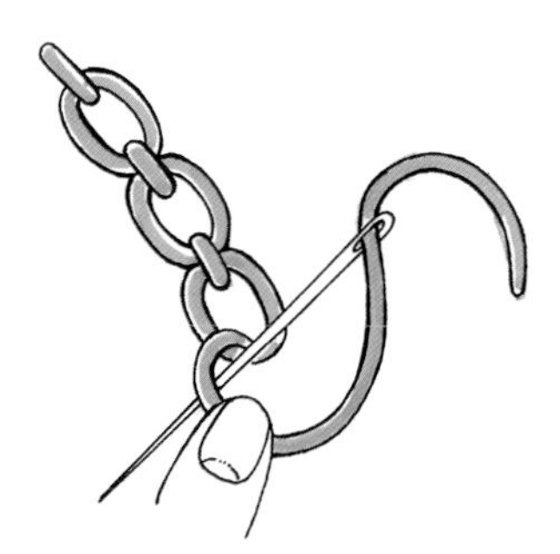

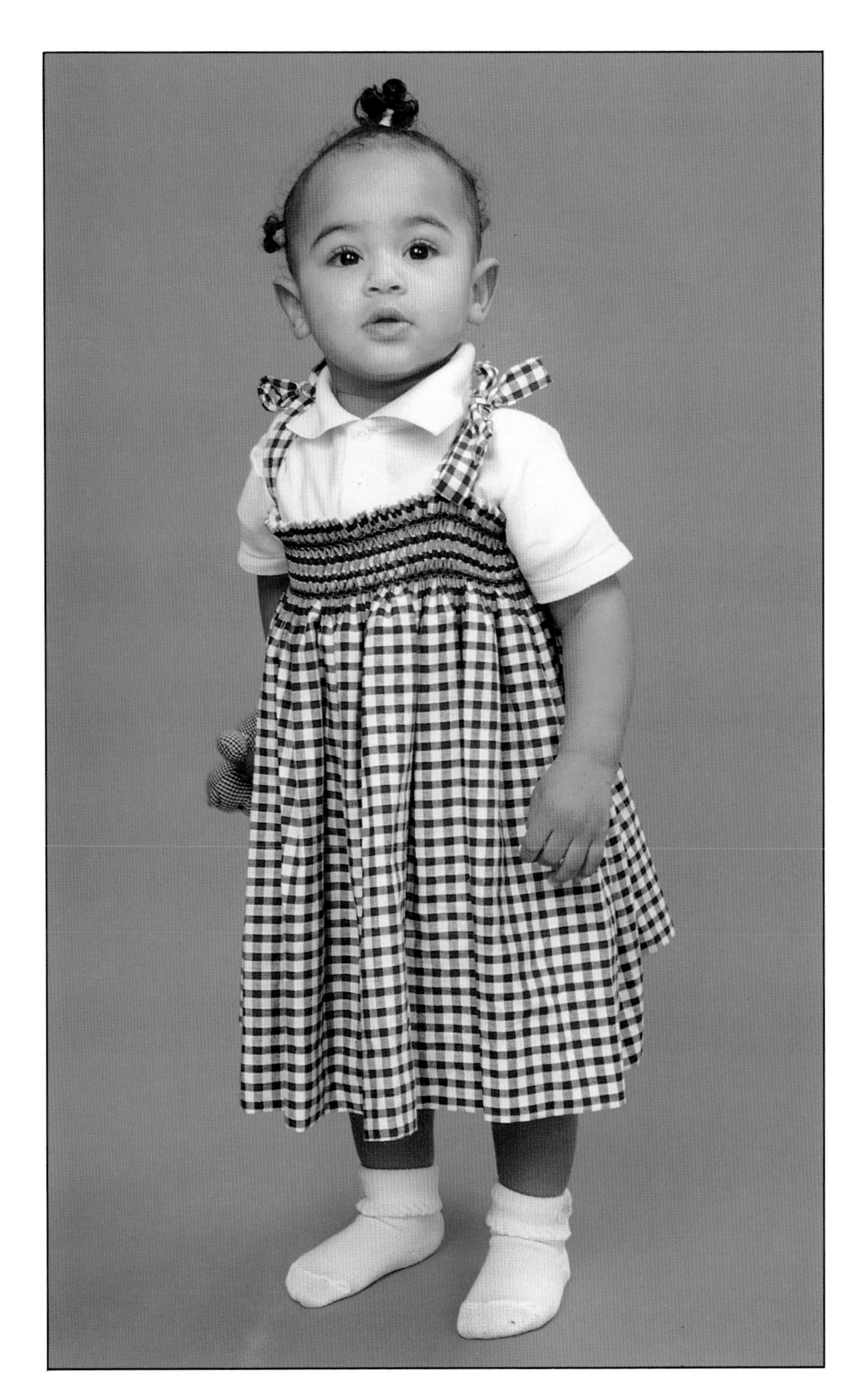

Toddler's Overall

THESE DIMENSIONS ARE FOR A 15-MONTH CHILD, BUT CAN EASILY BE ADJUSTED

YOU WILL NEED ■ *Paper and pencil if you need to re-scale dimensions* ■ *Tape measure* ■ *Strong cotton fabric in a plain colour* ■ *Scissors* ■ *Striped cotton fabric which will be cut on the bias* ■ *Pins* ■ *Needle and thread* ■ *Iron* ■ *Scrap of fabric to co-ordinate with striped fabric*

1 Using the plain cotton fabric, cut 1 front piece 30 × 42 cm (12 × 16½ in), 2 back pieces 30 × 21 cm (12 × 8½ in) and a yoke section 22 × 74 cm (8¾ × 29½ in). Cut 4 undersleeves from striped fabric, each 10 × 21 cm (4 × 8½ in), ensuring that the bias-cut stripes run the correct way.

Pin, tack (baste) and sew the 2 undersleeves to the top front of the overall, right sides together. Trim the seam allowance along the 10 cm (4 in) seam edge to 6 mm (¼ in) and oversew. Press the seam towards the sleeve end.

2 Turn back 5 cm (2 in) on one long edge of each back section and stitch down the raw edges. Placing right sides together, join the neatened edges in a seam, leaving a 9 cm (3½ in) opening. Press flat.

Join the 2 other undersleeve sections to the back section as before. With a pin, mark the centre of the front. Run a gathering thread along the top edge, starting 8 cm (3¼ in) from the undersleeve seams. Gather the back on each side, to 2 cm (¾ in) from the opening.

3 Fold the yoke section across its narrow, vertical width and mark the centre front. Also mark the centre of the yoke running horizontally. Cut an opening vertically in the centre front as far as the horizontal centre. Cut a neck opening 8 cm (3¼ in) in each direction from the centre and 16 cm (6½ in) long, to form a 'T' shape.

Lay all the pieces flat, wrong sides up and with the yoke central, matching the vertical opening on the yoke to the back opening seam and the centre front of the yoke to the centre of the front section. Pin the 4 sleeve ends to the yoke, right sides together.

4 Pulling the gathering threads on the front and back, draw up the sections to fit the yoke. Adjust the gathers evenly and secure. Pin, tack (baste) and stitch the 3 seams. Press the seams flat towards the top, trim the raw edges and oversew them together.

Fold the garment into a 'T' shape, right sides together, and pin and tack (baste) each side and underarm seam in one. Stitch both sides, working a curve at the corner. Check that the undersleeve seam is completely concealed from the outside, then trim the seam and oversew the edges together. Press firmly.

5 Prepare 60 cm (24 in) of 3 cm (1¼ in) wide bias binding from the striped fabric. Enclosing all raw edges, bind the back openings on the yoke by sewing the binding to the yoke right sides together and turning to the inside to hem. Bind the neck in the same way, enclosing the back opening binding ends as you start and finish. Take care not to pucker the yoke at the outer corners of the neck opening. Press firmly.

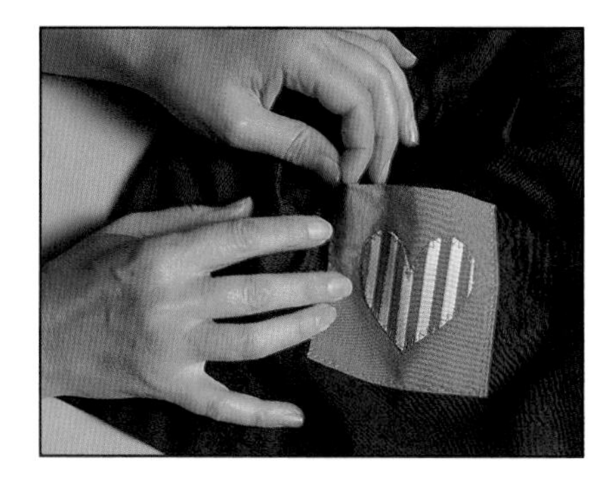

6 Make a small neatened square from the scrap of co-ordinating fabric for a pocket, and appliqué a striped heart to match the undersleeves and bindings. Stitch it to the overall front. Make some ties from striped fabric to tie the neck opening at the back.

Fairy Dress and Wand

THIS OUTFIT IS A DREAM COME TRUE FOR ANY 2–3-YEAR-OLD

YOU WILL NEED For dress: ■ *10 silver satin roses* ■ *Frilly vested petticoat* ■ *Pins* ■ *Needle and thread* ■ *75 cm (30 in) silver sequin strip* ■ *12 small bows made from silver braid* ■ *Rubber-based glue* ■ *Gold and green glitter* ■ *Star sequins in different colours* ■ *Scissors* ■ *1 m (40 in) white and gold ribbon, 2.5 cm (1 in) wide*
For wand: ■ *White card* ■ *Pencil* ■ *Scissors* ■ *Gold spray paint* ■ *Paper glue* ■ *Silver, gold and green glitter mixed together* ■ *Length of silver ribbon* ■ *Green garden cane* ■ *Sticky tape* ■ *Gold metallic strips*

1 Lay the roses around the neck of the dress, spacing them evenly. Pin, and sew on. Remove the pins. Mark the centre front point at the waist with a pin. Lay the sequin strip from the shoulder seam to the pin and pin in place to form a 'V'. Turn the dress wrong side out. Holding the sequin strip tightly against the fabric, slip stitch it in place.

2 Sew a silver braid bow at each end of the sequins and one at the centre of the 'V' at the waistline. Sew the remaining silver bows on the gathered skirt. Using the rubber-based glue, paint a pattern on the sides of the bodice and scatter gold glitter over it. Leave this to dry. Add green glitter dots to the design and a dot between each rose at the neckline using the same technique. Allow to dry thoroughly.

Sew the star sequins in a random fashion in the centre of the bodice. Finally, cut the white and gold ribbon in half and tie each length into a bow, leaving long ends. Decorate the ends by painting down the centre with the glue and sprinkling with the gold glitter. Sew each bow at the waistline on the side seam.

3 To make the wand, use the template to cut 2 star shapes from card. Spray with the gold paint. Leave to dry. Spread glue over the star and sprinkle on the glitter. Start winding the ribbon around the cane, securing the end with sticky tape. When you have covered the cane, cut off any excess; tape in place. Stick the metallic gold strips to the top end.

4 Lay the stick on the wrong side of one star shape and use the sticky tape to secure. Spread paper glue over back of the star. Press the second star shape on top, 'sandwiching' the stick. Make sure the metallic strips do not get caught inside.

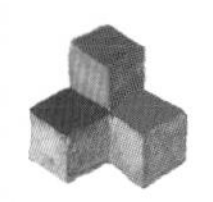

Beetle Hat

THIS LOVABLE BEETLE HAT WILL FIT INFANTS AGED 1–2 YEARS

YOU WILL NEED ■ *3.5 mm (E) and 3 mm (D) crochet hooks* ■ *40 g (1½ oz) black double knitting (sport) cotton* ■ *10 g (½ oz) white double knitting (sport) cotton* ■ *Scissors* ■ *40 g (1½ oz) red double knitting (sport) cotton* ■ *Large darning needle* ■ *Tailor's chalk* ■ *Pins*

HEAD AND BODY

Starting with a 3.5 mm (E) hook and using black cotton, work the beetle's head as follows:

3 ch, join with 1 ss in first ch to form a ring.

1st row: 1 ch, 6 dc (sc) into ring, join with 1 ss.

2nd row: 1 ch, 2 dc (sc) in each of next 5 sts, 1 ch, turn.

3rd row: 1 dc (sc) in each of first 3 sts, 2 dc (sc) in next st, 1 dc (sc) in next 2 sts, 2 dc (sc) in next st, 1 dc (sc) in each of last 3 sts, 1 ch, turn.

4th row: 1 dc (sc) in each of first 3 sts, 2 dc (sc) in next st, 1 dc (sc) in next 4 sts, 2 dc (sc) in next st, 1 dc (sc) in last 3 sts, 1 ch, turn.

5th row: 1 dc (sc) in first 2 sts, 2 dc (sc) in next st, 1 dc (sc) in next 2 sts, 2 dc (sc) in next st, 1 dc (sc) in next 2 sts, 2 dc (sc) in next st, 1 dc (sc) in next 2 sts, 2 dc (sc) in next st, 1 dc (sc) in last 2 sts, 1 ch, turn.

6th row: 1 dc (sc) in each of first 3 sts, 2 dc (sc) in next st, 1 dc (sc) in next 2 sts, 2 dc (sc) in next st, 1 dc (sc) in next 4 sts, 2 dc (sc) in next st, 1 dc (sc) in next 2 sts, 2 dc (sc) in next st, 1 dc (sc) in last 3 sts, 1 ch, turn.

7th row: 1 dc (sc) in each of first 6 sts, 2 dc (sc) in next st, 1 dc (sc) in next 2 sts, 2 dc (sc) in next st, 1 dc (sc) in next 2 sts, 2 dc (sc) in next st, 1 dc (sc) in next 2 sts, 2 dc (sc) in next st, 1 dc (sc) in last 6 sts, 1 ch, turn.

8th row: 1 dc (sc) in each of first 7 sts, 2 dc (sc) in next st, 1 dc (sc) in next 10 sts, 2 dc (sc) in next st, 1 dc (sc) in last 7 sts, 1 ch, turn.

9th row: 1 dc (sc) in each of first 11 sts, 2 dc (sc) in next st, 1 dc (sc) in next 4 sts, 2 dc (sc) in next st, 1 dc (sc) in last 11 sts, 1 ch, turn.

10th row: 1 dc (sc) in each of first 3 sts, 2 dc (sc) in next st, 1 dc (sc) in next 22 sts, 2 dc (sc) in next st, 1 dc (sc) in last 3 sts, 1 ch, turn.

11th row: 1 dc (sc) in each of first 13 sts, 2 dc (sc) in next st, 1 dc (sc) in next 4 sts, 2 dc (sc) in next st, 1 dc (sc) in last 13 sts, 1 ch, turn.

12th row: 1 dc (sc) in each of first 3 sts, 2 dc (sc) in next st, 1 dc (sc) in next 26 sts, 2 dc (sc) in next st, 1 dc (sc) in last 3 sts, 1 ch, turn.

13th row: 1 dc (sc) in each of first 15 sts, 2 dc (sc) in next st, 1 dc (sc) in next 4 sts, 2 dc (sc) in next st, 1 dc (sc) in last 15 sts, 1 ch, turn.

14th row: 1 dc (sc) in each of first 13 sts, 2 dc (sc) in next st, 1 dc (sc) in next 10 sts, 2 dc (sc) in next st, 1 dc (sc) in last 13 sts, 1 ch, turn.

Cut black cotton and join red cotton. Work body as follows:

15th row: 1 dc (sc) in each of next 40 sts, 1 ch, turn.

16th row: Repeat 15th row.

17th row: 1 dc (sc) in each of first 15 sts, 2 dc (sc) in next st, 1 dc (sc) in next 8 sts, 2 dc (sc) in next st, 1 dc (sc) in last 15 sts, 1 ch, turn.

18th row: 1 dc (sc) in each of first 16 sts, 2 dc (sc) in next st, 1 dc (sc) in next 8 sts, 2 dc (sc) in next st, 1 dc (sc) in last 16 sts, 1 ch, turn.

19th row: 1 dc (sc) in each of first 6 sts, 1 ht in each of next 4 sts, 1 tr (dc) in each of next 24 sts, 1 ht in each of next 4 sts, 1 dc (sc) in each of last 6 sts, 1 ch, turn.

20th row: 1 dc (sc) in each of first 4 sts, 2 dc (sc) in next st, 1 dc (sc) in next 34 sts, 2 dc (sc) in next st, 1 dc (sc) in last 4 sts, 1 ch, turn.

21st row: 1 dc (sc) in each of first 5 sts, 1 ht in each of next 5 sts, 1 tr (dc) in each of next 26 sts, 1 ht in each of next 5 sts, 1 dc (sc) in each of last 5 sts, 1 ch, turn.

22nd row: 1 dc (sc) in each of first 17 sts, 2 dc (sc) in next st, 1 dc (sc) in next 10 sts, 2 dc (sc) in next st, 1 dc (sc) in last 17 sts, 1 ch, turn.

23rd row: 1 dc (sc) in each of first 5 sts, 1 ht in next 5 sts, 1 tr (dc) in next 28 sts, 1 ht in next 5 sts, 1 dc (sc) in last 5 sts, 1 ch, turn.

24th row: 1 dc (sc) in each of next 48 sts, 1 ch, turn.

25th row: 1 dc (sc) in each of first 5 sts, 1 ht in each of next 5 sts, 1 tr (dc) in each of next 28 sts, 1 ht in each of next 5 sts, 1 dc (sc) in each of last 5 sts, 1 ch, turn.

26th row: start decreasing to form the back of the beetle. 1 dc (sc) in each of first 18 sts, miss 1 st, 1 dc (sc) in next 10 sts, miss 1 st, 1 dc (sc) in last 18 sts, 1 ch, turn.

27th row: 1 dc (sc) in each of first 5 sts, 1 ht in each of next 5 sts, 1 tr (dc) in each of next 26 sts, 1 ht in each of next 5 sts, 1 dc (sc) in each of last 5 sts, 1 ch, turn.

28th row: 1 dc (sc) in each of first 16 sts, miss 1 st, 1 dc (sc) in each of next 12 sts, miss 1 st, 1 dc (sc) in

each of last 16 sts, 1 ch, turn.
29th row: 1 dc (sc) in each of first 6 sts, 1 ht in each of next 4 sts, 1 tr (dc) in each of next 24 sts, 1 ht in each of next 4 sts, 1 dc (sc) in each of last 6 sts, 1 ch, turn.
30th row: 1 dc (sc) in each of first 15 sts, miss 1 st, 1 dc (sc) in each of next 12 sts, miss 1 st, 1 dc (sc) in each of last 15 sts, 1 ch, turn.
31st row: 1 dc (sc) in each of first 14 sts, miss 1 st, 1 dc (sc) in each of next 12 sts, miss 1 st, 1 dc (sc) in each of last 14 sts, 1 ch, turn.
32nd row: 1 dc (sc) in each of next 40 sts, 1 ch, turn.
33rd row: 1 dc (sc) in each of first 13 sts, miss 1 st, 1 dc (sc) in each of next 12 sts, miss 1 st, 1 dc (sc) in each of last 13 sts, 1 ch, turn.
34th row: 1 dc (sc) in each of first 12 sts, miss 1 st, 1 dc (sc) in each of next 12 sts, miss 1 st, 1 dc (sc) in each of last 12 sts, 1 ch, turn.
35th row: 1 dc (sc) in each of first 11 sts, miss 1 st, 1 dc (sc) in each of next 12 sts, miss 1 st, 1 dc (sc) in each of last 11 sts, 1 ch, turn.
36th row: 1 dc (sc) in each of first 10 sts, miss 1 st, 1 dc (sc) in each of next 12 sts, miss 1 st, 1 dc (sc) in each of last 10 sts, 1 ch, turn.
37th row: 1 dc (sc) in each of first 9 sts, miss 1 st, 1 dc (sc) in each of next 12 sts, miss 1 st, 1 dc (sc) in each of last 9 sts, 1 ch, turn.
38th row: 1 dc (sc) in each of first 8 sts, miss 1 st, 1 dc (sc) in each of next 12 sts, miss 1 st, 1 dc (sc) in each of last 8 sts, 1 ch, turn.
39th row: 1 dc (sc) in each of first 7 sts, miss 1 st, 1 dc (sc) in each of next 12 sts, miss 1 st, 1 dc (sc) in each of last 7 sts, 1 ch, turn.
40th row: 1 dc (sc) in each of first 6 sts, miss 1 st, 1 dc (sc) in each of next 12 sts. miss 1 st, 1 dc (sc) in each of last 6 sts, 1 ch, turn.
41st row: 1 dc (sc) in each of first 5 sts, miss 1 st, 1 dc (sc) in each of next 12 sts, miss 1 st, 1 dc (sc) in each of last 5 sts, 1 ch, turn.
42nd row: 1 dc (sc) in each of first 4 sts, miss 1 st, 1 dc (sc) in each of next 4 sts, miss 1 st, 1 dc (sc) in each of next 2 sts, miss 1 st, 1 dc (sc) in next 4 sts, miss 1 st, 1 dc (sc) in each of last 4 sts, 1 ch, turn.
43rd row: 1 dc (sc) in each of first 3 sts, miss 1 st, 1 dc (sc) in each of next 3 sts, miss 1 st, 1 dc (sc) in each of next 2 sts, miss 1 st, 1 dc (sc) in next 3 sts, miss 1 st, 1 dc (sc) in each of last 3 sts, 1 ch, turn.
44th row: * 1 dc (sc) in each of next 2 sts, miss 1 st. Repeat from * 3 more times, 1 dc (sc) in each of last 2 sts, 1 ch, turn.
45th row: 1 dc (sc) in first st, miss 1 st, 1 dc (sc) in next st, miss 1 st, 1 dc (sc) in next 2 sts, miss 1 st, 1 dc (sc) in next st, miss 1 st, 1 dc (sc) in last st, 1 ch, turn.
46th row: 1 dc (sc) in first st, miss 1 st, 1 dc (sc) in each of next 2 sts, miss 1 st, 1 dc (sc) in last st; turn, work 1 ss into first st. Cast (bind) off last stitch. Sew in all the ends.

Hat band
Change to a 3 mm (D) hook. Using red cotton measure 2 m (6 ft 6 in) from the end of cotton; starting at this point and working with the 2 m (6 ft 6 in) length, work 1 in ss around edge of hat over the red part (approx 60 sts), until you reach the black part. Using black cotton measure 1.5 m (60 in) from end of cotton; starting at this point and working with the 1.5 m (60 in) length, continue with the row of ss until you reach the start.

Change back to red cotton, 3 ch, 1 tr (dc) in each ss until you reach the black, pick up black yarn and continue to work 1 tr (dc) in each ss until you reach the red. Ss in first tr (dc), cast (bind) off last st.

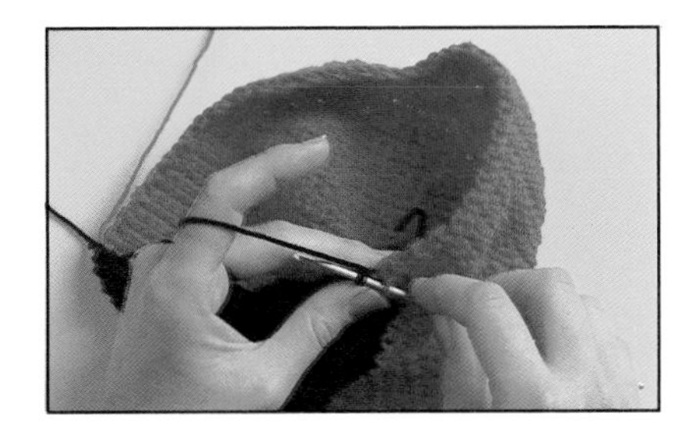

Spots
(Make 6 alike)
Use 3 mm (D) hook and black cotton.
1st step: 3 ch, ss in first chain to make a ring, 1 ch, 6 dc (sc) into ring, join with 1 ss in first st.
2nd step: 2 ch, 2 dc (sc) in each of next 6 sts, ss in first st.
3rd step: 2 ch, * 2 dc (sc) in first st, 1 dc (sc) in next st. Repeat from * 5 more times, ss in 1st st. Cast (bind) off, leaving a 15 cm (6 in) end.

EYES
(Make 2 alike)
Use 3 mm (D) hook and black cotton.
1st step: 3 ch, ss in first chain to make a ring, 1 ch, 6 dc (sc) into ring, join with 1 ss in first st.
2nd step: Cut black cotton and join white cotton. Using white cotton, work 2 ch, 2 dc (sc) in each of next 6 sts, ss in first st.
3rd step: 1 ch, ss in each of next 2 sts, 1 dc (sc) in each of next 2 sts, 2 dc (sc) in each of next 4 sts, 1 dc (sc) in each of next 2 sts, 1 ss in each of last 2 sts.
Cast (bind) off last st, leaving a 15 cm (6 in) end of cotton for attaching eye to hat.

TO MAKE UP
Fold hat in half lengthwise. Mark a line along the centre back of body and chain stitch along line with doubled black cotton.

Now arrange 3 spots equally on each side of the chain-stitched line. Pin in position and sew, using ends attached to spots. Lastly pin eyes onto head and stitch, using white cotton still attached to eyes.

T-Bar Shoes

THESE COMFORTABLE SHOES FIT BABIES UP TO 6 MONTHS

YOU WILL NEED ■ 1 pair 3 mm (US 3) knitting needles ■ Oddments of double knitting (sport) yarn in red, yellow, pink and turquoise ■ 2 buttons (or suitable beads) ■ Large darning needle

Tension (Gauge)
Using 3 mm (US 3) needles, 21 sts and 30 rows to 10 cm (4 in) (st st).

Sole
Using red yarn, cast on 37 sts.
Work 2 rows garter st.
1st row: inc 1, k 35 sts, inc 1.
2nd row: k to end.
3rd row: inc 1, k 37 sts, inc 1.
4th row: k to end.
5th row: inc 1, k 39 sts, inc 1.
6th row: k to end.
7th row: inc 1, k 41 sts, inc 1.
8th row: k to end.
Break yarn, change to pink.
9th row: inc 1, k 43 sts, inc 1.
10th row: p to end (47 sts).

To shape top
11th row: k 16, sl 1, k 1, psso, k 11, k 2 tog, k 16.
12th row: p to end.
13th row: k 16, sl 1, k 1, psso, k 9, k 2 tog, k 16.
14th row: p to end.
15th row: k 16, sl 1, k 1, psso, k 7, k 2 tog, k 16.
16th row: p to end.
17th row: k 16, sl 1, k 1, psso, k 5, k 2 tog, k 16.
18th row: p to end.

To shape strap
K 7, cast (bind) off 10 sts, k 5 (including st on needle after cast (bind) off). Cast (bind) off 10 sts, k 7 sts, work 4 rows st st on these 7 sts. Cast (bind) off. Return to centre 5 sts (for bar). Starting with a p row and yellow yarn, work 7 rows st st.
Next row: k 2 tog, k 1, k 2 tog.
Work a further 5 rows st st.
Next row: k 3 tog, fasten off.
Return to remaining 7 sts and using turquoise yarn cast on 15 sts (onto same needle as 7 sts), p across these sts then p across the group of 7 sts.
Next row: k 18, ynfwd, k 2 tog (for buttonhole).
Work 2 rows st st. Cast (bind) off.

SECOND SHOE
Make the same as the first shoe reversing the shaping of strap.

TO MAKE UP
Join sole and back seams.
Fold yellow T-bar over turquoise strap and sew to inside.
Attach button to side of shoe.

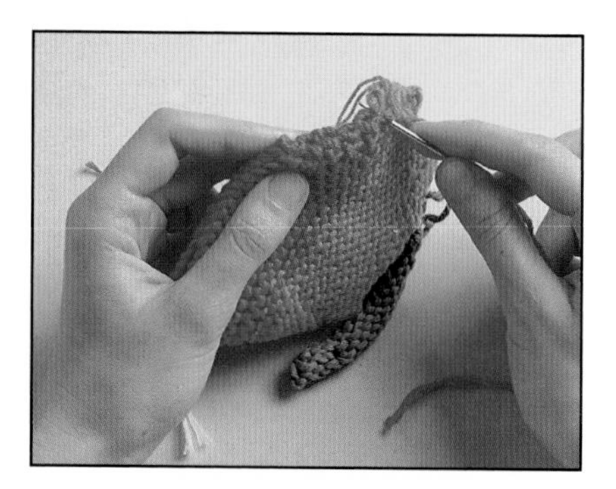

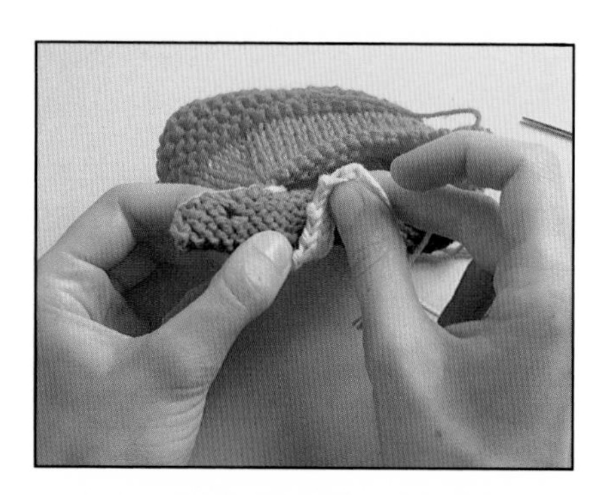

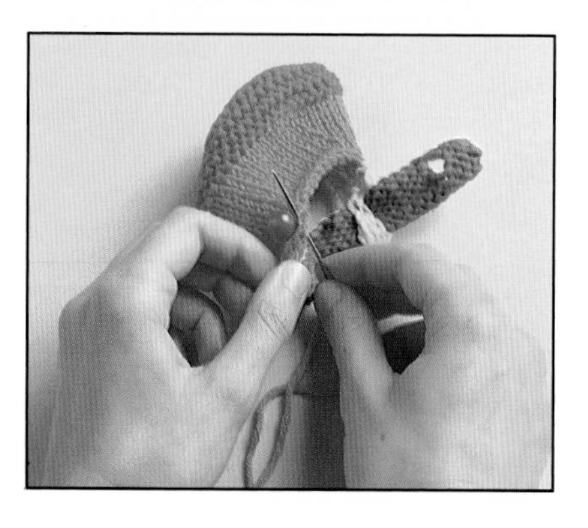

Imp Hat

THIS COSY LITTLE HELMET WILL LOOK CUTE ON ANY BABY

YOU WILL NEED ■ *50 g (2-ounce skein) red 4-ply baby yarn* ■ *Pairs of 3 mm (US 3) and 3.5 mm (US 4) knitting needles* ■ *Stitch holder* ■ *Tape measure* ■ *Large darning needle* ■ *Scissors* ■ *Non-toxic, flame retardant polyester filling (batting)*

Tension (Gauge)
Using 3.5 mm (US 4) needles, 22 sts and 28 rows to 10 cm (4 in) (st st).

EAR PIECES
(Knit 2 alike)
Using 3 mm (US 3) needles, cast on 2 sts.
1st row: inc in 1st st, k 1.
2nd row: k 1, p 1, k 1.
3rd row: inc in first st, p 1, inc in last st.
4th row: *p 1, k 1. Repeat from * to last st, p 1.
5th row: inc in first st, k 1, p 1, k 1, inc in last st.
6th row: k 1, *p 1, k 1. Repeat from * to end.
7th row: inc in first st, *p 1, k 1. Repeat from * to last 2 sts, p 1, inc in last st.
8th row: p 1, *k 1, p 1. Repeat from * to end.
9th row: inc in first st, *k 1, p 1. Repeat from * to last 2 sts, k 1, inc in last st.
Repeat rows 6–9 twice (19 sts).
Leave sts on a stitch holder.

Main part
Using 3 mm (US 3) needles, cast on 9 sts. With wrong side facing, work across 19 sts from first ear piece as follows:
(k 1, p 1) 9 times, k 1; cast on 31 sts, work across 19 sts from second ear piece as for first ear piece, cast on 9 sts (87 sts).
Continue in moss stitch as follows:
Next row: p 1, *k 1, p 1. Repeat from * to end. Repeat last row until main part measures 4 cm (1½ in), ending with right side facing for next row and inc 1 st at centre of last row (88 sts).
Change to 3.5 mm (US 4) needles and st st, starting with a knit row and work until main part measures 10 cm (4 in), ending with a p row. Shape crown as follows:
1st row: (k 6, k 2 tog) 11 times (77 sts).
2nd row and every alternate row: p.
3rd row: (k 5, k 2 tog) 11 times (66 sts).
5th row: (k 4, k 2 tog) 11 times (55 sts).
7th row: (k 3, k 2 tog) 11 times (44 sts).
9th row: (k 2, k 2 tog) 11 times (33 sts).
11th row: (k 1, k 2 tog) 11 times (22 sts).
13th row: (k 2 tog) 11 times (11 sts).
Break yarn, thread through remaining 11 sts, draw up tightly and fasten off.

Border
Using 3 mm (US 3) needles and with right side facing, start at centre back and work as follows:
Knit up 9 sts from cast-on sts, 15 sts along first side of ear piece and 15 sts up other side, k up 31 sts from cast-on sts, 15 sts along first side of second ear piece and 15 sts up other side, then k up 9 sts from cast-on sts (109 sts).
K 2 rows. Cast (bind) off.

HORNS
(Knit 2 alike)
Knit as for ear pieces. Cast (bind) off the 19 sts.

TO MAKE UP
Sew up the back seam. Fold each horn shape in half and oversew the seams leaving the bottom edge open. Stuff and sew to the hat. Using 5 strands of yarn, make 2 twisted cords 35 cm (13½ in) long. To do this, knot the 5 strands to a hook or drawer knob. Stretch them out and knot at the other end. Place a pencil in the loop and twist in one direction to make a firm cord. Knot both ends, and sew to the border at the bottom of each ear piece.

Fringed Bootees

THESE COSY FRINGED BOOTEES ARE PERFECT FOR COLDER WEATHER

YOU WILL NEED ■ *White paper* ■ *Black felt-tip pen* ■ *Piece of cotton jersey fabric* ■ *Pinking shears* ■ *Pins* ■ *Needle and thread* ■ *Elastic thread* ■ *Scissors* ■ *32 cm (12½ in) cotton fringing*

1 Transfer the template onto white paper. Draw around the template and cut out 4 pieces of jersey fabric for the bootees using pinking shears.

2 Fold over and pin the top edge of each piece of fabric and sew down. Sew the 2 sides of each bootee together.

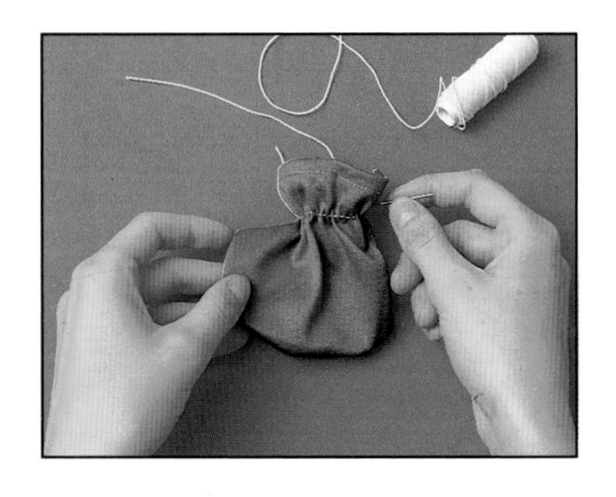

3 Sew a line of narrow elastic thread around the top of the bootee about 2.5 cm (1 in) in from the opening.

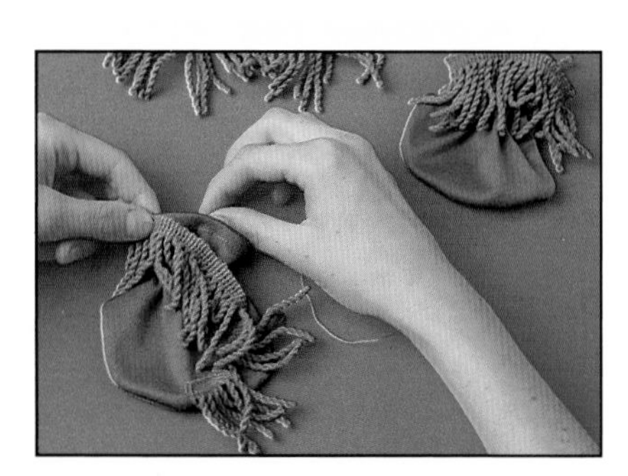

4 Cut the fringing in half and sew around the opening edge of the bootee.

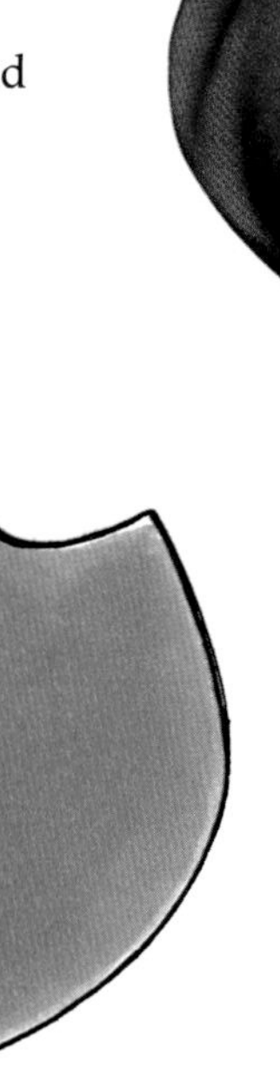

Painted Shoes

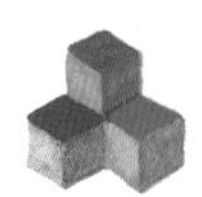

TRANSFORM PLAIN SHOES IN MINUTES WITH THESE BRIGHT PAINTS

YOU WILL NEED ■ *Pair of black or white canvas shoes* ■ *Newspaper* ■ *Old fabric* ■ *Puffy fabric paints in 5 colours* ■ *Hairdrier*

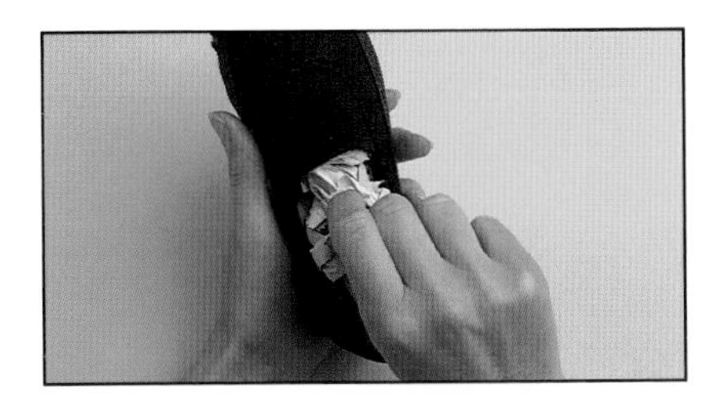

1 Stuff the toe of each canvas shoe with newspaper. It is a good idea to test puffy paints on an old piece of fabric before you start. This will reduce the chance of mistakes and also ensure that the paint is flowing freely without any air bubbles.

2 Start by drawing different coloured flowers on the front of the shoes, adding one to the back seam. Then add a different coloured dot to each flower. Leave to dry.

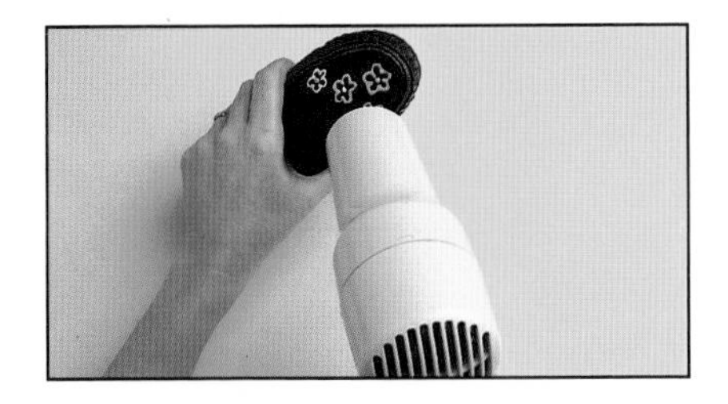

3 Finally, puff up the paint by using a hairdrier, following the manufacturer's instructions. Avoid holding the shoe too close to the heat.

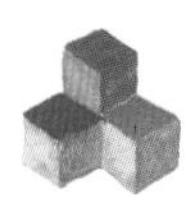

Feely Play Mat

A LARGE MAT TO PROVIDE BRIGHT COLOURS, TEXTURES AND SOUNDS

YOU WILL NEED ■ *Paper* ■ *Pencil* ■ *Tape measure* ■ *Selection of washable fabrics in different patterns, colours and textures, e.g. towelling (terrycloth), fur fabric, satin, velvet, corduroy and vinyl* ■ *Scissors* ■ *Scraps of yarn* ■ *Card* ■ *Pins* ■ *Needle and thread* ■ *Narrow ribbons in different colours* ■ *Iron-on interfacing* ■ *Non-toxic, flame retardant polyester filling (batting)* ■ *Toy bells* ■ *Dried peas in a secure plastic container* ■ *Old blanket (optional)*

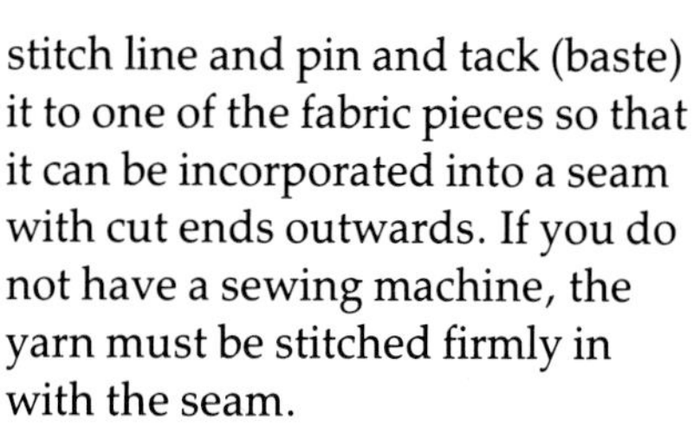

1 The mat is constructed in 3 strips joined together by 2 seams. The final arrangement of colours, patterns and textures is limited only by your imagination! Draw a rough plan on paper to help you keep track of your design and cut the shapes correctly. Remember to calculate with a generous seam allowance.

To insert yarn into a seam, first wind some yarn around a card about 8 cm (3¼ in) wide. Cut along the fold and feed the cut yarn through a sewing machine, sewing a line through the centre of the strips. Fold the yarn along the stitch line and pin and tack (baste) it to one of the fabric pieces so that it can be incorporated into a seam with cut ends outwards. If you do not have a sewing machine, the yarn must be stitched firmly in with the seam.

To make a knotted ribbon strip, cut several 24 cm (9½ in) lengths of satin ribbon, fold in half and tack (baste) to the edge of the fabric, so that they can be incorporated into the required seam in the form of loops. Once the seam is made the ribbons can be knotted in order to make them stand upright.

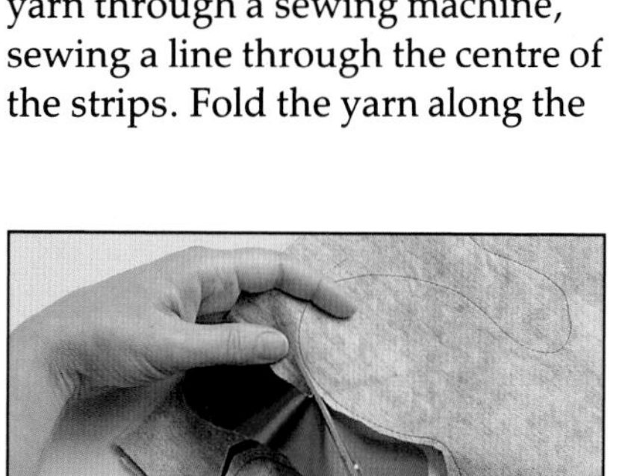

2 Make the satin flaps with a different colour on each side. Use a cool iron and iron-on interfacing to back 2 satin rectangles, slightly shorter than your final strip. Place right sides together and stitch wavy freehand shapes in and out of the satin, starting at one end of the rectangle and ending at the other. Trim, and clip major curves. Turn right side out and press. The finished flap can be incorporated into your chosen seam.

3 Make a 'rattly bag' from 2 contrasting squares, appliquéd with shapes on the outside if you wish, sewn right sides together and with one side left open. Stuff with polyester filling (batting) and incorporate the open end into your chosen seam. Bells can be added in with the filling but should first be enclosed in a small cotton bag. A small pea-filled container will make a good rattle but the container must be secure.

4 Additional play elements can be incorporated into the 2 final seams. Small loops sewn into the mat seam can be used to attach a favourite rattle or teddy when the baby is playing. When all elements are ready, pin, tack (baste) and sew the mat together. Turn under the outer edges and hem. The mat can be used as it is, or it can be backed with an old cut-down blanket.

Clutch Ball

A SOFT AND SAFE JINGLY BALL FOR A BABY TO HOLD OR THROW

YOU WILL NEED ■ *Pencil* ■ *Paper* ■ *Scissors* ■ *Plain cotton fabrics in several colours* ■ *4 contrasting patterned cotton fabrics* ■ *Pins* ■ *Needle and thread* ■ *Non-toxic, flame retardant polyester filling (batting)* ■ *2 toy bells*

1 Using the templates as a guide, cut paper patterns for the outer and inner segments. Cut 8 fabric shapes from the inner segment pattern in plain colours. Cut 4 fabric shapes from the outer segment pattern in the patterned fabrics. With right sides together, pin 1 outer segment to 1 inner, easing the curve as you go. Tack (baste) and stitch together 10 mm (⅜ in) from the edge.

Repeat for the second side of the outer segment, using a second inner segment to form a boat shape. Stop the second stitch line where it meets the first at the pointed ends, and secure all thread ends. Make up the 3 other segments in the same way.

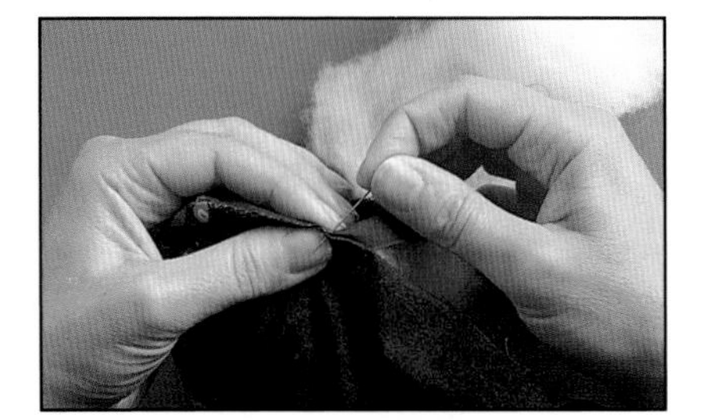

2 Turn each segment right side out. Folding in the straight segment sides about 10 mm (⅜ in) as you sew, oversew each segment closed. Stuff the segments with filling (batting) as you go but don't fill the pointed ends too tight. Enclose each bell in a small cotton bag and insert them in 2 of the segments.

3 Pinch the tops of 2 separate segments together and oversew them together about 4 cm (1½ in) down the straight edges at the top and bottom. Repeat for the second pair of segments.

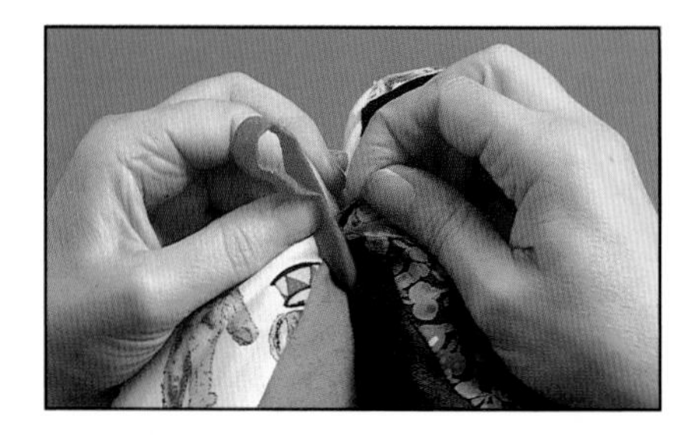

4 Make a narrow tie from plain fabric about 30 cm (12 in) long. Cut a length of 20 cm (8 in). Hold the 2 pairs of joined segments together and pass the tie between them, threading the 2 sets together. Sew the loop closed by overlapping its ends and conceal the sewn end neatly within the ball.

Pinch the segment tops, draw the loop tight and sew to itself just above the ball, securing all the segments and leaving a looped end. Using the remaining tie, thread the bottom of the ball but sew the tie without leaving a loop. Conceal the sewn ends in the ball.

Holding Ring

A VERY BASIC FIRST TOY FOR A YOUNG BABY TO HOLD

YOU WILL NEED ■ Pencil ■ Card ■ Ruler ■ Pair of compasses ■ Scissors ■ Gingham or similar cotton fabric ■ Needle and thread ■ 2 patterned cotton fabrics ■ Iron ■ Non-toxic, flame retardant polyester filling (batting) ■ 2 plain cotton fabrics

1 Draw 2 circles on card about 10 cm (4 in) in diameter and cut them out. Cut slits from the circle edges to the centre. Cut a circle of gingham about 12 cm (4¾ in) in diameter and place the card centrally over the gingham. Overlap the fabric edge and tack (baste) round the circle, drawing up the fabric to make a neat hem. Press firmly. Repeat with one of the patterned fabrics.

2 Using the slit, carefully remove the cards. Cut circular holes in the centre of both fabrics about 2 cm (¾ in) in diameter. Place the circles right sides together and stitch around the centre hole, about 6 mm (¼ in) from the edge. Clip the seam carefully and pull one of the circles through the centre hole, easing out the seam with your fingers. Press flat.

3 Oversew the 2 tacked (basted) circular hems together and stuff the doughnut-shaped ring firmly as you go.

4 Cut 2 × 7 cm (2¾ in) diameter circles from the 2 plain fabrics and a small flower shape about 5 cm (2 in) across. Cut a gingham centre to the flower. Appliqué the flower and its centre to 1 circle. Make a narrow tie from the second patterned fabric and stitch it firmly to the right side centre of the other small circle. Place the circles right sides together and tack (baste) them, leaving the ties protruding from a small opening on one side.

5 Stitch the circles together, following the outline of the flower which you can gauge from the appliqué stitch line, and leaving the end where the ties are open. Clip excess fabric from the flower corners and turn it to the outside. Stuff the flower shape and oversew the opening closed.

6 Wrap the tie around the stuffed ring, cutting away any excess and tucking the raw edges under to neaten, and stitch very firmly to the ring, leaving the flower facing outwards.

Bright-finned **F**ish

THIS FISH CAN BE MADE FLAT FOR A CUSHION OR DOUBLE-SIDED FOR A TOY

YOU WILL NEED ■ *Pencil* ■ *Paper* ■ *Scissors* ■ *Striped cotton fabric* ■ *Pins* ■ *Needle and thread* ■ *Tape measure* ■ *Satin fabric in red and green* ■ *Iron* ■ *Iron-on interfacing* ■ *Non-toxic, flame retardant polyester filling (batting)* ■ *2 patterned cotton fabrics* ■ *Scrap of white fabric* ■ *Embroidery thread* ■ *2 plain cotton fabrics*

1 Make paper patterns for each of the pieces, using the templates as a guide. Cut 2 sets of opposite shapes in striped cotton for the fish body, lining up the fabric stripes with the pattern edge at the tail end of the fish.

Pin, tack (baste) and sew the body sides right sides together along the straight central seam using a 1 cm (3⁄8 in) seam allowance and stopping 1 cm (3⁄8 in) short of the tail end. Turn back the raw edges by 1 cm (3⁄8 in) at the tail ends, press and tack (baste) the hems.

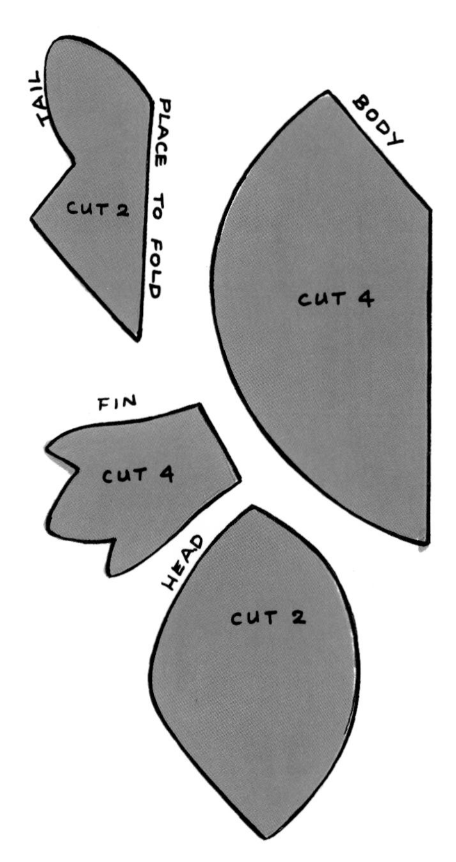

2 Back the red satin fabric with iron-on interfacing using a cool iron. Cut out 4 fin shapes. Pin and tack (baste) two of them with right sides together, and sew 6 mm (1⁄4 in) from the edge. Clip carefully into the inner corners and turn right side out. Repeat for the other pair of fin shapes. Stuff firmly, pushing the filling down into the points with a pencil, but leave them loosely filled at the open end.

3 Cut out 2 pieces of patterned fabric for the head and 2 of green interfaced satin for the tail. Cut 8 small dark patterned circles for spots. (If the fish will be used as a cushion, you only need decorate one side.) Appliqué the spots to the side. Position the patterned cotton for the head and insert 1 of the fins midway round the seam. Tack (baste) then appliqué the seam in place, enclosing the fin.

Cut circles for the eyes, and appliqué them in place. Embroider a smiley mouth. Overlay the wrong side of the V-shaped end of the striped section 1 cm (3⁄8 in) onto the right side of the green fish tail. Tack (baste) in place and appliqué them together. Repeat for the other side.

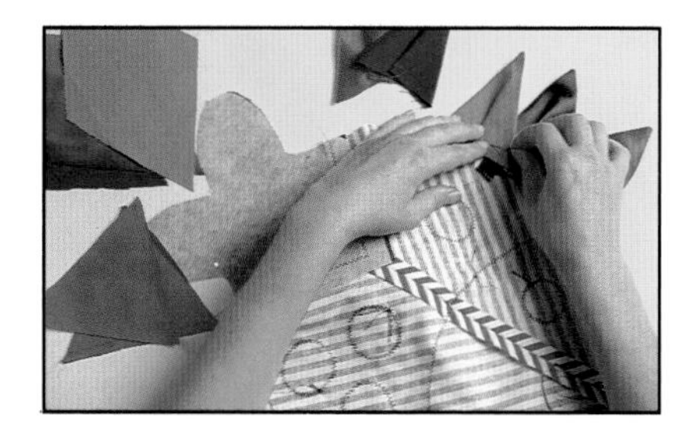

4 Cut 10 diamond shapes for back fins from the satins and the plain cottons. The diamonds should fold in half to form triangles with 13 cm (5¼ in) sides. Fold and stitch 1 side seam of each fin and turn the fins right side out to press. Pick the points with a pin to make them sharp.

Tack (baste) a vertical tuck in each fin so they measure about 8 cm (3¼ in) across the open ends. Pin each fin in position within the striped area of the top and bottom of each side, turning in the striped raw edges 1 cm (3⁄8 in) as you go. The fins must overlap and should fan out around the fish. Tack (baste) and stitch into position.

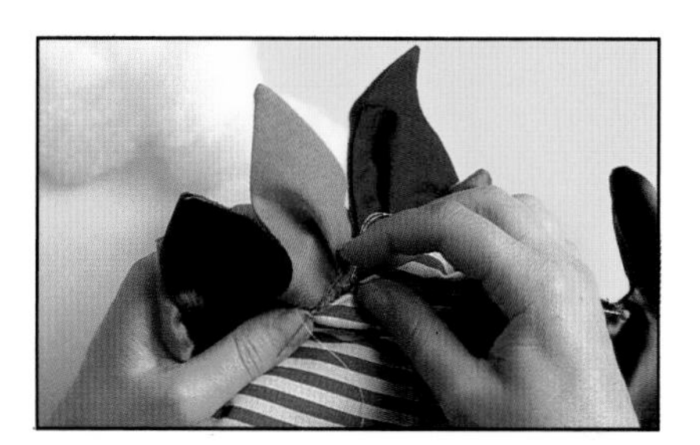

5 Position both sides together with right sides facing. Pin and tack (baste) tail and head up to the stitching lines with the striped area. Stitch the seam 1 cm (3⁄8 in) from the edge. Clip the tail curves. Turn right side out and press the seams firmly.

Stuff the tail, pushing the filling well into the ends. Stitch the top and under seams together by turning under the striped raw edges on the sides without fins, and hemming them securely to the backs of the fins on the opposite side. Fill the fish as you sew the last seam.

Appliquéd Toys

SHAPES AND TEXTURES TO DELIGHT AND AMUSE A BABY

YOU WILL NEED ■ *Pair of compasses* ■ *Ruler* ■ *Pencil* ■ *Scissors* ■ *Pins* ■ *Oddments of fabric in bright colours, patterns and textures* ■ *Needle and thread* ■ *Ribbon in assorted colours* ■ *Non-toxic, flame retardant polyester filling (batting)* ■ *Large wooden beads* ■ *2 wooden rings*

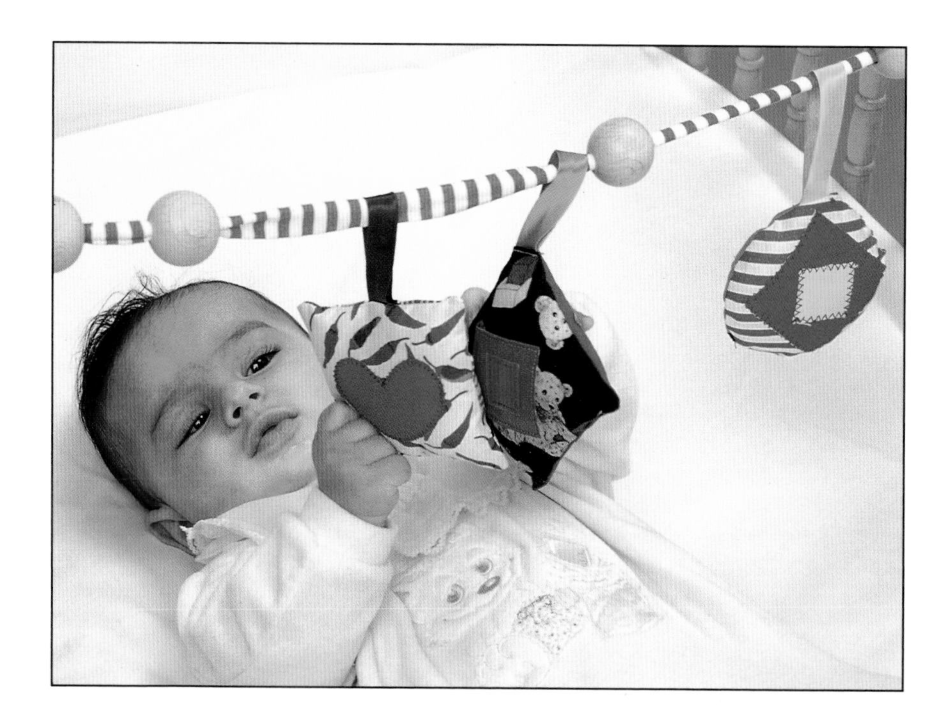

1 Each of the 3 different hanging shapes is made in the same way. The appliqué decorations are simply triangles, squares, hearts and circles which you can arrange as you please. To make the shapes, first draw, cut and assemble your chosen elements and motifs. Use a pair of compasses to draw the circles accurately.

2 Appliqué the decorative elements to the right sides of your hanging shape. Cut a length of ribbon about 7 cm (2¾ in) long, fold it in half and tack (baste) it to the seam edge within the shape so that it will be incorporated into the seam. Leaving an opening to turn, tack (baste) and sew around the shape with right sides together.

3 Turn the shape right side out and stuff it firmly with polyester filling (batting). Oversew the opening to close. Repeat with the other shapes.

4 Make a strong fabric tie of sufficient length to reach across the cot (crib) or pram. Thread on the wooden beads. Sew a wooden ring very securely to each end of the tie. Thread the shapes onto the tie, with a bead between each. Make 2 short ties in contrasting colours and thread one through each ring, sewing firmly across close to the ring to hold them in place. Use these to tie the toy to the cot (crib) edge. Do not leave excessive lengths of loose tie near a small baby.

Denim Bear

BABY'S FIRST BEAR: A SIMPLE-TO-MAKE CUDDLY TOY

YOU WILL NEED ■ *Pen* ■ *Paper* ■ *Scissors* ■ *Strong cotton fabric such as denim or broadcloth* ■ *Patterned cotton fabric* ■ *Pins* ■ *Needle and thread* ■ *Safety eyes* ■ *Non-toxic, fire retardant polyester filling (batting)* ■ *Knitting needle or pencil* ■ *Embroidery thread*

1 Scale up the template to the size required and make a paper pattern for the bear. Cut 2 bear shapes from the strong cotton. Cut 4 shapes for paws and 2 for ears from the patterned cotton and position them 1 cm (3/8 in) in from the raw edges of the bear's body. Pin and then tack (baste) them in place, and sew onto the bear's body front.

Make a vertical slit in the centre of the body back 8 cm (3¼ in) long. Place the right sides of the bodies together and stitch around the outside. Clip the main curves and turn the body to the right side through the slit.

2 Mark the positions for the safety eyes and attach them according to the manufacturer's instructions. Lightly stuff the bear's ears and stitch diagonally across to give them shape. Stuff the head, ensuring there is plenty of filling (batting) behind the eyes.

Make 3 backstitches from the front through to the back across the neck to keep the filling (batting) in place and also to give shape. Stuff the remainder of the body firmly, pushing the filling (batting) down to the ends of the paws with a knitting needle or a pencil. Oversew the opening.

3 Embroider the nose and mouth onto the bear. Sew a 'belly button' by making stitches back and forth through the centre of the bear, pulling the thread tight to give a dimpled shape. Make a narrow tie from the patterned cotton fabric. Trim the ends in a forked shape and then tie the tie round the bear's neck with a proper tie knot. Sew the back tie end firmly to the bear so that it cannot be pulled undone.

Bedtime Friends

THIS FAMILY OF DELIGHTFUL COMPANIONS WILL ENTRANCE ANY BABY

YOU WILL NEED ■ *1 pair of 3 mm (US 3) knitting needles* ■ *Oddments of double knitting (sport) yarn in 5 different colours:* Boy *Colour A – Shoes; Colour B – Trousers; Colour C – Sweater stripe; Colour D – Skin; Colour E – Hair;* Girl *Colour A – Shoes, Body, Hair and Arms; Colour B – Skin; Colour C – Skirt* ■ *Stitch holder* ■ *Large darning needle* ■ *Non-toxic, flame retardant polyester filling (batting)* ■ *Oddments of yarn for facial embroidery* ■ *Length of round cord elastic* ■ *Wooden beads* ■ *Bells*

BOY DOLL

Legs, body and head
Using yarn A, cast on 4 sts for the shoe.
Inc row: double sts (k twice into each st) 8 sts.
Next row: P to end. Break yarn. Change to yarn B and work 10 rows garter st (every row knit) for leg. Break yarn and leave these sts on a holder. Work other leg as the first, but do not break yarn.
Next row (body): k 8 sts then k 8 sts from holder: 16 sts. Work 3 rows in garter st. Join in yarn C for jumper stripe pattern. Garter st: 2 rows C 2 rows B. Work 12 rows in stripe pattern.
Change to yarn D and work 10 rows st st (k 1 row p 1 row) for the head.
Dec row: (k 2 tog) to end. Break yarn, thread end through remaining sts, pull up and secure.

Arms
(Knit 2 alike)
Using yarn D, cast on 8 sts. Work 2 rows st st. Break yarn, change to

stripe pattern (2 rows C, 2 rows B) and work 7 rows garter st. Cast (bind) off.

TO MAKE UP

Join leg, body and head seams leaving an opening. Stuff and close opening. Fold arms lengthwise (right sides together) and join seam. Stuff and sew arms to body. Tie a length of yarn tightly around neck. Embroider facial features.*** Using D yarn knot short lengths into top and back of head for hair. Separate lengths of yarn and trim.

GIRL DOLL

Legs, body and head

Using yarn A, cast on 4 sts for shoe.

Inc row: (knot twice into each st) 8 sts.

Next row: p to end. Break yarn. Change to yarn B and work 9 rows st st, change to yarn A and p 1 row (for leg). Break yarn, leave these sts on a holder.

Work other leg as given for first leg, but do not break yarn.

Next row (body): k 8 sts then k 8 sts from holder (16 sts).

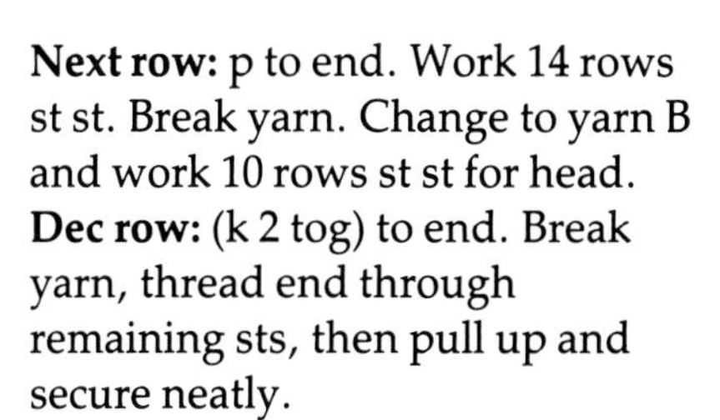

Next row: p to end. Work 14 rows st st. Break yarn. Change to yarn B and work 10 rows st st for head.

Dec row: (k 2 tog) to end. Break yarn, thread end through remaining sts, then pull up and secure neatly.

Arms

(Knit 2 alike)

Using yarn B, cast on 8 sts. Work 2 rows st st. Change to yarn A and work 7 rows st st. Cast (bind) off.

Skirt

Using yarn A, cast on 35 sts. Work 2 rows garter st.

Change to yarn C and work 8 rows st st. Break yarn. Thread end through remaining sts.

TO MAKE UP

Make up as instructed for boy doll to ***. Join back seam of skirt, gather up stitches to fit around waist and sew to body.

Hair: cut yarn C into 11 cm (4½ in) lengths. Knot each length into centre of head starting at front and finishing at centre back of head. Separate each length of yarn. Tie into 2 pigtails, secure with an oddment of yarn B and trim if required.

Make 2 boy and 2 girl dolls. Thread elastic carefully through the arms, inserting a large bead between each doll and a large bell in the centre. Make a loop with the elastic threading a bead through the end. Secure firmly with a large knot. Thread the end of the elastic back through the doll.

Sun Toy

THIS HAPPY SUN WILL BRIGHTEN UP A BABY'S DAY

YOU WILL NEED ■ *Pinking shears* ■ *2 fabric circles* ■ *Pins* ■ *6 felt triangles* ■ *18 cm (7 in) yellow fringing* ■ *30 cm (12 in) red cord* ■ *Scissors* ■ *Needle and thread* ■ *Oddments of felt* ■ *Rubber-based glue* ■ *Plastic squeaker* ■ *Oddments of fabric* ■ *Non-toxic, flame retardant polyester filling (batting)*

1 Cut out the fabric circles using pinking shears. Pin the triangles on 1 of the round pieces of fabric so that they are pointing towards the centre. Pin the fringing around the top, with the cord ends, to make a loop.

2 Place the other round fabric piece on top, with right sides facing, and sew around the edge leaving a gap at one side. Turn the shape right side out.

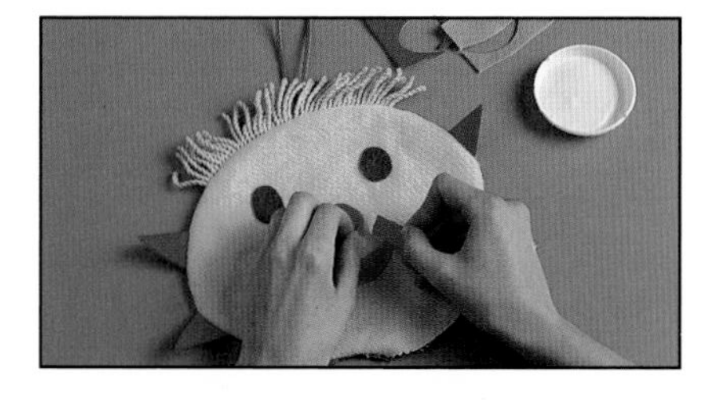

3 Remove all the pins. Cut out 2 eyes, a nose and a mouth from oddments of felt and glue them down onto the front to make a face. Add a few stitches to each piece to secure them down.

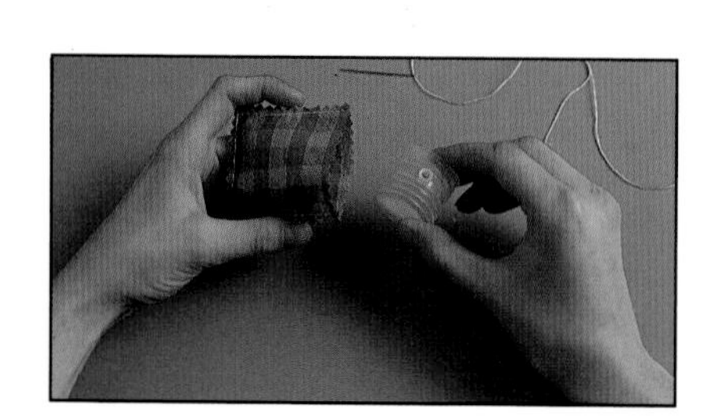

4 For safety, make a small fabric case for the squeaker from 2 pieces of fabric, place the squeaker inside it and sew up.

5 Wrap the squeaker inside some polyester filling (batting) and stuff the toy lightly. Finish by sewing up the gap.

Surprise Play Cube

A RATTLY ROLL-AROUND CUBE WITH A SURPRISE BEHIND THE DOOR

YOU WILL NEED ■ *Assorted fabrics in bright colours, textures and patterns* ■ *Scissors* ■ *Tape measure* ■ *Pencil* ■ *Card* ■ *Iron-on (fusible) interfacing* ■ *Needle and thread* ■ *Pins* ■ *Wadding (batting)* ■ *Embroidery thread* ■ *Non-toxic, flame retardant polyester filling (batting)* ■ *Dried peas in a plastic container* ■ *Iron* ■ *Velcro*

1 Cut out sufficient fabric in assorted textures, patterns and colours to make up 6 sides of the cube. Some of the sides can be pieced from a patchwork of 4 smaller squares or from 2 triangles joined diagonally. Each square should be 14 × 14 cm (5½ × 5½ in) to include a 1 cm (⅜ in) seam allowance all round.

2 Make a template for a simple bird shape from a piece of card. Trace around it onto a piece of interfaced cotton and cut it out. Appliqué it to your chosen top 'surprise' square and embroider an eye and feet onto the bird. Join 4 squares edge to edge, right sides together, and join the fourth side to the first to make an open box shape.

3 Arrange the open box with wrong sides outwards. Pin and tack (baste) a fifth square to make the base of the box, sewing the right sides together. Stitch the base, easing gently as you turn the corners to avoid puckers. Still with wrong sides out, sew 3 sides of the top square and just turn the corner on the fourth. Leave the remainder of this side open .

4 To make the 'door', prepare 2 further squares and place them right sides together with a piece of wadding (batting) on the top. Insert a small flat fabric loop into the centre of one edge which should be the centre of the 3 sides you will stitch. Stitch around the 3 sides, turn out and press firmly. Stitch the open edge, which will be the door 'hinge', closed along the seam allowance.

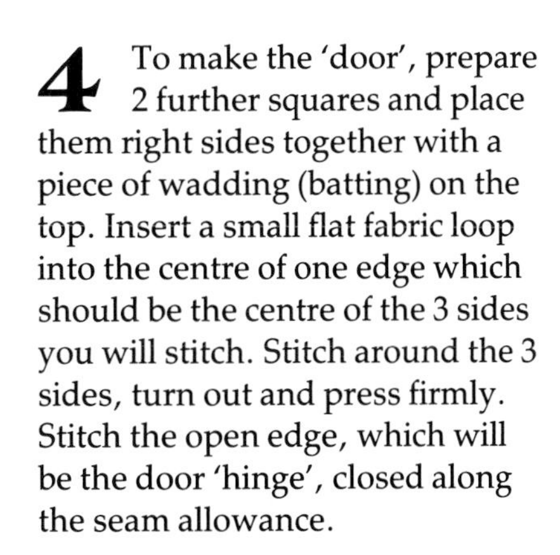

5 Turn the cube right side out and stuff firmly, especially into the corners. A small pea-filled container can be buried in the cube centre to make it rattle. After stuffing the cube oversew the opening securely to close it. Oversew the door to the cube top along the hinge edge. Attach a piece of Velcro to the underside of the flat loop and another to the cube side so it can be fastened.

Sarah **S**ock **D**oll

A SOFT, SAFE FIRST DOLL USING AN ODD SOCK FROM THE LAUNDRY BASKET!

YOU WILL NEED ■ *Scissors* ■ *A large man's sock, clean and in good condition* ■ *Tape measure* ■ *Needle and strong cotton thread* ■ *Non-toxic, flame retardant polyester filling (batting)* ■ *Patterned cotton fabric* ■ *Pins* ■ *Iron* ■ *Pre-gathered broderie anglaise* ■ *Oddments of felt* ■ *Embroidery thread*

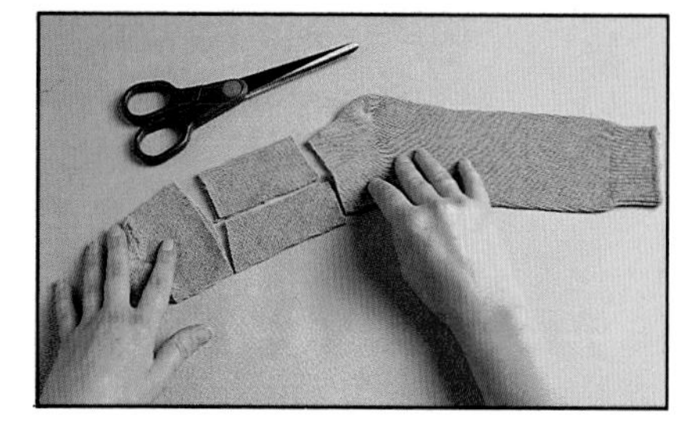

1 Cut the sock into 4 pieces as shown: the leg and heel section will be used for making the doll's body. Allow at least 4 cm (1½ in) beyond the curve of the heel before making the cut to separate the large section. The second cut should be about 8 cm (3¼ in) long. This is cut in half and used for the sleeves and arms. The toe is discarded.

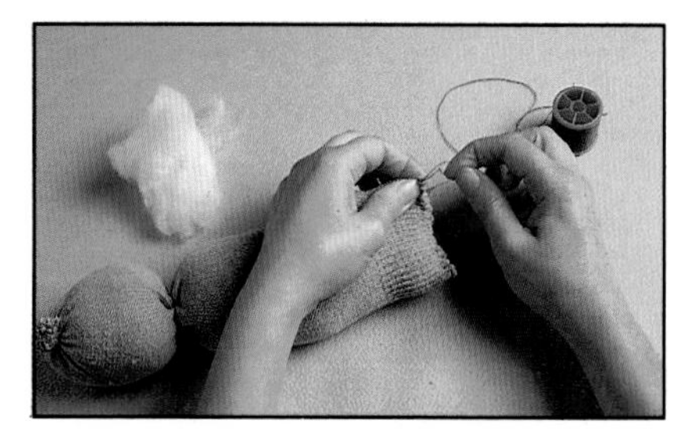

2 Using doubled strong cotton thread, secure a thread about 1 cm (⅜ in) below the cut top of the body section and gather round it, pulling it in tight. Pass the needle back and forth through the gathers to strengthen the closure and secure the thread. Stuff the head firmly and gather round as before to make a head about the size of a tennis ball. Secure the thread. Stuff the body section firmly and oversew the opening to close it.

3 Cut 2 sleeves 8 × 8 cm (3¼ × 3¼ in) from patterned cotton. Open up the remaining sock sections from the centre and select the least worn parts. Cut 2 pieces, 8 × 5 cm (3¼ × 2 in), with the grain of the knitting running along the short length. Pin the fabric to the sock piece right sides together along the long sides. Tack (baste) and stitch, then press the seam flat and oversew the raw edges on both arms. Fold in half lengthwise and press.

Round off the doubled corners of the sock ends. Tack (baste) and stitch, starting at the underarm and leaving a 1 cm (⅜ in) edge. Taper the seam into the folded edge. Turn the sleeves out, stuff firmly and oversew the ends to close. Attach them securely to the body sides.

4 Cut a piece of fabric for the dress about 65 × 20 cm (26 × 8 in). Sew a seam joining along the shorter sides and neaten the raw edges. Make a 1 cm (⅝ in) hem at one end for the neck, and run a doubled gathering thread around the neck just over 1 cm (⅜ in) down from the edge. Turn up the bottom hem of the dress and sew on the broderie anglaise.

Cut a piece of fabric for the bonnet measuring 20 × 10 cm (8 × 4 in). Turn the short sides of the fabric under and stitch down, then sew broderie anglaise to one long edge. Pin the bonnet to the doll with the broderie anglaise running around the front, and arrange the sides and back in even tucks and pleats before hemming the whole bonnet securely to the head.

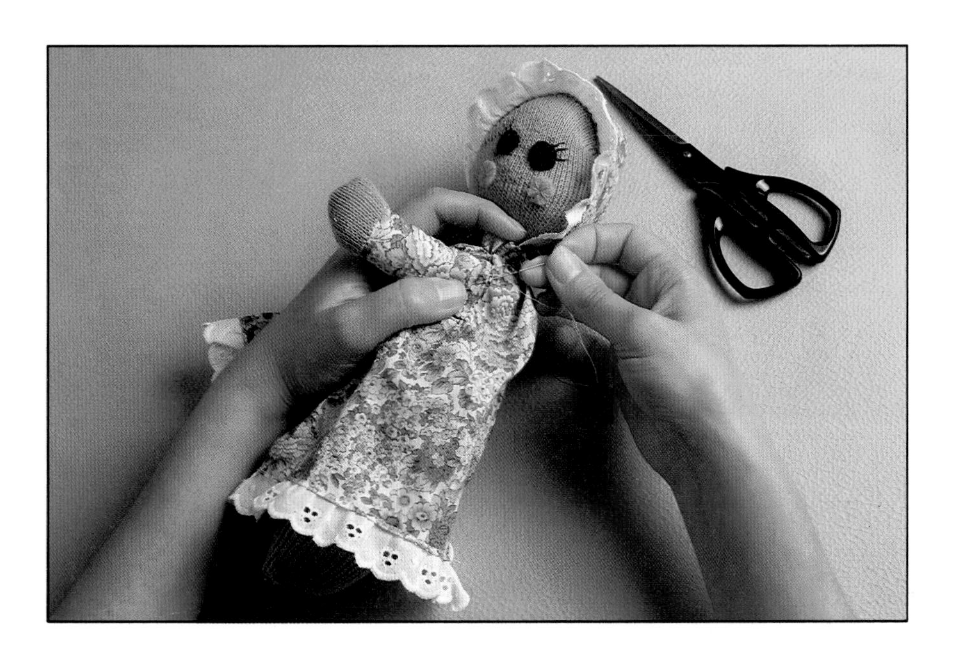

5 Put the dress on the doll with the seam down the back. Gather up the neck and draw it tight. Sew the gathering threads back and forth through the neck to ensure it cannot come undone. Arrange the gathers carefully before making two slits (the width of the arms) in the dress for the arms to emerge.

Turn under the raw edges of the slits as you sew the sleeves and slits together. Cut felt for the eyes and cheeks and embroider them to the head, stitching a star shape on each of the circles. Finally, embroider eyelashes, nostrils and a big smile.

Play Cube

A BRIGHT, FUN, SQUEEZY PLAY CUBE

YOU WILL NEED ■ *Pinking shears* ■ *6 assorted fabric squares 18 × 18 cm (7 × 7 in)* ■ *Needle and thread* ■ *16 cm (6½ in) cotton fringing in 2 different colours* ■ *Scissors* ■ *Non-toxic, flame retardant polyester filling (batting)*

1 Cut around the fabric squares with pinking shears. Sew 2 of the squares together trapping a piece of fringing in between them.

2 Attach a third square to the others and continue attaching the squares as shown, including fringing on 3 sides, until you have joined all the pieces together with the exception of a gap to allow the filling (batting) to be inserted.

3 Stuff the cube with the polyester filling (batting) until the cube is quite firm and sew up the gap.

Twirly Fish

HAVE FUN MAKING THIS DECORATIVE FISH TO HANG OVER A BABY'S COT

YOU WILL NEED ■ *Pencil* ■ *45 × 33 cm (18 × 13 in) card* ■ *Scissors* ■ *Drawing pins (thumb tacks)* ■ *60 × 60 cm (24 × 24 in) cotton fabric* ■ *Wooden frame* ■ *Wax and wax pot or bain-marie* ■ *Paintbrushes* ■ *Fabric dyes in red, yellow, green and blue* ■ *Iron* ■ *Newspaper* ■ *Paper* ■ *Pins* ■ *Needle and thread* ■ *Non-toxic, flame retardant polyester filling (batting)* ■ *Cord* ■ *2 wooden beads*

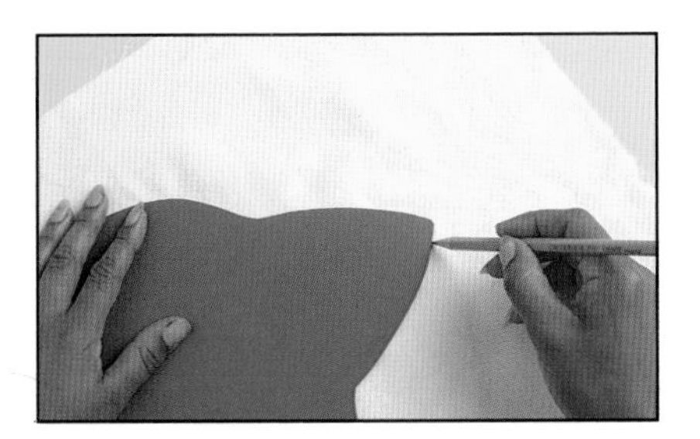

1 Scale up the template onto the card and cut it out. Pin the fabric onto a wooden frame or board using drawing pins (thumb tacks), ensuring that it is held firmly in place. Place the fish template onto the fabric and draw around it twice to produce 2 fish shapes.

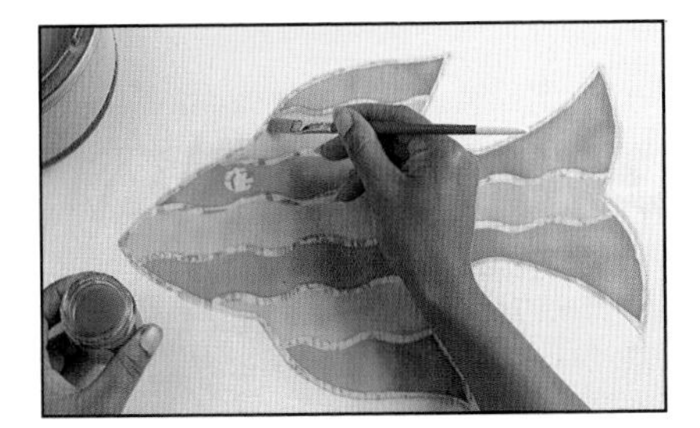

2 Melt the wax in a wax pot or in a bain-marie placed over a low heat. Use a brush to paint the wax around the 2 fish outlines. Then paint wax stripes onto the fish. Make up dyes following the manufacturer's instructions. You will have excess dye to use for another project as you need very little for painting the fish design. Paint both fish using 2 different colours for each. Allow to dry then cut out both fish shapes.

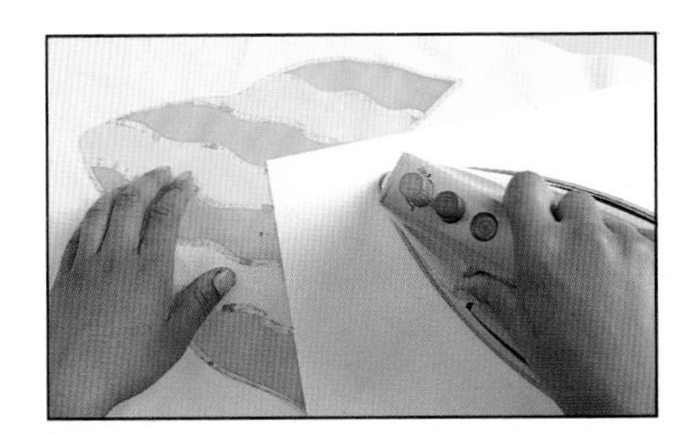

3 Set an iron to its highest setting and place some newspaper on an ironing board. Sandwich each fish between 2 sheets of paper and iron over the top, pressing evenly throughout. The paper will absorb most of the wax. Hand wash the batiked cloth in mildly soapy lukewarm water to remove the excess dye. To remove every trace of wax, dry cleaning is necessary.

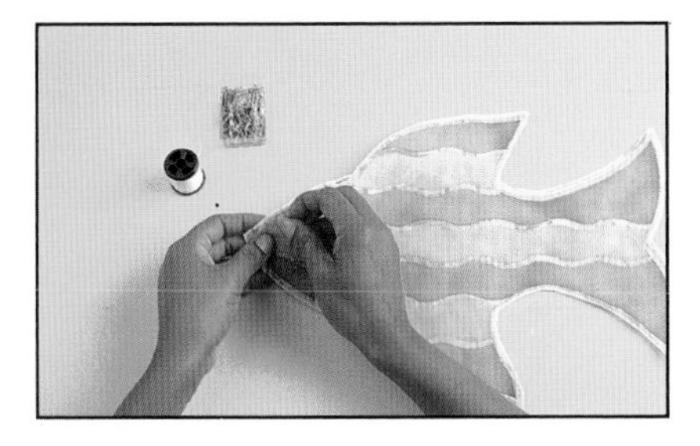

4 Place the 2 fish shapes right sides together. Pin, tack (baste) and sew them together, leaving the upper fin open for stuffing and to attach the cord.

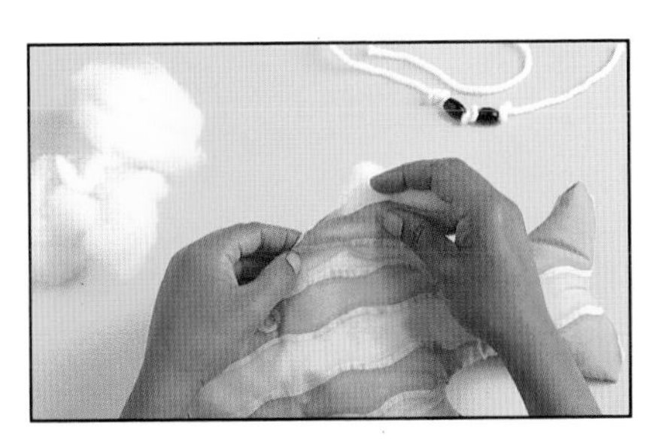

5 Turn right side out and stuff the fish from the open upper fin. Knot the length of cord and attach 2 beads in the centre with a knot between and on either side to ensure that they are held firmly in place. Turn in the fin edges and sew, placing one end in the centre of the cord and securing it in the final stitching.

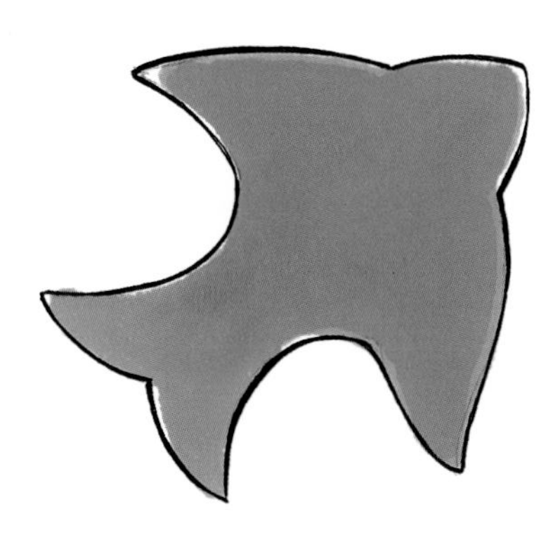

Cuddly Duck

THIS SOFT AND FRIENDLY DUCK CONTAINS A RATTLE

YOU WILL NEED ■ *Pencil* ■ *Paper* ■ *Scissors* ■ *Plain and patterned cotton fabrics in related shades* ■ *Pins* ■ *Needle and thread* ■ *Non-toxic, flame retardant polyester filling (batting)* ■ *Corduroy or needlecord fabric* ■ *Dried peas in a plastic container* ■ *Oddments of felt* ■ *Embroidery thread*

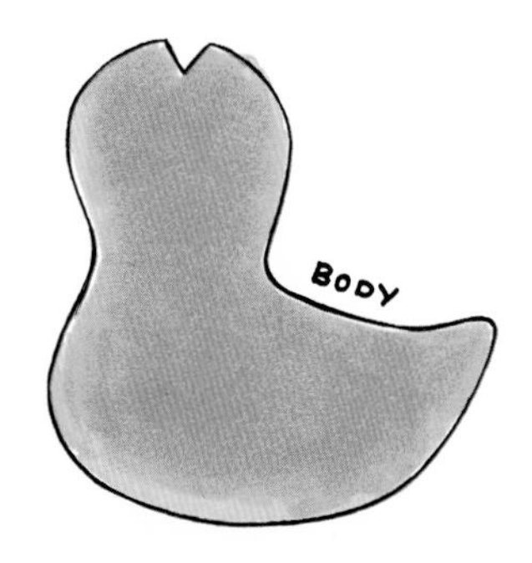

1 Make paper patterns for all pieces using the templates as a guide. Cut out 1 shape from the plain and 1 from the patterned cotton fabric for the feet. Tack (baste) them together and stitch, leaving the flat edge open. Clip into the central corner and turn right side out. Lightly stuff the feet with filling (batting).

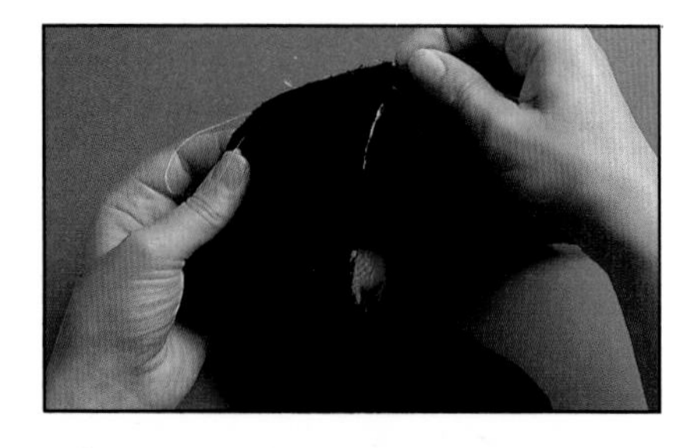

2 Cut the 2 gusset pieces from corduroy or needlecord. The longer piece will be for the front of the duck. Enclosing the feet within the seam, stitch the gussets right sides together along the flat edge. The patterned side of the feet must face upwards. Cut 2 opposite shapes for the duck's body. Stitch the small darts in the head on both sides.

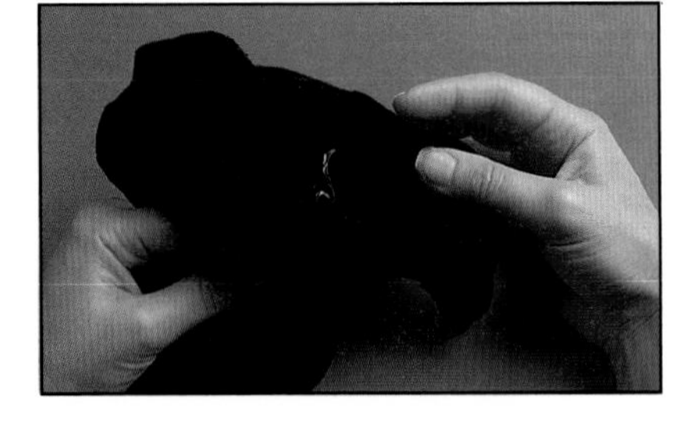

3 Starting at the duck's tail, pin the back point of the gusset to the duck, right sides together, and work forward under the duck until you reach the front of the gusset. Tack (baste) and stitch the seam. Repeat with the second body shape. Break off the stitching line and restart it, having first pressed the bodies flat so that the gusset is folded along its centre. Leave the duck's back open to turn but work 2 cm (¾ in) of the seam from the tail to allow you to achieve a neat point.

Turn the body right side out and stuff the duck firmly, enclosing a small pea-filled container. Oversew the opening. Cut 2 sets of wing shapes and stitch in pairs leaving the flat edges open. Turn right side out and stuff lightly, then turn in the flat edges and oversew them. Stitch the wings very firmly to the body.

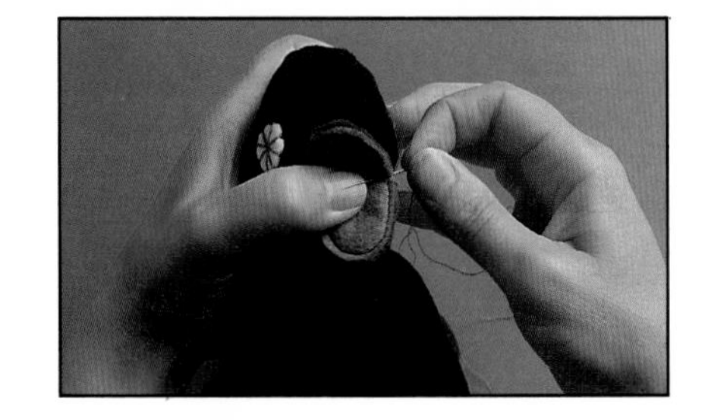

4 Cut 2 pieces of felt for the beak and stitch them together close to the edge. Fold the beak through the centre and stitch it firmly to the head. Cut 2 white felt circles for eyes and attach them to the head as shown. Cut a triangle of patterned fabric for a headscarf, neaten the edges and sew it to the head, tying in a knot under the chin.

Smiley Toys

THESE FUNNY LIPS WILL KEEP ANY BABY SMILING

YOU WILL NEED ■ *Fine black felt-tip pen* ■ *Thin card* ■ *Scissors* ■ *Coloured felt* ■ *Black embroidery yarn* ■ *Large darning needle* ■ *Length of narrow ribbon* ■ *Needle and thread* ■ *Non-toxic, flame retardant polyester filling (batting)* ■ *Squeaker or bell (optional)*

1 Using the template as a guide, draw a lip shape onto thin card. Cut it out and place it on the coloured felt. Draw around the shape twice and cut out.

2 Using the embroidery yarn, sew a line of chain stitch through the middle of one of the felt lip shapes.

3 Cut a short length of ribbon, fold in half to make a loop and sew the ends to the top of the other felt lip shape.

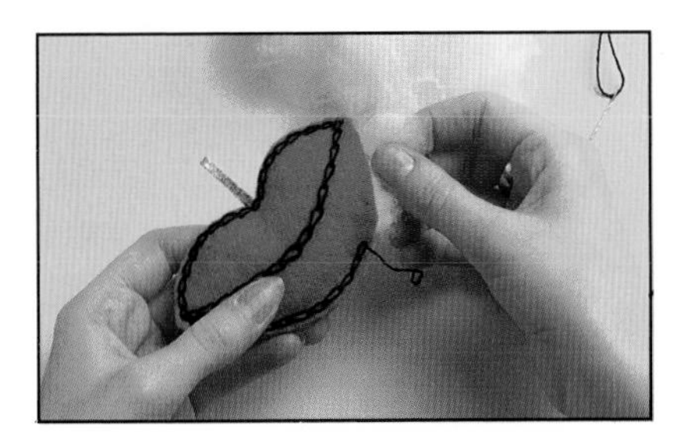

4 Put the lips wrong sides together and chain stitch them together using the embroidery yarn and leaving a small gap for stuffing. Stuff gently. If you want to insert a squeaker or bell, be sure to enclose it in a tightly-sewn cotton bag as a safety measure. Chain stitch the gap together.

Crocheted **D**olls

THESE CHARMING CROCHETED COTTON DOLLS MAKE IDEAL COMPANIONS

YOU WILL NEED ■ 3.5 mm (E) crochet hook ■ 25 g (1 oz) green double knitting (sport) cotton ■ Scissors ■ 25 g (1 oz) yellow double knitting (sport) cotton ■ 15 g (3/4 oz) pink double knitting (sport) cotton ■ 2 handfuls of non-toxic, flame retardant polyester filling (batting) ■ Tape measure ■ 15 g (3/4 oz) black double knitting (sport) cotton ■ Large darning needle ■ Oddments of red, dark green and blue double knitting (sport) cotton

MEASUREMENTS

Crocheted with a 3.5 mm (E) hook, the finished dolls will measure 25 cm (10 in) from head to toe. Using a larger crochet hook will produce a larger doll.

BODY AND HEAD

Starting at the bottom of the body, and using green cotton, work 3 ch, then join into a ring with a ss in first chain.

1st step: 1 ch, 5 dc (sc) into ring. Close with a ss in first dc (sc).

2nd step: 1 ch, now working in a spiral fashion, 2 dc (sc) in each st until you have 24 sts on work.

3rd step: * 1 dc (sc) in each st. Repeat from * 23 more times.

4th step: * 1 dc (sc) in each of next 11 sts, miss 1 st. Repeat from * 1 more time.

5th step: * 1 dc (sc) in each st. Repeat from * 109 more times.

6th step: Cut green cotton and join yellow cotton. Keep short ends inside work. With yellow cotton work upper body as follows:

* 1 dc (sc) in each st. Repeat from * 65 more times.

7th step: 1 dc (sc) in each of the next 5 sts, miss 1 st, 1 dc (sc) in each of next 10 sts, miss 1 st.

8th step: 1 dc (sc) in each of next 54 sts, miss 1 st, 1 dc (sc) in each of next 9 sts, miss 1 st (you now have 18 sts on the work).

9th step: * 1 dc (sc) in first st, miss next st, 1 dc (sc) in following st. Repeat from * 5 more times.

10th step: Cut yellow cotton and join pink cotton. Keep ends inside the work.

With pink cotton work neck and head as follows:

* 1 dc (sc) in each st. Repeat from * 11 more times.

Take a handful of polyester filling (batting) and stuff the body.

11th step: * 1 dc (sc) in first st, miss next st. Repeat from * 5 more times.

12th step: * 2 dc (sc) in first st, 1 dc (sc) in next st. Repeat from * 5 more times.

13th step: * 1 dc (sc) in each st. Repeat from * 11 more times.

14th step: * 2 dc (sc) in first st, 1 dc (sc) in each of next 2 sts. Repeat from * 7 more times.

15th step: * 1 dc (sc) in each st. Repeat from * 19 more times.

16th step: * 1 dc (sc) in each of next 2 sts, miss 1 st, 1 dc (sc) in next st. Repeat from * 4 more times.

17th step: * 1 dc (sc) in each st. Repeat from * 29 more times.

18th step: Cut pink cotton and join black cotton. Keep short ends inside work. With black cotton work hair as follows:

* 1 dc (sc) in each st. Repeat from * 29 more times.

Take some polyester filling (batting) and stuff the head.

19th step: * miss first st, 1 dc (sc)

in each of next 2 sts. Repeat from * 4 more times.
20th step: * miss first st, 1 dc (sc) in next st. Repeat from * 4 more times. Cast (bind) off last st. Sew end of cotton into the head.

ARMS

1st step: using yellow cotton work 3 ch, approx 60 cm (24 in) from end of cotton. (This will be used later to attach arm to body.)
Join into a ring with a ss in first ch.
2nd step: 1 ch, 5 dc (sc) into ring, close with a ss in first dc (sc). Hook the 60 cm (24 in) end of cotton through centre of the ring so it hangs on the right side of work.
3rd step: Working in a spiral fashion, * 2 dc (sc) in first st, 1 dc (sc) in next. Repeat from * 2 more times (you now have 8 sts on the work).
4th step: * 1 dc (sc) in each st. Repeat from * 95 more times.
5th step: Cut yellow cotton and join pink cotton. Keep short ends inside work. With pink cotton work hands as follows:
* 1 dc (sc) in first st, miss next st. Repeat from * 3 more times.
6th step: * 2 dc (sc) in first st, 1 dc (sc) in next st. Repeat from * 3 more times.
7th step: * 1 dc (sc) in each st. Repeat from * 15 more times.
8th step: * miss first st, 1 dc (sc) in each of next 3 sts. Repeat from * 1 more time.
Cast (bind) off last st. Sew end of cotton into hand.
Repeat steps 1–8 for other arm.

LEGS

1st step: using green cotton work the legs by following steps 1–3 as given for the arms.
4th step: * 1 dc (sc) in each of next 3 sts, 2 dc (sc) in following st. Repeat from * 1 more time.
5th step: * 1 dc (sc) in each st. Repeat from * 149 more times.
6th step: Cut green cotton and join pink cotton. Keep short ends inside work. With pink cotton work feet as follows:
* 1 dc (sc) in each st. Repeat from * 9 more times.
7th step: * 1 dc (sc) in each of next 2 sts, miss 1 st. Repeat from * 2 more times.
8th step: * 1 dc (sc) in each st. Repeat from * 8 more times (you now have 7 sts to work).
9th step: 1 dc (sc) in each of next 2 sts, 2 dc (sc) in each of next 4 sts, 1 dc (sc) in next st.
10th step: Cut pink cotton and join black cotton. With black cotton work shoe as follows: 1 dc (sc) in each of next 3 sts, 2 dc (sc) in each of next 6 sts, 1 dc (sc) in each of next 3 sts.
11th step: * 1 dc (sc) in each st. Repeat from * 21 more times.
12th step: Miss first st, 1 dc (sc) in each of next 4 sts, miss 1 st, 1 dc (sc) in each of next 6 sts.
13th step: * ss in each st. Repeat from * 14 more times.
Cast (bind) off last st. Sew end of cotton into shoe.
Repeat steps 1–13 to make the remaining leg.

TO MAKE UP

Attach the arms and legs to the doll's body as follows:

Using 60 cm (24 in) cotton ends, work several slightly loose stitches. Make a shank by twisting the cotton tightly around the stitches. Fasten off.

EARS AND NOSE

Cut a piece of pink cotton measuring approximately 80 cm (32 in) in length. Using it double, embroider as follows:

Starting at the bottom of the ear, make a 1 cm (3/8 in) long back stitch, bringing needle out at the starting position (to form a loop). Bind the loop with 3–4 blanket stitches. Repeat on other side of head for remaining ear and in the centre for the nose.

MOUTH

Using a single strand of red cotton, sew mouth in the same way as for the ears.

EYES

Using a single strand of dark green cotton, work several small back stitches in the same place, either side of the nose. Fasten off.
Decorate neck edge and cuffs of the doll's body with simple running stitches.

Hoppy **C**ushion

HOPS HAVE TRADITIONALLY BEEN USED FOR THEIR SOPORIFIC EFFECT!

YOU WILL NEED ■ *Ruler* ■ *Pencil* ■ *Paper* ■ *Tracing paper* ■ *Pins* ■ *Strong cotton fabric* ■ *Scissors* ■ *Contrasting velvet fabric* ■ *Non-toxic, flame retardant polyester filling (batting)* ■ *Oddments of red, white and black felt* ■ *Needle and thread* ■ *Oddments of yarn* ■ *Bodkin or large needle* ■ *Hops*

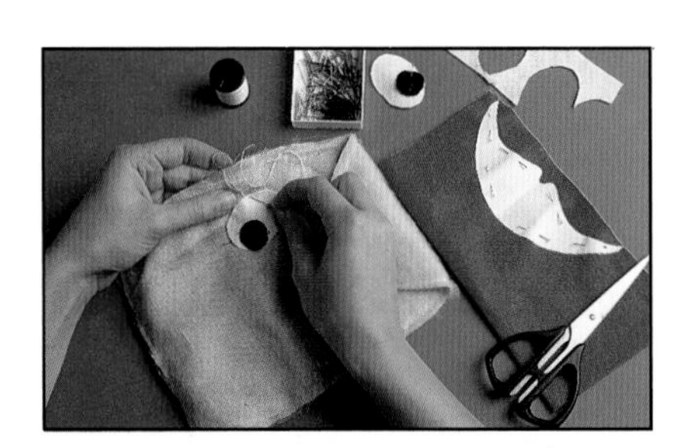

1 Scale up the templates to the required size and trace over and mark positions for eyes and mouth. Pin the paper patterns to the cotton fabric and cut out 4 side panels and 2 centre panels. Cut 1 base and 2 arms from the velvet fabric. Cut out matching pieces in filling (batting). Sew each piece of filling (batting) to reverse side of each piece of matching fabric. Cut the mouth and eye pieces from felt. Tack (baste) them to the front section and then zigzag stitch them securely in position.

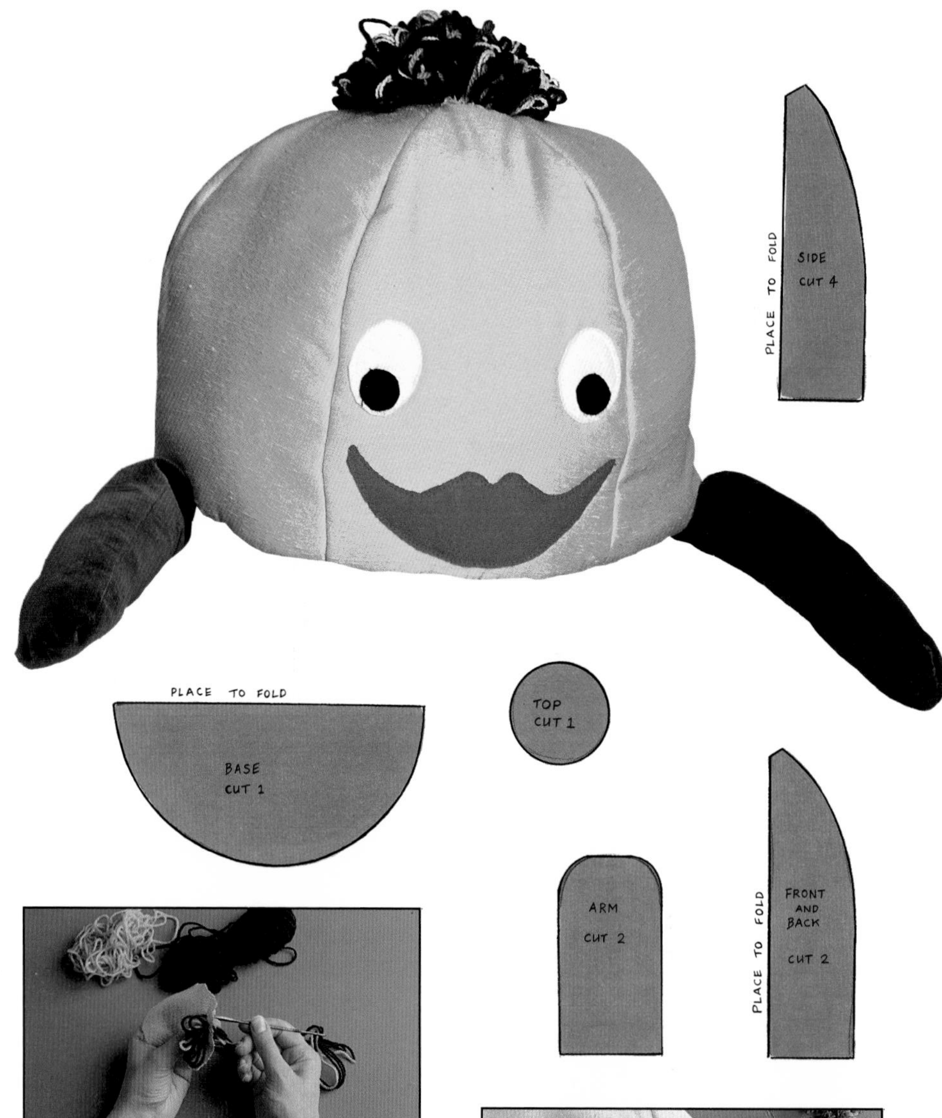

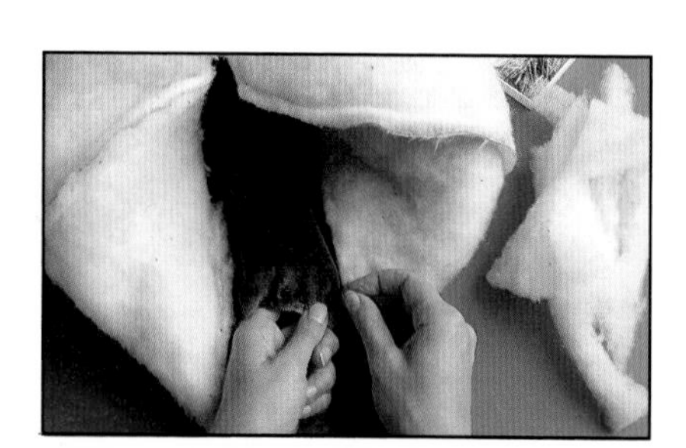

2 Making a 12 mm (½ in) seam, join all sides right sides together, leaving 1 back seam half open for filling. Fold the arms in half lengthwise with right sides together and sew. Turn right side out. Pin the top section to the base, wrong sides out, and push both arms into position. Double stitch round to join. Turn right side out.

3 To make the hair, push lengths of yarn through a small circle of fabric using a bodkin or large needle to form loops. Leave a 1.5 cm (⅝ in) seam allowance around the edges. When the circle is completely covered with looped lengths of yarn, fold in the seam allowance and sew the circle to the top of the cushion.

4 Stuff the cushion through the back seam with a mixture of filling (batting) and hops. Finally, sew up the seam to close the gap.

Pompon **M**obile

THIS EYE-CATCHING MOBILE WILL FASCINATE THE SMALLEST CHILD

YOU WILL NEED ■ *2 green garden stakes, 37 cm (14½ in) long* ■ *Florist's wire* ■ *Scissors* ■ *Lengths of red, blue, yellow and green yarn* ■ *Large darning needle* ■ *4 red pompons; 4 blue pompons; 4 yellow pompons; 4 green pompons; all 5 cm (2 in) in diameter* ■ *Needle and thread* ■ *Curled ribbon in matching colours*

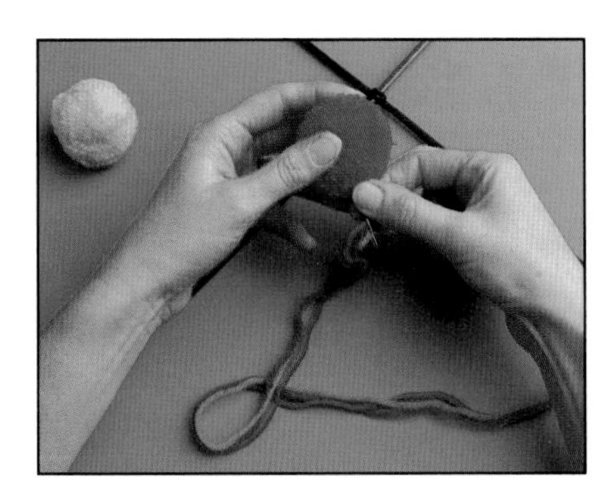

1 Lay the stakes to form a cross. Secure in the centre using florist's wire. Thread 3 lengths of yarn, approximately 51 cm (20 in) long, onto the darning needle. Sew the yarn through the first pompon, tying a knot at the end to secure.

Continue to thread the yarn through the next pompon. Knot the yarn 8 cm (3¼ in) from the first pompon and slide the pompon down to the knot. Continue until all 4 colours have been used. Tie the end of the yarn to the centre of the stake leaving 12 cm (4¾ in) between the pompon and stake.

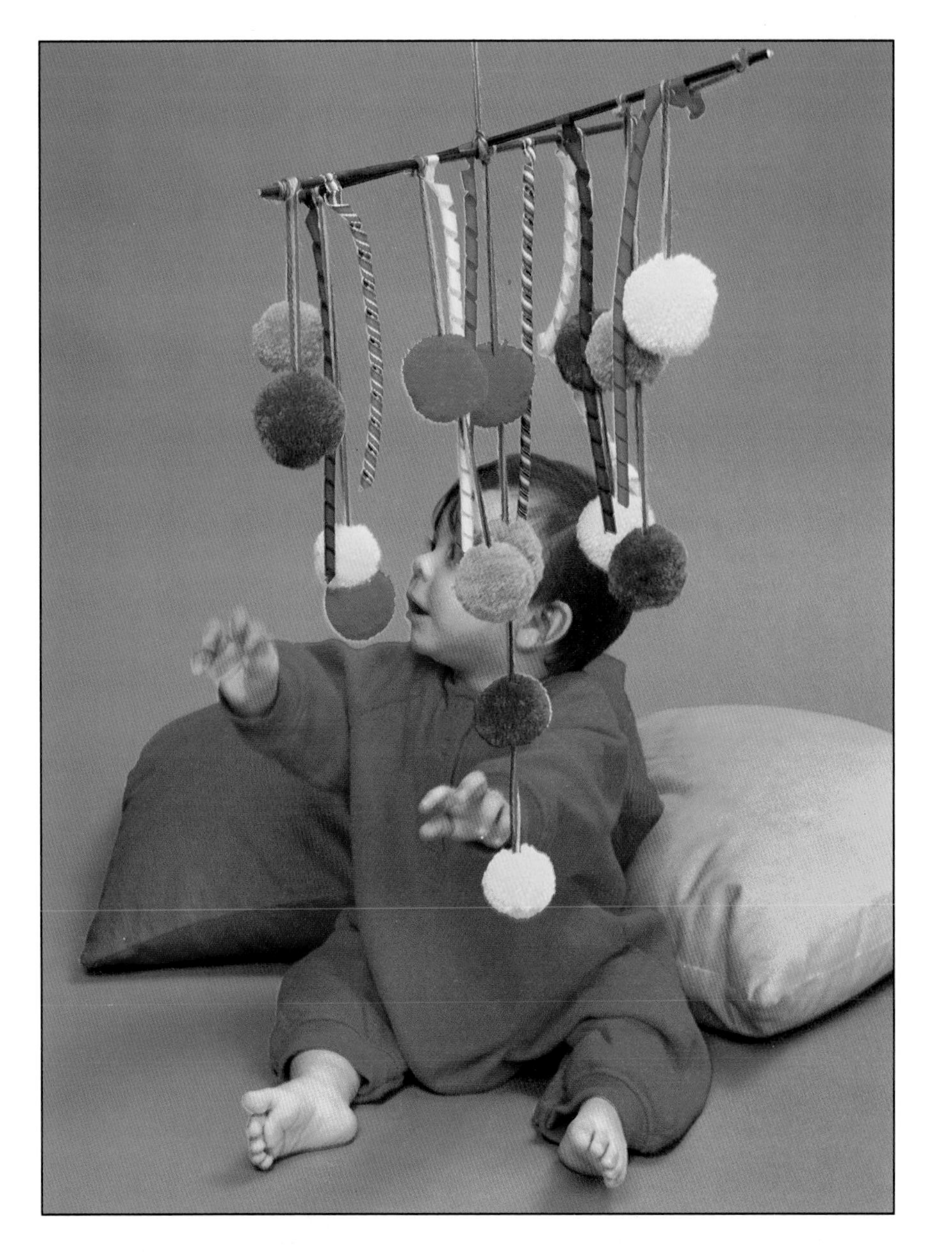

2 Next, thread 2 pompons onto the yarn as before. Repeat 4 times, using a different colour combination each time. Tie onto the stake 8 cm (3¼ in) from the centre. Thread each remaining pompon onto the yarn and tie at each end of the stake. Sew the ribbon between each hanging pompon. Tie a length of yarn from the centre to allow the mobile to be hung from the ceiling.

Turtle Jigsaw

THIS SIMPLE TO MAKE JIGSAW IS AN ATTRACTIVE TOY FOR 1½ TO 3-YEAR-OLDS

YOU WILL NEED ■ White paper ■ Pencil ■ Piece of plywood, 12 mm (½ in) thick ■ Chalk ■ Fretsaw (scroll saw) ■ Sandpaper ■ Matt white emulsion (flat latex) paint ■ Small paintbrush ■ Non-toxic acrylic paints ■ Non-toxic clear acrylic varnish

1 Draw the simple tortoise shape onto white paper. Transfer the design onto the piece of plywood by chalking the back of the paper and then drawing over the outline on the front.

2 Cut out the shapes with a fretsaw (scroll saw). Work carefully, especially when cutting the line inside the tortoise. Sand all the edges.

3 Prime each piece with a coat of white emulsion (flat latex) paint. Allow to dry, then paint each section a different colour. Rub down the edges of each piece to ensure a good fit.

4 Finish with a coat of clear acrylic varnish.

Ribbons and Bells

THIS COLOURFUL DECORATION WILL JINGLE AS IT MOVES

YOU WILL NEED ■ *Lengths of different coloured ribbon* ■ *Scissors* ■ *Bells* ■ *20 cm (8 in) length of dowelling, 5 mm (3/16 in) thick* ■ *Rubber-based glue*

1 Taking 3 different coloured lengths of ribbon at a time, attach them to a bell using a strong double knot.

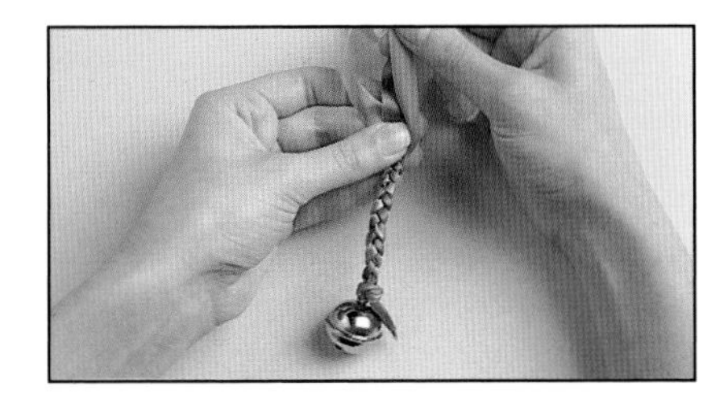

2 Braid the lengths together, leaving enough ribbon free to knot around the dowelling. Finish off the braiding by tying a strong double knot.

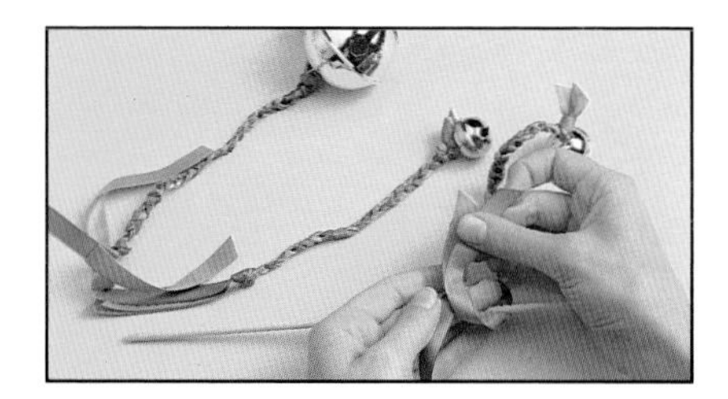

3 Tie each braid securely onto the dowelling using another double knot and a dab of glue to stop the bells slipping along the dowelling. Tie a length of ribbon on to either end of the dowelling and suspend from a high point. The decoration can then be spun around and the ribbons will wind around each other.

Clown Carousel

THIS HAND-OPERATED CAROUSEL WILL PROVIDE ENDLESS AMUSEMENT

YOU WILL NEED ■ Thin plywood ■ Thick plywood ■ Pair of compasses ■ Pencil ■ Fretsaw (scroll saw) ■ Hand drill ■ Ruler ■ Length of wood, 4 cm (1½ in) wide and 2 cm (¾ in) thick ■ Sandpaper ■ Non-toxic enamel paints ■ Paintbrushes ■ Wood glue ■ 24 cm (9½ in) dowelling ■ Scissors ■ Lengths of different coloured ribbons ■ Drawing pin (thumb tack)

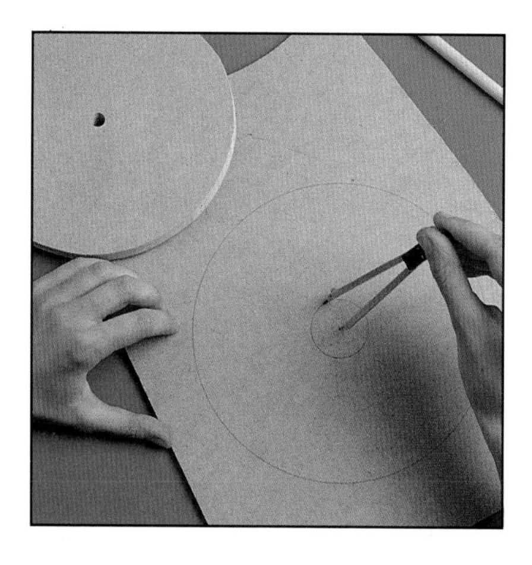

1 Using a pair of compasses, draw out the smaller circle onto the thick plywood and the larger one onto the thin plywood. Cut out carefully using a fretsaw (scroll saw). Drill a hole in each circle to fit the dowelling. Enlarge the hole in the larger circle a little with a fretsaw (scroll saw) to allow movement.

2 Transfer the clown shape on the template onto a piece of thick plywood and cut out 3 clown shapes using a fretsaw (scroll saw). Drill a small hole in each of the hats so that ribbon can be threaded through later. To make the knob for the top of the carousel, mark off a line to make a square at the end of the length of wood. Draw 2 diagonals on the cut square of wood to find the centre of the square. Drill a hole the same diameter as the dowelling in the centre, about 1 cm (⅜ in) deep. Next saw off the square with the hole in the centre from the rest of the length of wood. Sand all the edges of the wooden pieces until smooth with sandpaper.

3 Paint all the pieces of wood with enamel paint in an assortment of bright colours. Paint the main colours first with a fairly large brush, and allow to dry before adding the details with a small brush. When the paint is dry, glue the piece of dowelling into the base (the smaller circle) with wood glue.

Glue the 3 clowns around the platform. Place the platform over the dowelling so that it rests on top of the base. Place a thin piece of plywood or some folded paper between the 2 circles so that there will be a gap between them while you attach the ribbons.

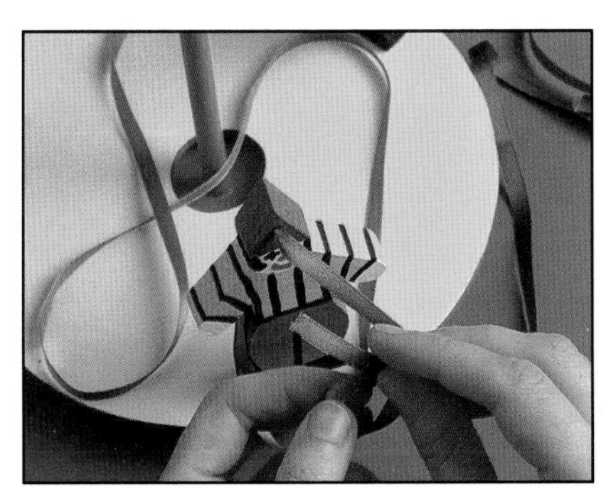

4 Cut 3 lengths of ribbon in different colours and thread through the top of the clowns' hats, securing with a knot at the front. Bring the 3 lengths of ribbon together at the top of the piece of dowelling and secure with wood glue and a drawing pin (thumb tack). Make sure that there is equal tension in the taut ribbon.

Finally, glue the knob onto the top of the dowelling, hiding the pin and the ribbon ends. Leave the glue to dry for at least 2 hours, then remove the thin plywood or paper from between the platforms. Swing the platform in one direction and the ribbons will wind and unwind, moving the clowns backwards and forwards.

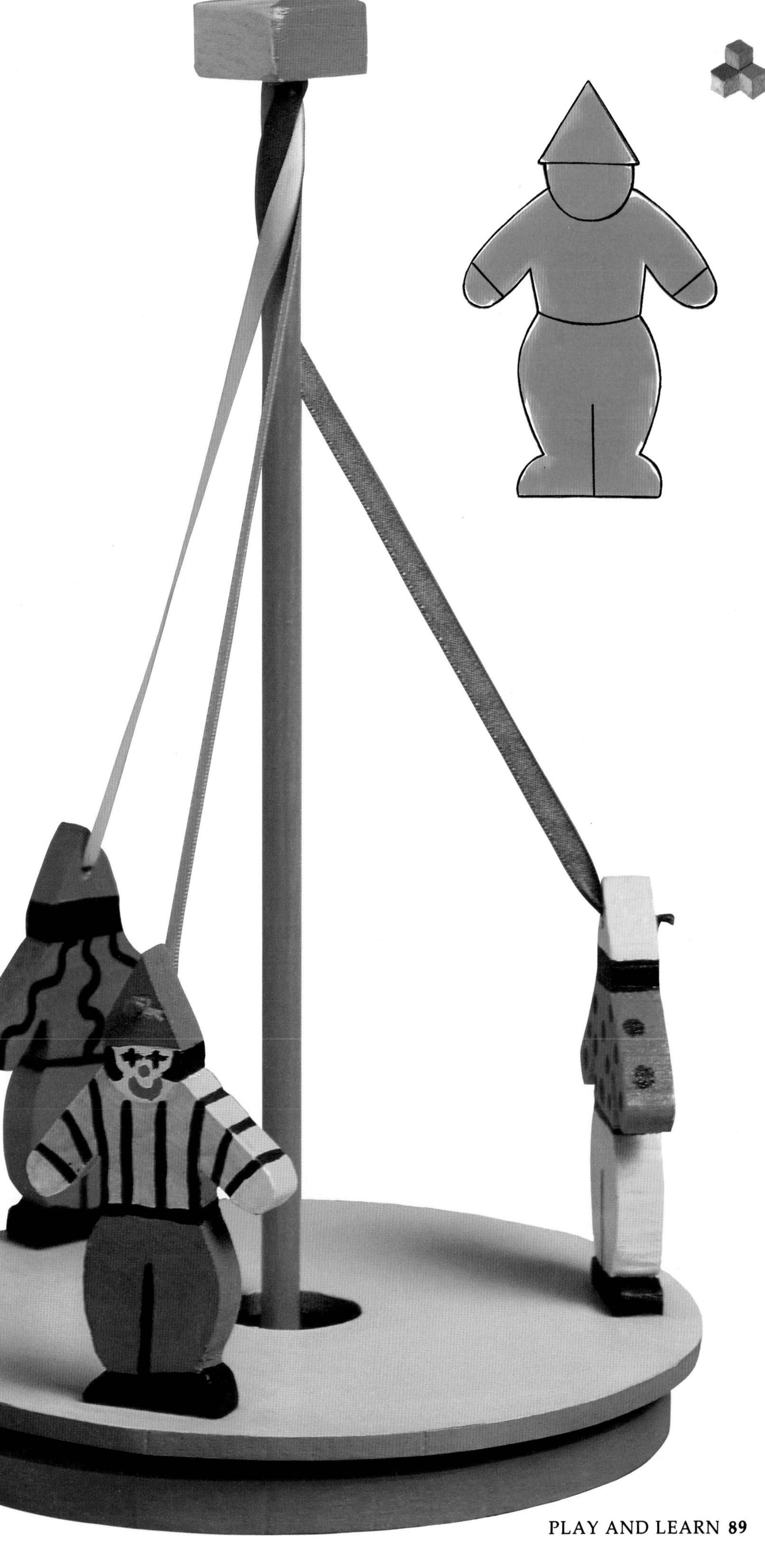

Tugboat

THIS TUG CAN BE USFD AS A PUSH-ABOUT TOY

YOU WILL NEED ■ *Pen* ■ *Paper* ■ *Scissors* ■ *40 × 7.5 cm (16 × 3 in) wood, 2.5 cm (1 in) thick* ■ *Hand saw* ■ *Sandpaper* ■ *10 × 4.5 cm (4 × 2 in) wood, 12 mm (½ in) thick* ■ *4 × 4 cm (1½ × 1½ in) woodscrews* ■ *Screwdriver* ■ *Plastic wood* ■ *6 × 4.5 cm (2¼ × 2 in) and 4.5 × 4.5 cm (2 × 2 in) wood, all 2 cm (¾ in) thick* ■ *Wood glue* ■ *Panel pins (finishing nails)* ■ *Hammer* ■ *7.5 cm (3 in) dowelling, 3 cm (1¼ in) in diameter* ■ *Hand drill* ■ *Paintbrush* ■ *Non-toxic acrylic paints*

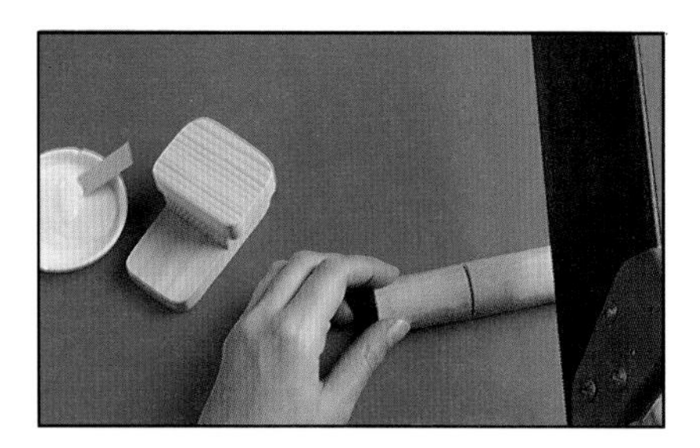

1 Scale up the hull shape from the template. Cut it out and draw around the outline onto the large piece of wood. Saw round the outline and sand the edges. Use this hull shape to trace out the front 10 cm (4 in) of the bow and the rear 5 cm (2 in) sections on the remaining larger piece of wood.

Cut these 2 pieces at an angle from front to rear to make a slope. Cut out a 'V' from the inside edges. Sand them smooth and screw them onto the hull, through the base, counter-sinking the screws and covering with plastic wood. Sand to match the shape of the bow and stern of the hull.

2 Sand the corners of the other 3 blocks of wood, but leave 2 square corners on the square block. Assemble with the largest piece at the bottom, the square in the middle front and the remaining piece on top.

Attach all pieces using wood glue and panel pins (finishing nails) to make the wheelhouse. Drill a hole in the dowelling to screw to the boat. Sand the base and top of the dowelling so that the funnel stands at a slight angle.

3 Paint all the pieces and leave to dry. Screw the funnel in place, then screw the whole assembly to the hull through the base of the hull, counter-sinking the screws and filling with plastic wood. Paint over the filler.

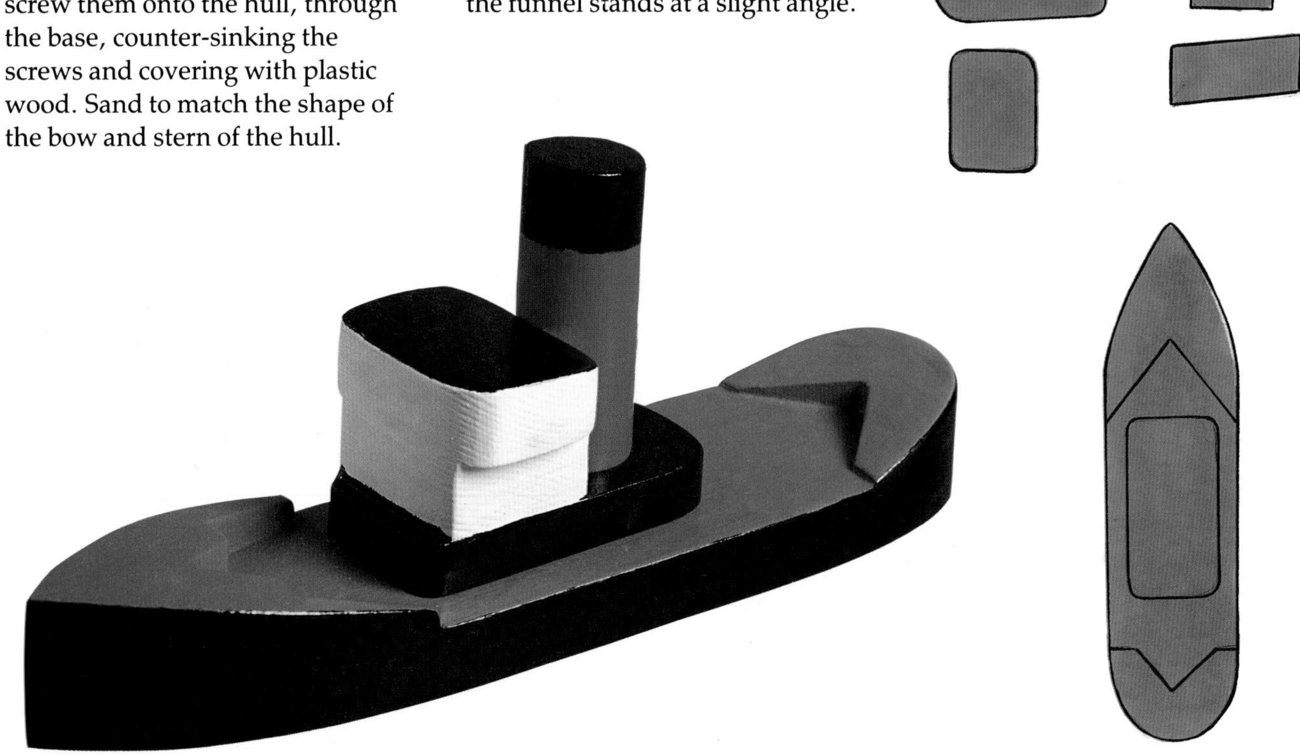

Rocking Parrot

GIVE THE PERCH A FEW TWISTS, AND THIS PARROT WILL SWING AROUND UNAIDED

YOU WILL NEED ■ Pencil ■ Paper ■ Scissors ■ 30 × 20 cm (12 × 8 in) plywood, 6 mm (¼ in) thick ■ Fretsaw (scroll saw) ■ Scrap wood ■ Hand drill ■ Sandpaper ■ Masking tape ■ 30 cm (12 in) dowelling ■ Paintbrushes ■ Acrylic paints ■ Wood glue ■ 90 cm (36 in) coloured string

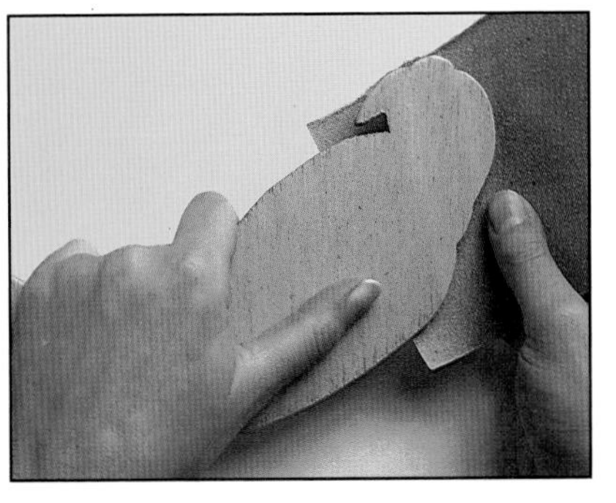

3 Smooth down any rough edges on the parrot shape with sandpaper.

1 Scale up the parrot template to the size required and draw the shape onto a sheet of paper. Cut it out and then draw around the outline onto the plywood sheet. Cut out carefully with the fretsaw (scroll saw).

2 Mark the centre of the hole where the dowelling perch is to be inserted. Place the parrot onto a piece of scrap wood and accurately drill a hole to exactly the same diameter as that of the piece of dowelling.

4 Starting from the centre, wind masking tape outwards to each end of the dowelling, leaving uncovered spaces between the tape. Paint the uncovered area and leave to dry before peeling off the tape. Paint the parrot in bright colours, section by section. Drill a 3 mm (⅛ in) hole at each end of the dowelling and slide it into the hole in the parrot. Glue it in the centre, with the 2 holes at the ends facing upwards. Thread the string through the 2 holes, wrap it around the ends and tie securely. Carefully knot a loop at the centre.

Snake **M**obile

THIS SIMPLE MOBILE SPIRALS ROUND IN A FASCINATING WAY

YOU WILL NEED ■ *Pencil* ■ *Coloured card* ■ *Scissors* ■ *Large darning needle* ■ *Fine cord* ■ *Dowelling, painted white (optional)*

1 Using the template as a guide, draw spiral snake designs onto different pieces of coloured card in a range of different sizes. Cut out the spirals with a sharp pair of scissors, following the lines precisely so that the shapes are accurate.

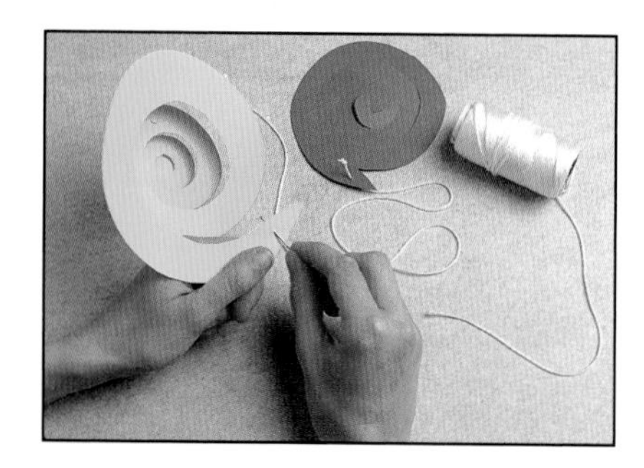

2 Using a needle threaded with the cord, pierce a hole through the head end of each 'snake'. Pull the thread through to the desired length and secure with a knot at the head end. Either hang the threaded snakes from a length of painted white dowelling or secure them individually from the nursery ceiling.

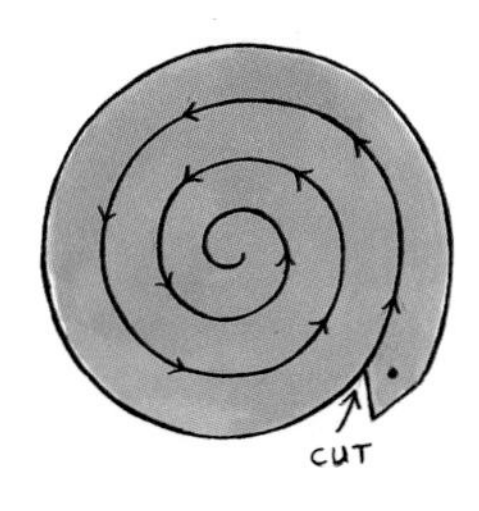

Geometric Mobile

THIS BRIGHT MOBILE WILL FASCINATE ANY CHILD

YOU WILL NEED ■ *Pair of compasses* ■ *Ruler* ■ *Pencil* ■ *White card* ■ *Scissors* ■ *Paintbrushes* ■ *Non-toxic acrylic paints* ■ *Gummed paper in several bright colours* ■ *Needle* ■ *Gold thread*

1 Using a pair of compasses, ruler and pencil, draw onto card all the shapes needed for this mobile. You will need a long narrow strip 8 × 40 cm (3¼ × 16 in) to form the coronet and 2 circles, a square, a diamond and a triangle, each 7 cm (2¾ in) across. Also draw 2 smaller circles. Cut out all of the shapes with a sharp pair of scissors.

2 Paint all the shapes different colours using the acrylic paints. Paint the long narrow strip, 1 large circle and the 2 small circles black. Cut out a range of smaller shapes from the coloured gummed paper.

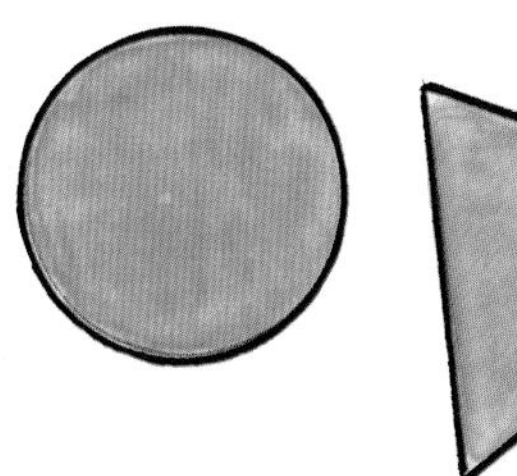

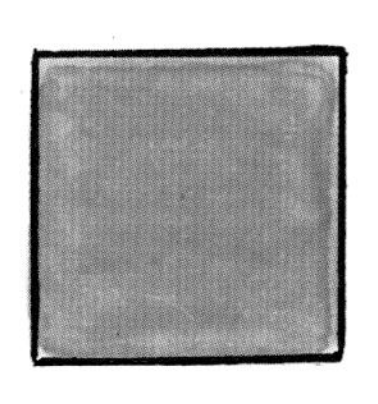

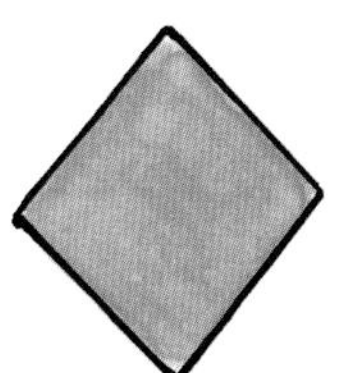

3 When the paint is dry, stick the gummed coloured shapes onto both sides of the black painted shapes. Glue the long narrow strip together at the ends to form a coronet. With a needle, pierce 4 pairs of holes into the top and bottom edges of the coronet. Also pierce a hole at the top of each shape.

Thread 10 cm (4 in) of gold thread through each of the 4 coloured shapes and secure them with a knot. Suspend each shape from the bottom of the coronet and secure each with a knot tied on the inside of the coronet.

4 Pierce the 3 black circles top and bottom and connect up with gold thread, spacing them out and securing them at each hole with a knot. Cut four 40 cm (16 in) lengths of gold thread and thread them through the holes at the top of the coronet. Then gather these 4 threads together with the central thread at the top and tie a knot. The mobile will now hang in a well-balanced display.

Tiger Stripes

THIS CRAZY TIGER IS IDEAL FOR A BEGINNER TO KNIT

YOU WILL NEED ■ *Oddments of brightly-coloured double knitting (sport) yarn* ■ *1 pair of 4 mm (US 5) knitting needles* ■ *Scissors* ■ *Darning needle* ■ *Fine black felt-tip pen* ■ *Thin card* ■ *White felt* ■ *Needle and thread* ■ *2 buttons or safety eyes* ■ *Non-toxic, flame retardant polyester filling (batting)*

Tension (Gauge)
This will differ according to the yarn used.

BODY
(*Knit 2 alike*)
Cast on 30 sts. Work in garter stitch (every row knit) throughout, changing yarn frequently for stripes. K 8 rows. Cast (bind) off 9 sts at the beg of the next row, k to end.
Cast (bind) off 7 sts at the beg of the next row, k to end. K 9 rows.
Cast on 7 sts at the beg of the next row, k across these 7 sts and the rest of row (21 sts). K 9 rows.
Cast (bind) off 7 sts at the beg of the next row, k to end (14 sts).
K 15 rows.
Cast on 7 sts at the beg of the next row, k across these 7 sts and the rest of row (21 sts).
Cast on 7 sts at the beg of the next row, k across these 7 sts and the rest of row (28 sts). K 5 rows.
Cast (bind) off 4 sts at the beg of the next row, k to end (24 sts).
K 2 rows.
Cast (bind) off 7 sts at the beg of the next row, k to end (17 sts).
K 6 rows.
Cast on 4 sts at the beg of the next row, k across these 4 sts and the rest of row (21 sts).
Cast on 7 sts at the beg of the next row, k across these 7 sts and the rest of row (28 sts). K 4 rows.
Cast (bind) off 4 sts at the beg of the next row, k to end (24 sts).
K 4 rows.
Cast (bind) off 7 sts at the beg of the next row, k to end (17 sts).
K 2 rows.
Cast (bind) off the remaining 17 sts. Sew in ends.

TO MAKE UP
Oversew the 2 body pieces together leaving an opening at the cast-off (bound-off) edges (the tiger's mouth). Using the template as a guide, cut out the shape for the tiger's teeth from the white felt. Finally sew 2 buttons on for eyes (if the tiger is intended for a very young child, use safety eyes instead of buttons). Stuff the tiger through the mouth opening. Place the felt teeth inside the mouth and sew up the gap using sewing cotton to complete.

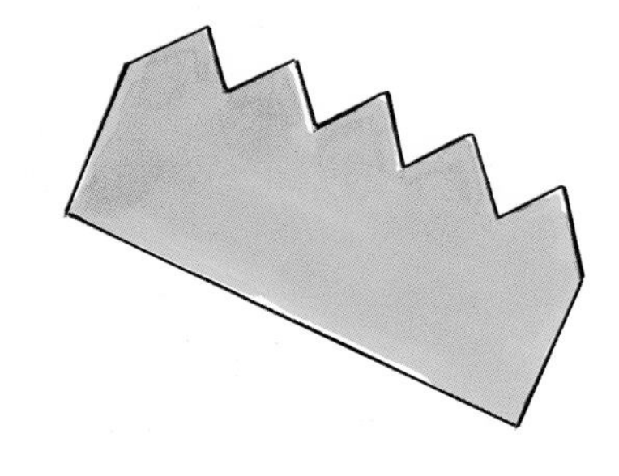

Pocketed Quilt

THIS COSY ACTIVITY QUILT HAS POCKETS FOR HIDING SURPRISE GIFTS

YOU WILL NEED ■ *Scissors* ■ *6 pieces of 25 × 25 cm (10 × 10 in) fabric for pockets* ■ *Pins* ■ *Needle and thread* ■ *Pinking shears* ■ *75 cm (30 in) fringing* ■ *2 pieces of 65 × 120 cm (26 × 47 in) fabric for quilt* ■ *64 × 120 cm (25½ × 47 in) light wadding (batting)* ■ *3.7 m (4 yd) bias binding*

1 Cut out the pocket pieces. Pin the squares together in pairs and sew round the edges. Trim the edges with pinking shears and turn right side out.

2 Cut 3 lengths of fringing 25 cm (10 in) long and sew one length along the top edges of each of the squares.

3 Sew the 3 pockets in a line down the length of one of the quilt pieces.

4 Sandwich the wadding (batting) between the 2 quilt pieces and sew the bias binding all around the edge.

Height Chart

KEEP TRACK OF YOUR CHILD'S GROWTH WITH THIS DECORATIVE CHART

YOU WILL NEED ■ *Metal ruler* ■ *Pencil* ■ *125 × 25 cm (50 × 10 in) coloured paper* ■ *Craft knife* ■ *Marker pens* ■ *Numerals stencil* ■ *Assorted animal pictures* ■ *Scissors* ■ *Strong clear glue* ■ *2 rolls iron-on protective laminating film, 4 m × 30 cm (5 × 1 ft)* ■ *Iron* ■ *60 cm (24 in) wooden dowelling* ■ *Rubber-based glue* ■ *String*

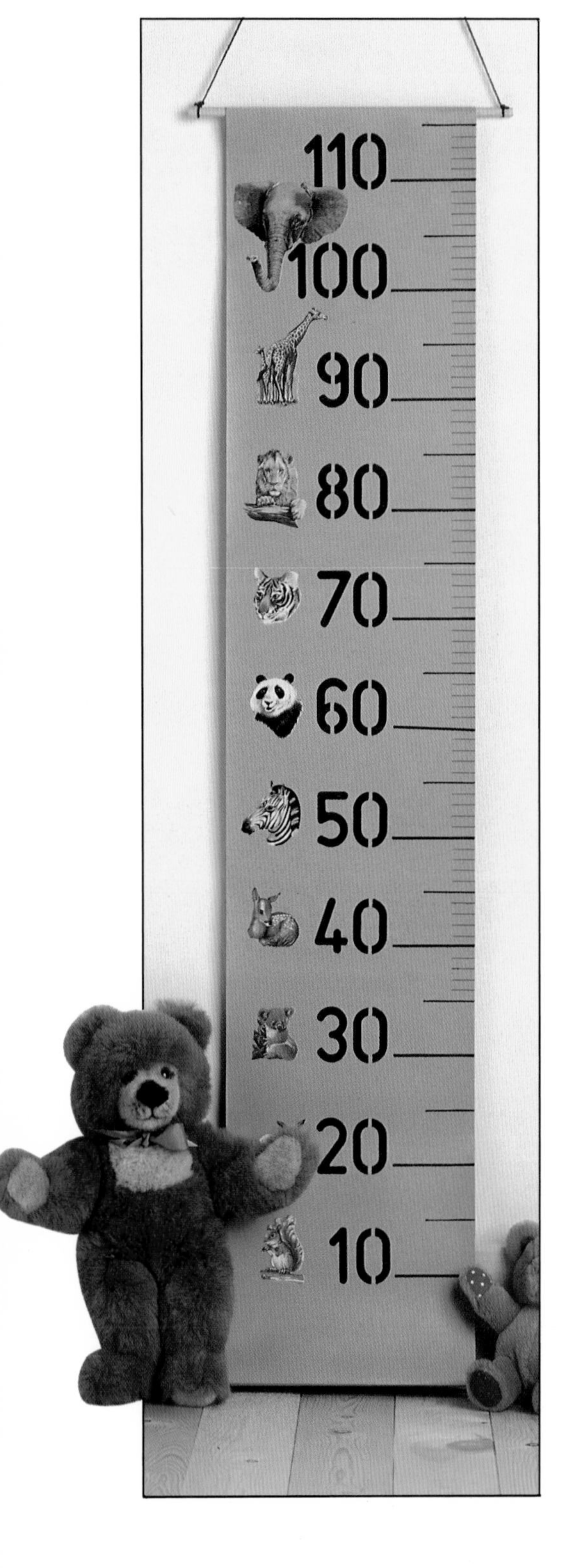

1 Using the metal ruler, mark out two lines 4 and 5 cm (1½ and 2 in) from the top and bottom ends of the paper, and lightly score across them using a craft knife. On the right-hand side of the paper measure from the lower score line and pencil in divisions of 5 and 10 cm or 3 and 6 in, starting at 10 cm or 6 in. Mark single units too after 35 cm or 12 in, making a longer mark for each 5th and 10th unit.

2 Use a thick marker pen to mark out 8 cm (3¼ in) lines at each of the 10 cm or 6 in divisions. Use a medium marker pen to mark out 5 cm (2 in) long lines at the intervening 5 cm or 3 in divisions and finally use a thin pen to mark out the remaining units with 1 cm (⅜ in) long lines.

Using the stencil, number each 10 cm or 6 in division from 10 cm to 110 cm, or each 6 in division from 6 in to 5 ft. Cut out pictures to fit each 10th division, working from the smallest at the first division to the largest at the highest division. Glue in place.

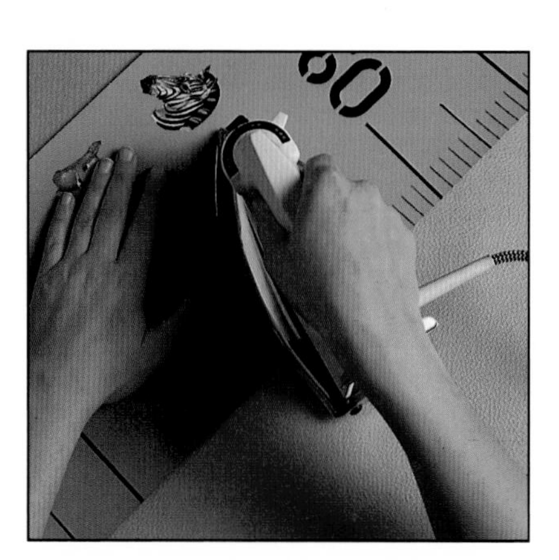

3 Spread the sheet out on an ironing board. Cover the top surface with the iron-on protective laminating film and iron down carefully according to the manufacturer's instructions. Turn the sheet over and repeat the process on the reverse side.

4 Fold the top and bottom of the chart at the score lines. Cut the wooden dowelling in half and glue one length at each end with rubber-based glue. Tie string to each end of the top dowelling and hang the chart so that the base rests on the floor.

Stripy **T**oy **S**ack

RECYCLE AN OLD PILLOW CASE TO MAKE THIS BRIGHT TOY SACK

YOU WILL NEED ■ White cotton pillow case ■ Yellow, red and blue dyes ■ Dye fix ■ Plastic bowl or bucket ■ Iron ■ Drawing pins (thumb tacks) ■ Newspaper ■ Large paintbrush ■ Short length of rope

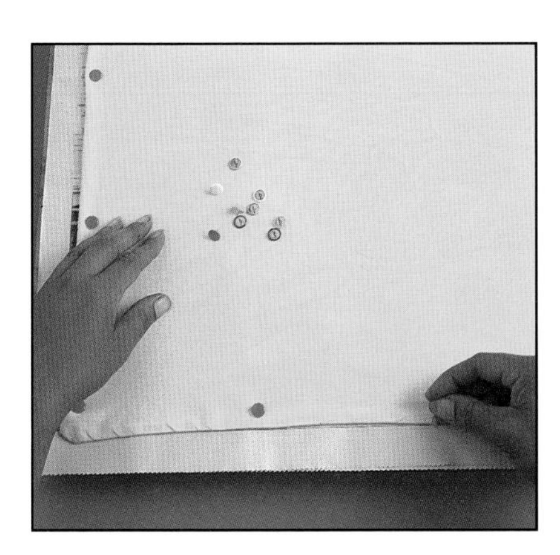

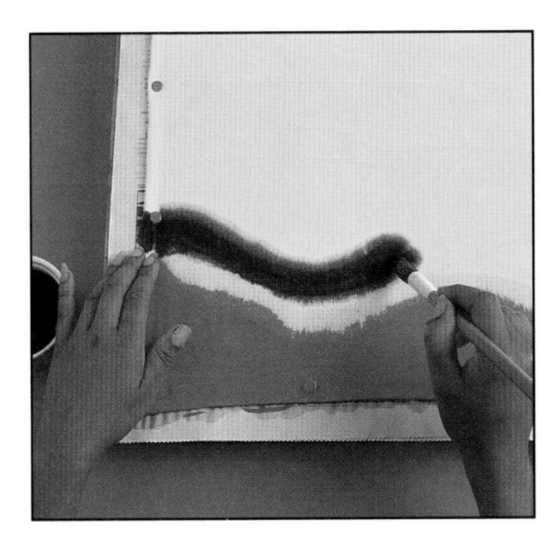

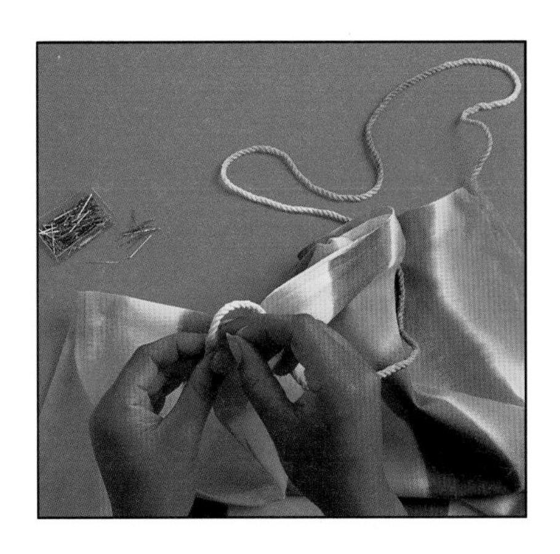

1 Wash the pillow case and allow to dry naturally. Mix the yellow dye following the manufacturer's instructions and add the dye fix. Pour the dye into a plastic bowl or bucket. Place the pillow case into the dye and leave for the recommended time. Rinse under running water and allow to dry naturally. Iron the pillow case, and pin it onto a clean even surface that has first been covered with a layer of newspaper to absorb any excess dye.

2 Using a large brush, paint bold stripes of red and blue dye onto the pillow case, leaving a gap of yellow between each stripe. Leave for at least 30 minutes to allow the dye to soak into the fabric. Remove, and hang up to dry naturally.

3 Use the leftover dyes to paint the rope in stripes. Pin the rope to the edges of the pillow case and stitch firmly. Do not leave excessive lengths of loose rope near a small baby.

Patchwork Quilt

ESSENTIAL FOR THE NURSERY, THIS TRADITIONAL QUILT IS SIMPLE TO MAKE

YOU WILL NEED ■ *Tape measure* ■ *Pencil* ■ *Graph paper* ■ *Ruler* ■ *Scissors* ■ *Traditional cotton fabrics in 8 different patterns* ■ *Pins* ■ *Needle and thread* ■ *Iron* ■ *Darker cotton fabric* ■ *Wadding (batting)* ■ *Patterned cotton for quilt back*

1 Measure the cot (crib) to find the overall quilt size required, and then draw up a simple plan on graph paper showing the finished border widths and square sizes. The design shown here uses 28 squares in all.

Start the centre patchwork squares by cutting 8 strips using the 8 different patterned cottons. The strip widths should be cut accurately to the width of your squares *plus* 2 × 6 mm (¼ in) seam allowances. Calculate the length in the same way, adding 2 sets of 6 mm (¼ in) seam allowances for *each square*. Arrange 2 sets of 4 strips keeping adjoining tones varied, and pin, tack (baste) and stitch 1 set of 4 together, following your seam allowance as accurately as possible. Secure all loose threads and press the seams open at the back. Repeat the same procedure to make up the second set of 4 strips.

Next, cut across the strips to make strips of squares. Remember when you cut that you will need to include the seam allowances for each square. You will need 4 strips from 1 set and 3 strips from the other to make a total of 28 squares for the quilt.

2 Arrange the strips side by side taking 1 from each set and reversing the direction each time so that the patterns are varied and no adjoining squares are the same. Pin, tack (baste) and stitch and secure all loose threads. Press all seams open at the back.

Make up the long border strips, using contrasting triangles at the corners to make squares and sewing the squares to the long border ends. Pin, tack (baste) and stitch the short border ends to the squared section and press, and then join the long borders to the quilt edges. Press firmly on the back and front.

3 Cut the wadding (batting) and a piece of fabric for the quilt back to the overall quilt size plus seam allowances. Place the patchwork onto the wadding (batting), right side up. Position the quilt back on top of both layers, right side down. Smooth the layers outwards from the centre and pin and tack (baste) all 3 layers together.

Stitch all round, rounding off the corners and leaving an open length on one edge for turning. Trim the corners and turn the quilt to the outside. Press firmly with a medium iron. Oversew the edge to close. Topstitch the quilt about 1.5 cm (⅝ in) all round the edge.

Waist Hold-all

THE IDEAL HOLD-ALL FOR PARENTS ON THE MOVE

YOU WILL NEED ■ *Scissors* ■ *27 × 43 cm (10½ × 17 in) fabric* ■ *20.5 × 43 cm (8¼ × 17 in) fabric in contrasting colour* ■ *Pinking shears* ■ *Needle and thread* ■ *126 cm (50 in) bias binding* ■ *126 cm (50 in) ribbon or fabric binding*

1 Cut out the 2 fabric pieces and trim the edges with pinking shears. On the smaller piece sew a line of bias binding along the longest edge.

2 Sew 2 lines of stitching down the smaller piece to divide it into 3 pockets. Sew the smaller fabric piece onto the large piece, around the 3 unbound edges, and leave the extra fabric at the top edge.

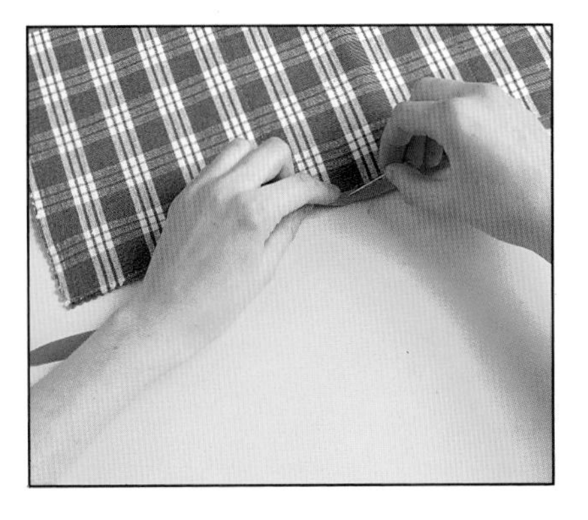

3 Sew a length of bias binding round the bottom and side edges of the hold-all.

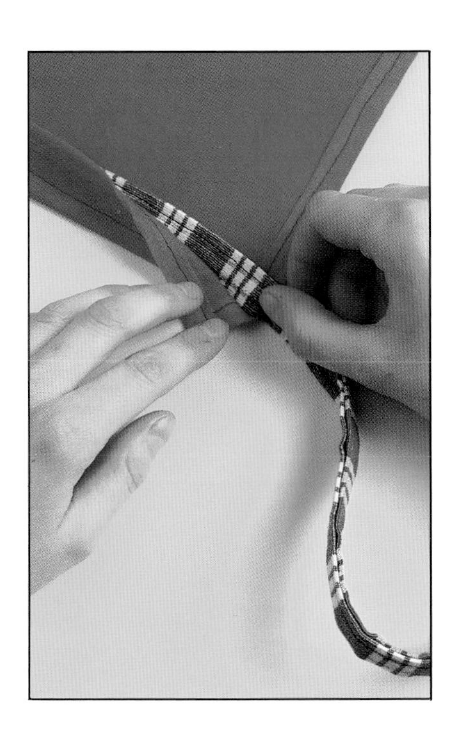

4 Sew the length of ribbon or fabric binding just below the top edge of the reverse side of the hold-all, to make the waist ties. Fold over the top edge and sew down over the waist tie.

Bedroom Tidy

A BRIGHT AND CHEERFUL HOLDER FOR BEDROOM CLUTTER

YOU WILL NEED ■ *Scissors* ■ *1.5 m (1½ yd) of red cotton fabric, 90 cm (36 in) wide* ■ *Tape measure* ■ *Pins* ■ *Needles and thread* ■ *Iron* ■ *20 cm (8 in) yellow cotton fabric, 90 cm (36 in) wide* ■ *46 cm (18 in) dowelling* ■ *80 cm (32 in) length of red braid* ■ *Pieces of felt in various colours* ■ *Rubber-based glue*

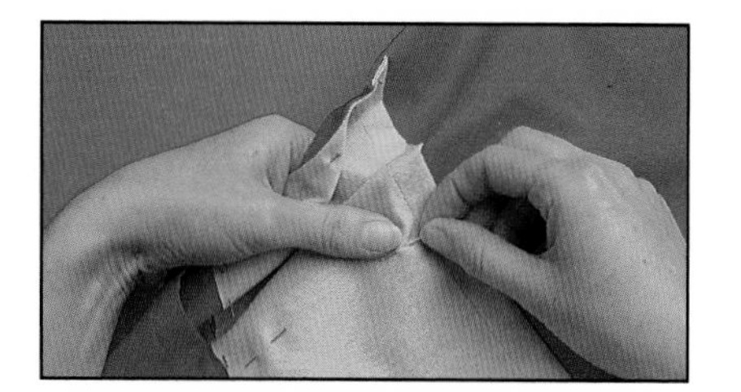

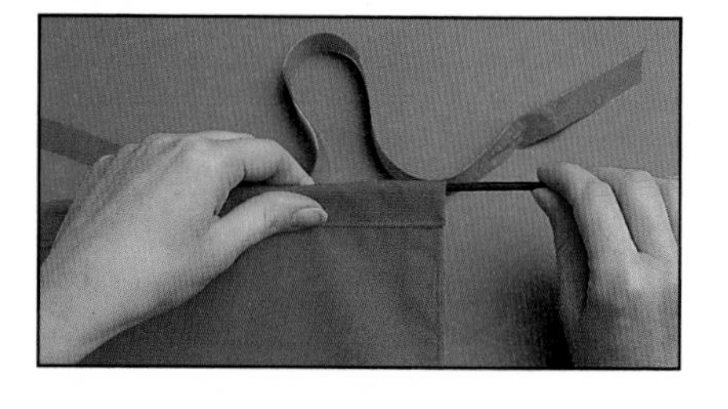

1 Cut a piece of red cotton fabric 1.1 m × 40.5 cm (43 × 16 in). With right sides together, fold in half widthways and pin together. Tack (baste) down each side. Remove the pins and stitch with a 1.5 cm (⅝ in) seam allowance. Trim, turn through the open top seam and press.

Next, cut 2 pieces of red cotton fabric to 39.5 × 18 cm (15½ × 7 in) plus 1 piece of yellow cotton the same size. Turn under 1.5 cm (⅝ in) on 3 edges and fold 1 long length over an extra 1.5 cm (⅝ in). Pin and tack (baste). Remove the pins. Stitch along the long double folded edge.

2 Place the first red pocket at the bottom of the large piece of fabric. Pin in place. Lay the yellow pocket above it, leaving a 5 mm (¼ in) gap between them and pin. Repeat with the next red pocket and pin. Measure 12 cm (4¾ in) in from each side to divide each long pocket into 3, and mark the position with pins along the length. Tack (baste) along all pin lines and remove the pins. Sew and remove tacking (basting).

3 Make a casing at the top of the bedroom tidy by turning down a hem 2 cm (¾ in) wide. Pin, tack (baste) and sew. Slip the piece of dowelling through the casing. Tie one end of the braid to each end of the dowelling.

4 Cut out coloured motifs from the felt. Glue into place, one on each pocket, and leave to dry.

Changing **B**ag

A HANDY PADDED CHANGING MAT AND BAG WITH LARGE POCKETS

YOU WILL NEED ■ *Plain cotton fabric* ■ *Scissors* ■ *Tape measure* ■ *Pins* ■ *Needle and thread* ■ *Iron* ■ *Towelling (terrycloth)* ■ *Patterned cotton fabric* ■ *Medium-weight wadding (batting)* ■ *Toggle*

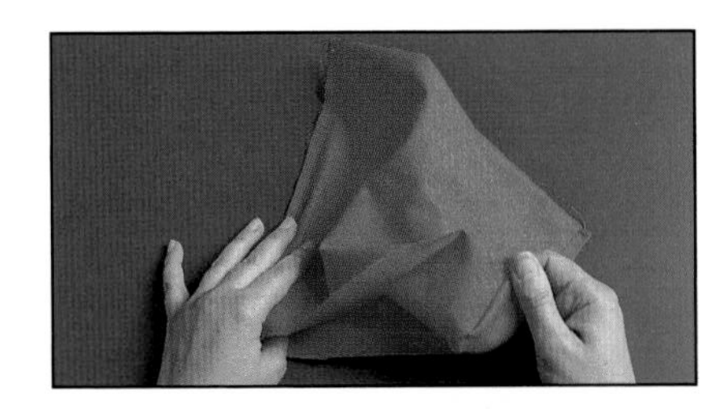

1 From the plain cotton cut 2 pocket flaps each 46 × 26 cm (18¼ × 10¼ in). Fold each flap in turn across its longest edge to make a shape 23 × 26 cm (9 × 10¼ in). Stitch along the 2 shorter edges, making a bag. Turn the seams to the inside and press.

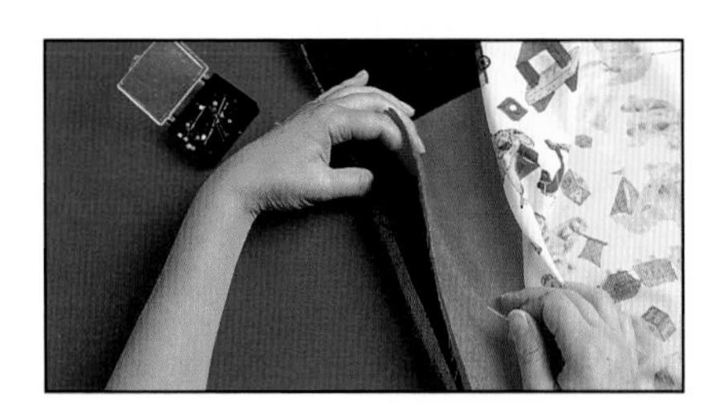

2 To make the mat, cut 1 piece each of towelling (terrycloth), patterned cotton fabric and wadding (batting) to 80 × 46 cm (32 × 18¼ in). Place the towelling (terrycloth) right side up on the wadding (batting). Make a narrow loop of patterned fabric for the toggle and tack (baste) it in place at the centre bottom of the mat so that the ends can be stitched into the seam.

Tack (baste) the pocket flaps 6 cm (2¼ in) from the top of the mat. Position the patterned cotton right side down on top. Pin and tack (baste), then stitch, leaving a 20 cm (8 in) gap on a long side for turning. Turn right side out and press lightly. Oversew the opening neatly.

3 Cut 2 facings of patterned fabric 40 × 13 cm (16 × 5¼ in) and 2 pieces of plain fabric 40 × 23 cm (16 × 9 in) for the pockets. Turn under 1 long edge to the wrong side and hem. Place the hemmed facing right side down onto the wrong side of 1 pocket, matching the raw top and side edges of the facing to the pocket. Pin, tack (baste) and stitch the facing to the pocket top on 3 sides. Snip into the pocket seam allowance where the facing hem meets the pocket side.

Tack (baste) a hem on the pocket bottom, with the facing/pocket stitch line and the fold of the pocket hem on the sides forming a continuous line. Trim the facing/pocket seam edges, turn the facing to the right side and press firmly with an iron on a medium setting. Stitch the facing to the pocket front. Fold a box pleat in pocket so that its finished width is about 20 cm (8 in). Tack (baste) the pleat in place, pressing firmly. Repeat the same procedure to make up the second pocket.

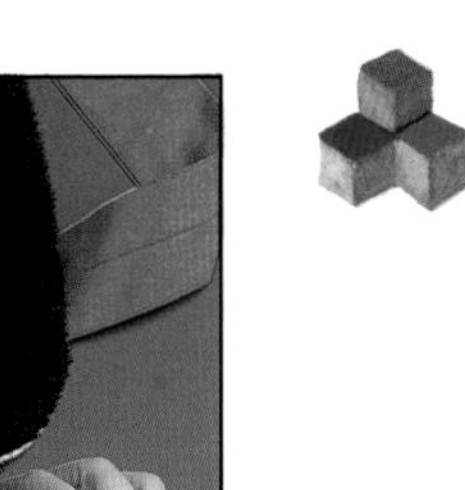

4 Make 2 lengths of fabric for the straps about 5 cm (2 in) wide and approximately 70 cm (28 in) long. Fold the pocket flaps in and fold the mat up just below the flaps. Turn the mat over. The bottom of the mat with the loop folds down to overlap the front, becoming the top of the bag. Pin the loop temporarily to the front and also mark the correct position for the toggle with a pin. Pin the straps in position, adjusting until the bag hangs well and the straps are even. Turn under the raw edges at the ends and stitch the straps in place through all thicknesses of the mat.

5 Pin and tack (baste) and hem the pockets to the pocket backs. Oversew at the top pocket corners for strength. Fold the pocket flaps in. Make 2 ties from patterned fabric and stitch 1 to each flap where their edges meet so that when tied the pocket flaps will stay in position. Sew the toggle to the bag front.

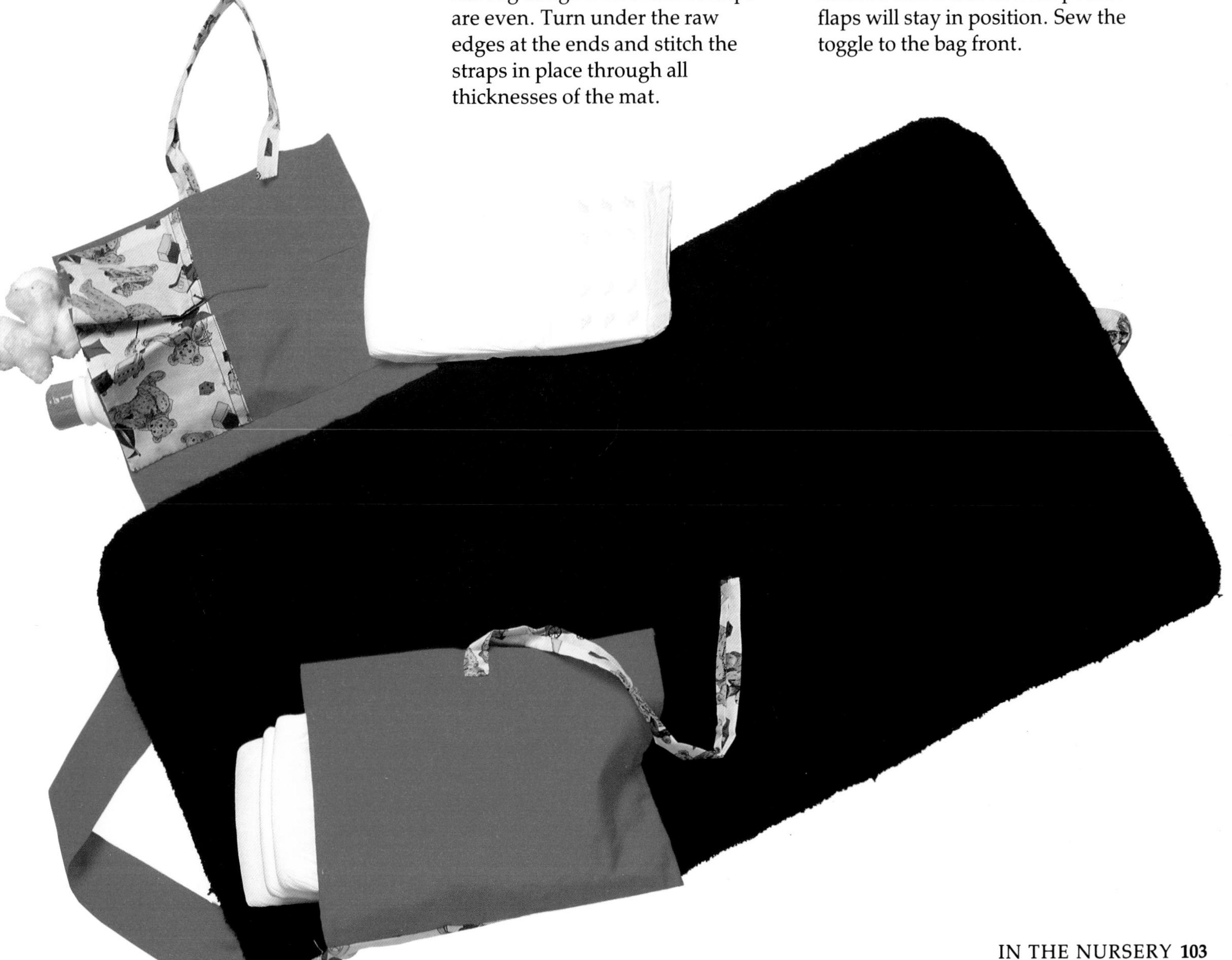

Reversible **B**umper

ADD TO THE COMFORT OF A BABY'S COT OR CRIB WITH THIS SIMPLY-MADE BUMPER

YOU WILL NEED ■ *Tape measure* ■ *2 pieces contrasting fabric* ■ *Scissors* ■ *Pins* ■ *Needle and thread* ■ *Thick wadding (batting)* ■ *3 m (3 yd) narrow bias binding* ■ *Wide bias binding*

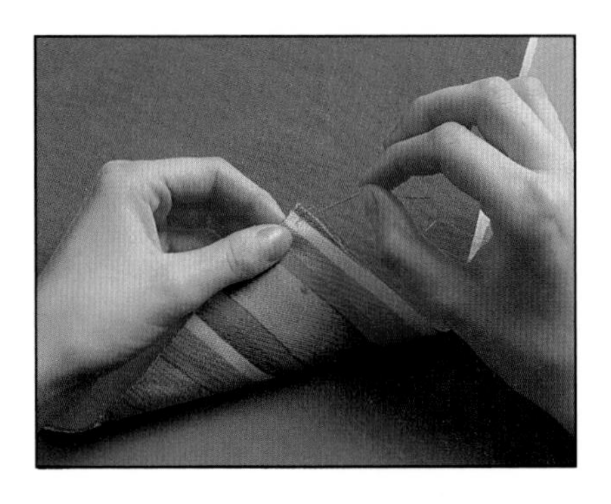

1 Measure the end and halfway along the sides of the cot (crib). Cut 2 side pieces and 1 end piece from the contrasting fabrics. Join the 3 pieces by pinning, tacking (basting) and sewing 2 seams right sides together. Cut 1 backing piece to match the front.

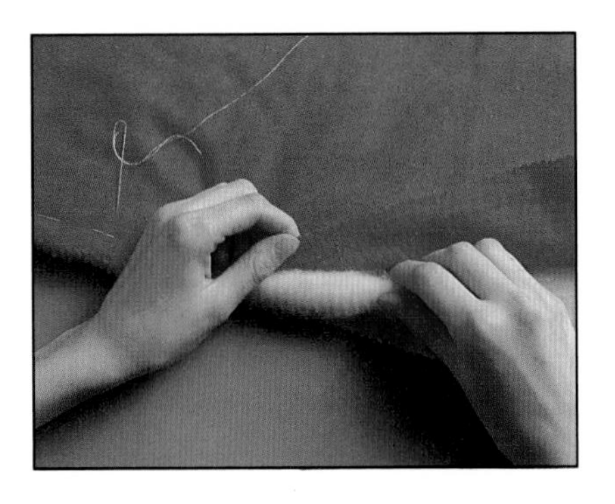

2 Cut wadding (batting) to fit and sandwich between the backing and the main fabric. Where the 3 front pieces of fabric join, sew down those seams to secure all 3 layers. Tack (baste) around the edge of the bumper.

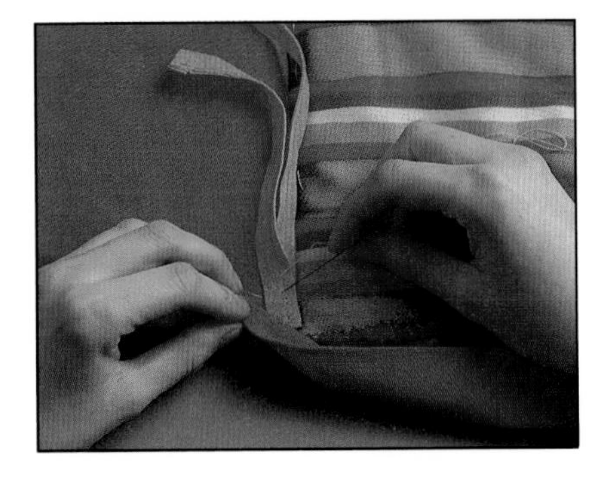

3 Cut 8 × 36 cm (14 in) ties from the narrow bias binding. Fold and stitch. Sew the wide bias binding around the edge of the bumper, trapping the ties in the appropriate places to fit the bars of the cot (crib).

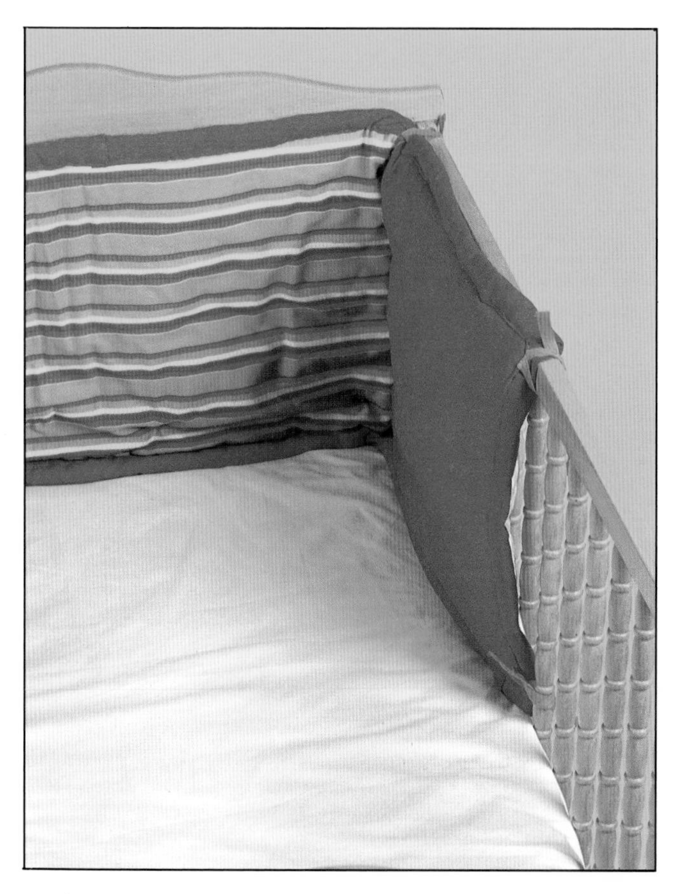

Nursery Basket

AN ATTRACTIVE CONTAINER FOR A BABY'S TOILETRIES

YOU WILL NEED ■ *Wicker basket with handle* ■ *Tape measure* ■ *Cotton gingham* ■ *Scissors* ■ *Needle and thread* ■ *Elastic* ■ *Pre-gathered lace with ribbon eyelets* ■ *Length of narrow ribbon* ■ *Ribbon for handle* ■ *Sticky tape*

1 Measure the basket from rim to rim, taking the tape measure under the basket, and add on 5 cm (2 in). Using this measurement as the diameter, cut out a circle of gingham. Turn the edge under by 1.5 cm (⅝ in) and tack (baste). To gather the edge, sew the elastic along the hem, hiding the raw edge, stretching it as it is being stitched. Remove the tacking (basting).

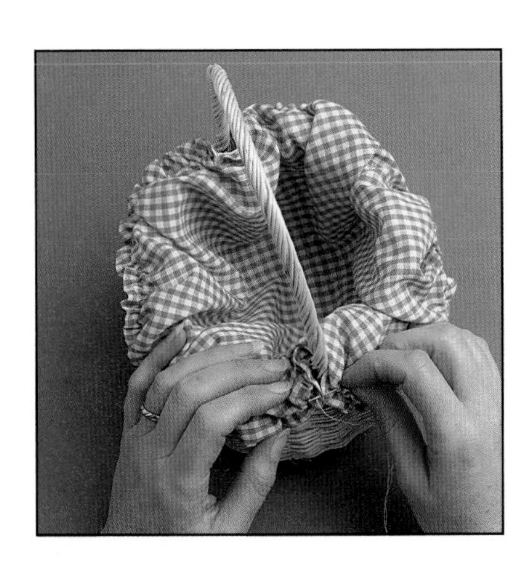

2 Tuck the gingham into the basket and stitch the fabric around each side of the handle to keep it in place.

3 Cut a length of pre-gathered lace to the measurement of the basket rim plus half again. Thread the ribbon through the lace and gather. Position the gathered ribbon around the basket rim to cover the elastic stitching and adjust the gathering to fit. Tie the ribbon securely and knot. Cut off ends. Wind the remaining ribbon around the handle. Secure at each end with sticky tape and tie a bow at each side to cover the tape.

Baby Changing Bag

USE THIS BAG TO STORE NAPPIES OR DIAPERS

YOU WILL NEED ■ *Scissors* ■ *Tape measure* ■ *Stiff board* ■ *1 m × 115 cm (1¼ yd × 45 in) fabric* ■ *Rubber-based glue* ■ *Pins* ■ *Needle and thread* ■ *2.5 m (2½ yd) ribbon, 6 mm (¼ in) wide* ■ *2.5 m (2½ yd) ribbon, 2.5 cm (1 in) wide*

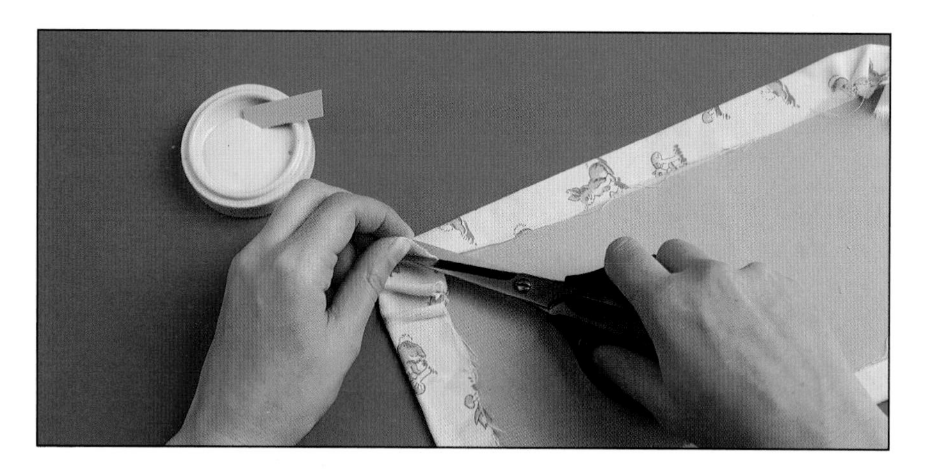

1 Cut out a piece of board 32 × 18 cm (12½ × 7 in) and round the corners. Cut out 2 pieces of fabric 35 × 20 cm (13½ × 8 in). Lay the board on the wrong side of one piece of fabric then spread glue 2.5 cm (1 in) around the edge of the board. Pull the fabric over the edges and press down. Trim the spare fabric at the corners.

2 Cut a piece of fabric 77 × 115 cm (31 × 45 in) and fold in a 2.5 cm (1 in) seam along each short edge. Join the sides along this fold to a depth of 10 cm (4 in). Now pin this end to the second piece of base material right sides together, and double stitch together allowing a 12 mm (½ in) seam allowance. Trim the seam and turn right side out.

3 Fold the top edge over 7.5 cm (3 in); pin. Stitch close to the edge and again 2 cm (¾ in) above to make a ribbon casing. Cut a slit in the back centre of the basing and buttonhole stitch all the way round. Cut the narrow ribbon in half. Thread one piece through the casing and sew the ends together where they meet at the back. Repeat with the second piece of ribbon, this time joining the ends at the front.

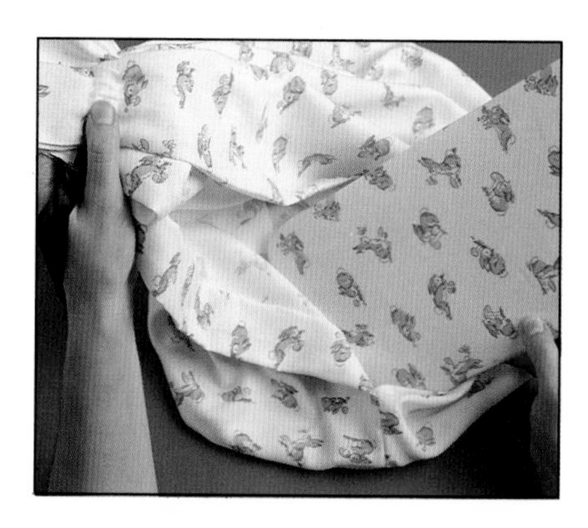

4 Fit the firm base inside the bag, material side up. Pull up the drawstrings and tie the wide ribbon around the top to form a bow.

Tissue Box Cover

THIS COVER CAN BE ADAPTED TO FIT DIFFERENT SIZES OF BOX

YOU WILL NEED ■ *Scissors* ■ *0.5 m (20 in) pretty cotton fabric* ■ *Tape measure* ■ *Medium-weight wadding (batting)* ■ *Pink bias binding* ■ *Needle and thread* ■ *Pins* ■ *1 m (40 in) pink ribbon, 1 cm (3/8 in) wide* ■ *1 m (40 in) pink ric-rac braid*

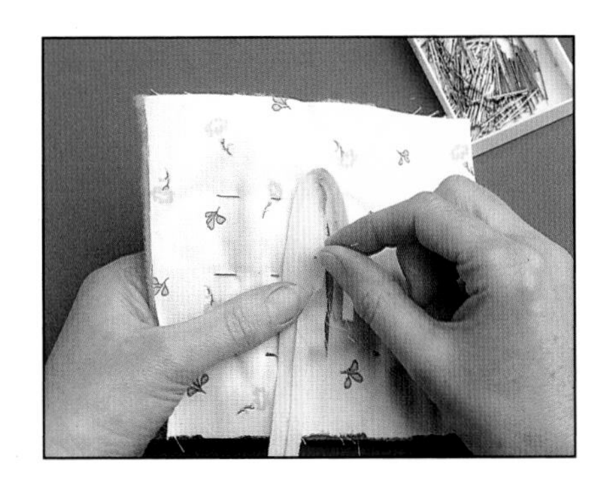

1 Cut out 2 pieces of fabric, one 15 × 15 cm (6 × 6 in) and the other 16 × 46 cm (6¼ × 18¼ in). Cut 2 pieces of wadding (batting) to the same size as each piece. Pin together the squares of fabric and wadding (batting). Cut through the centre of both layers to make a 7 cm (2¾ in) opening. Lay a small piece of bias binding along the cut edge. Stitch along the fold line around the opening. Trim off any excess and fold through to the wrong side. Slip stitch into place.

2 Lay the remaining piece of fabric on top of the wadding (batting) and pin together. Sew the ribbon along the centre line, catching the wadding (batting) at the same time. Pin a length of ric-rac braid on each side and sew into place. Remove the pins.

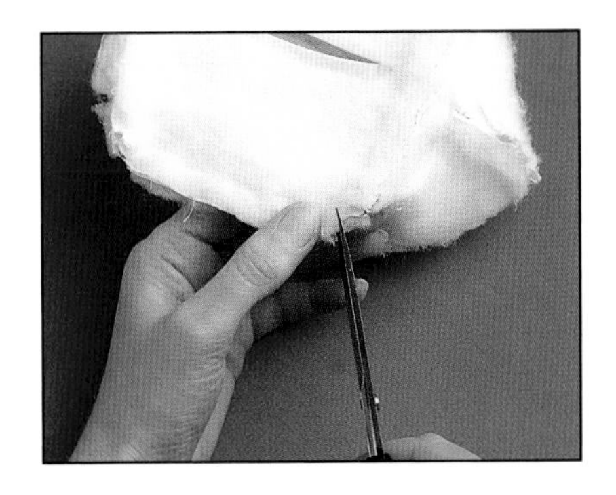

3 With right sides together, sew the material down the side seam with a 1.5 cm (5/8 in) seam allowance. Trim. Carefully pin the sides to the top and tack (baste). Remove pins and stitch together. Trim the seams and clip the corners. Turn through. Hem the bottom. Make two small bows with the remaining ribbon and sew at the top opening.

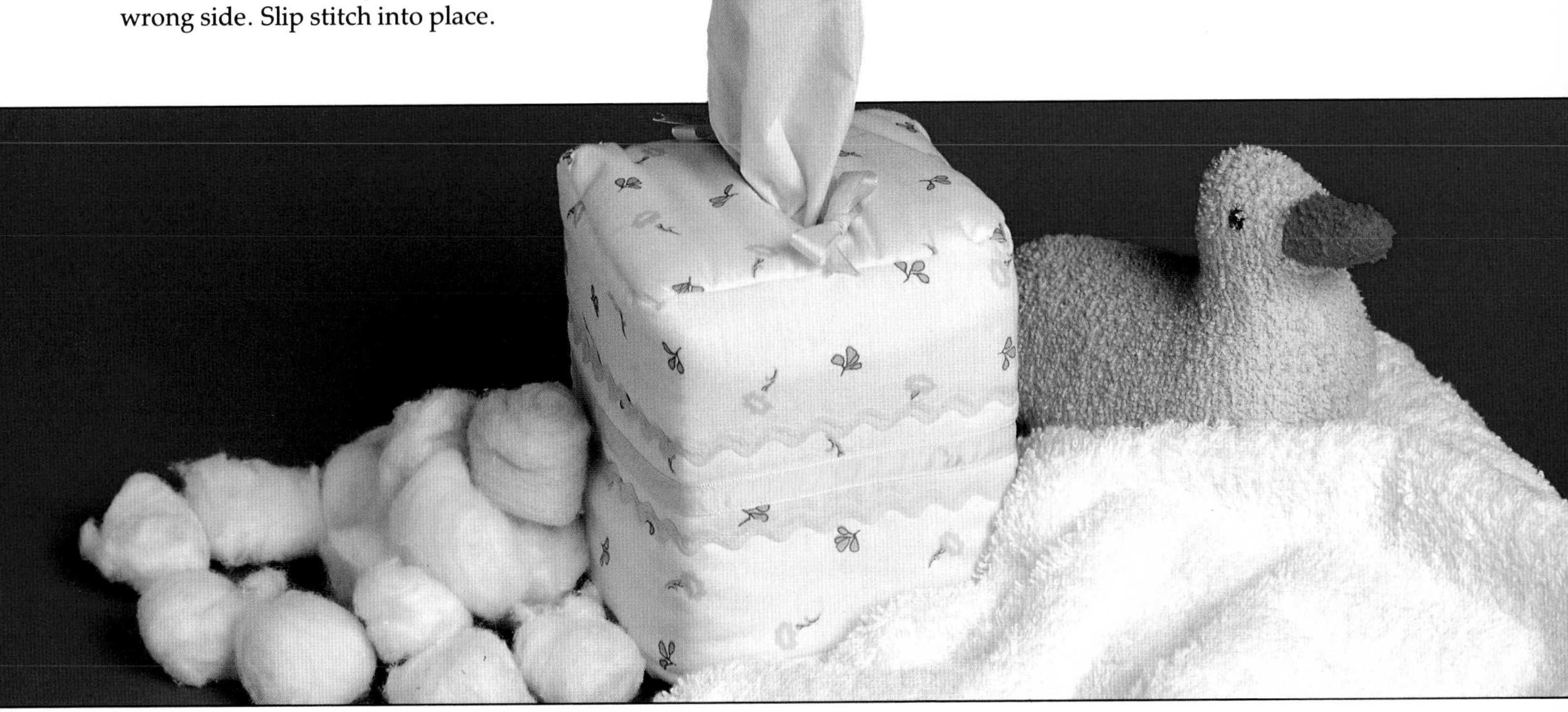

Bathtime **A**pron

A PRACTICAL APRON TO KEEP PARENTS DRY AT BATHTIME

YOU WILL NEED ■ *Scissors* ■ *Bright cotton fabric* ■ *Tape measure* ■ *Pins* ■ *Needle and thread* ■ *Safety pin* ■ *Pencil* ■ *White paper* ■ *Towelling (terrycloth) fabric* ■ *Iron*

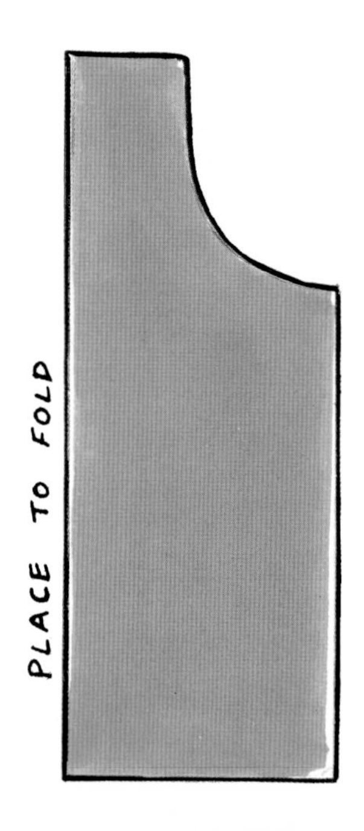

1 Cut 3 strips of cotton fabric about 6 cm (2¼ in) wide and of sufficient length to make into the 2 apron ties and a neck loop. Make up the strips by folding each one in half along its length, with the right sides together. Pin and sew up each strip. Carefully turn each tube through to the right side using a safety pin.

2 Scale up the template onto white paper and cut out. Fold the fabric in half and pin the template along the fold. Cut out one shape from cotton fabric and one from towelling (terrycloth). Pin the neck-loop ends to the fabric 15 cm (6 in) in from the top edge and at right angles to it. Tack (baste) into place.

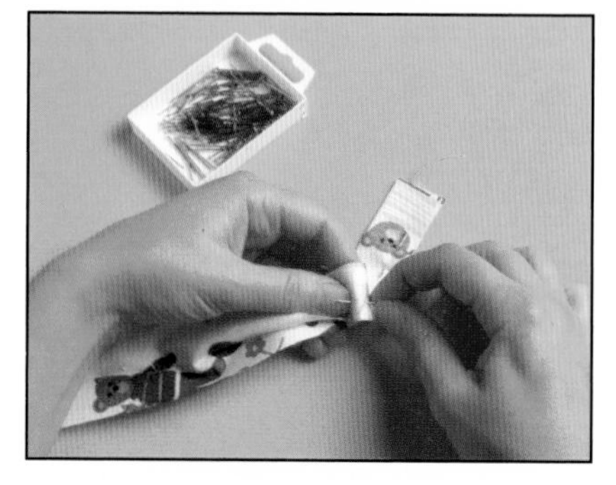

3 Position the apron ties at the top of the apron sides. Place the patterned cotton and the towelling (terrycloth) right sides together, and pin and tack (baste) all round the edge, enclosing the ends of the ties and rounding off the bottom corners as you stitch.

Leave an open length on one straight edge. Trim the excess fabric on the rounded corners and turn the apron to the right side through the opening. Oversew the opening to close. Press and topstitch all round about 1 cm (⅜ in) from the edge.

Hooded Towel

THIS COSY HOODED TOWEL USES BRIGHT COTTON AND ABSORBENT FABRICS

YOU WILL NEED ■ *Scissors* ■ *Towelling (terrycloth) fabric* ■ *Bright cotton fabric* ■ *Tape measure* ■ *Pins* ■ *Needle and thread* ■ *Iron*

1 Cut 2 triangles, one each of towelling (terrycloth) and cotton. The edges on the right angle should be 27 cm (10½ in) long. Pin, tack (baste) and stitch right sides together on the diagonal to make a 27 cm (10½ in) square. Press the seam to one side and trim the excess fabric on the seam edges at the corners.

2 Press the square back into a triangle along the seam, with right sides out. Cut a piece of towelling (terrycloth) 80 cm (32 in) square. Pin and tack (baste) the hood to the right side of the towelling at one corner matching the raw edges, with the cotton side of the hood uppermost.

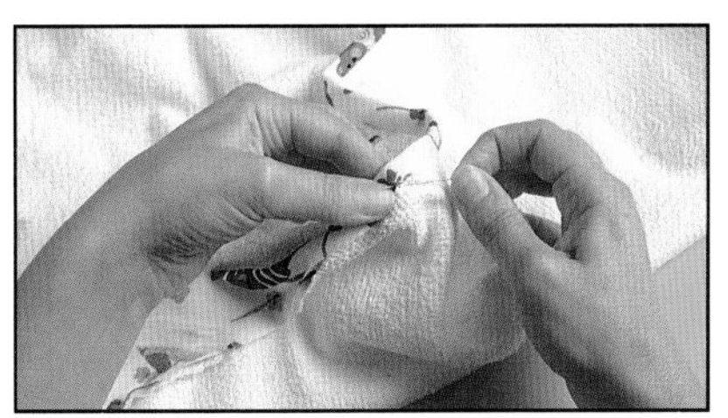

3 Cut a strip of cotton fabric about 4 cm (1½ in) wide to go around the whole towel. Turn back the raw edge of one binding end diagonally along the grain and pin and tack (baste) the right sides of the binding to the towel, stitching the hood to the towel on the corner. Round off all 4 corners.

Overlap the binding ends and turn back the second raw edge. Stitch the binding to the towel. Trim the excess fabric at all corners where the edges are rounded. Press, turn the binding to the wrong side and hem to enclose the raw edges. Press.

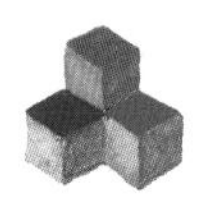

Folded Hold-all

THIS HOLD-ALL IS PERFECT FOR CARRYING BABY-CHANGING ITEMS

YOU WILL NEED ■ *Tape measure* ■ *Pre-washed strong cotton ticking* ■ *Scissors* ■ *Assorted plain and patterned cotton fabrics* ■ *Pair of compasses* ■ *Pencil* ■ *Iron-on interfacing* ■ *Iron* ■ *Pins* ■ *Needle and thread* ■ *Gingham fabric* ■ *Narrow ribbon*

1 Cut a piece of ticking 66 × 37 cm (26½ × 14½ in) with stripes running lengthwise. From the assorted fabrics, use a pair of compasses to cut a circle about 18 cm (7 in) across. Also cut 8 triangles about 6 cm (2¼ in) high.

Use iron-on interfacing on all appliquéd pieces. Position the circle and triangles onto the ticking to make a sun shape. Pin and tack (baste) each shape. The triangles should not cross the seam allowance at the top and sides. Appliqué the shapes into place and press.

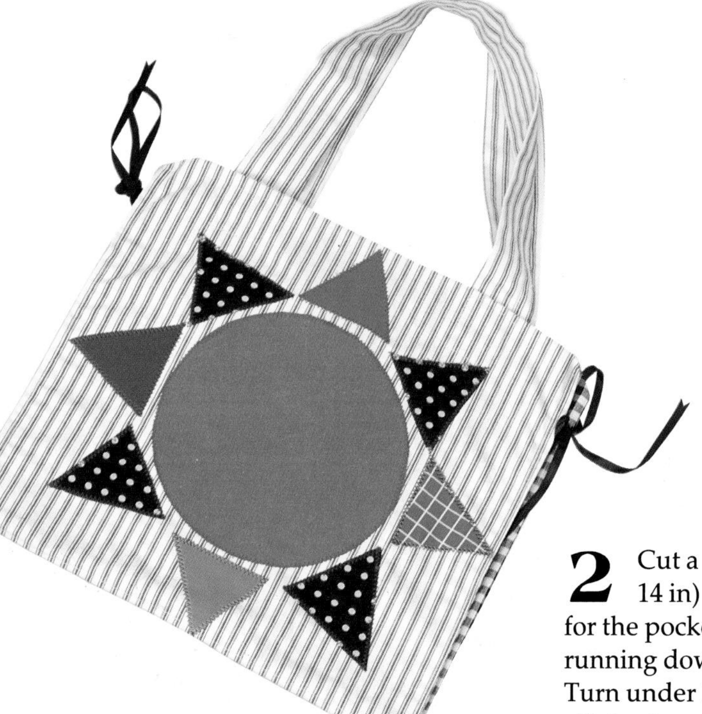

2 Cut a 40 × 36 cm (16 × 14 in) shape from the ticking for the pocket, with the stripes running down the longer side. Turn under 1 short raw edge and stitch a hem. Turn the hemmed edge to the front of the pocket, folding it about 8 cm (3¼ in) from the top, and stitch the 2 layers together at the sides to form the facing. Carefully snip into the pocket seam allowance where the facing hem meets the pocket side just as far as the stitching line. Then tack (baste) a hem on the pocket bottom with the facing/pocket stitch line and the fold of the pocket hem on the sides forming a continuous line. Turn the facing to the inside and press. Fold a box pleat in the pocket so that it will fit snugly within the width of the bag and tack (baste) it in place. Press well. Choosing another plain fabric, make up the second pocket in the same way.

3 Cut a piece of gingham 66 × 37 cm (26½ × 14½ in) for the bag lining. With right sides together, pin, tack (baste) and stitch the lining to the bag leaving an opening at the side for turning. Turn right side out, oversew the opening to close and press.

4 From the ticking, make 2 straps, each about 64 cm (25½ in) long and 5 cm (2 in) wide. Turn under the raw edges and pin both straps to the inside of the bag at both ends. Test and adjust their lengths and positions before stitching, noting that the stitched strap ends should eventually be concealed under the top edge of the pockets.

Pin, tack (baste) and stitch the pockets through all layers of the bag, stitching the pleat down at the same time. Cut and sew lengths of narrow ribbon to the pleat tops as ties. Sew more ribbon to the top sides of the bag so it can be tied closed when carried to keep the contents safe.

Practical Apron

AN ESSENTIAL PROTECTIVE LAYER FOR THE BUSY PARENT

YOU WILL NEED ■ *Tracing paper* ■ *Pencil* ■ *Ruler* ■ *White paper* ■ *Scissors* ■ *60 × 75 cm (24 × 30 in) fabric for apron* ■ *Pins* ■ *Needle and thread* ■ *180 cm (72 in) ribbon or fabric binding* ■ *2 pieces of 48 × 48 cm (19 × 19 in) fabric for pocket* ■ *Felt*

1 Scale up the apron and pocket shapes from the templates and transfer them onto white paper. Cut out the apron in fabric. Fold over and pin a neat edge all the way round the apron and sew down. Cut the ribbon or fabric binding into 3 pieces. Sew to the top and sides to make a neck loop and 2 waist ties.

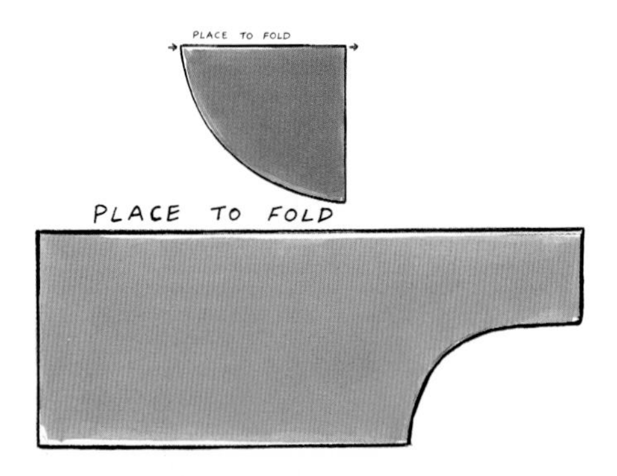

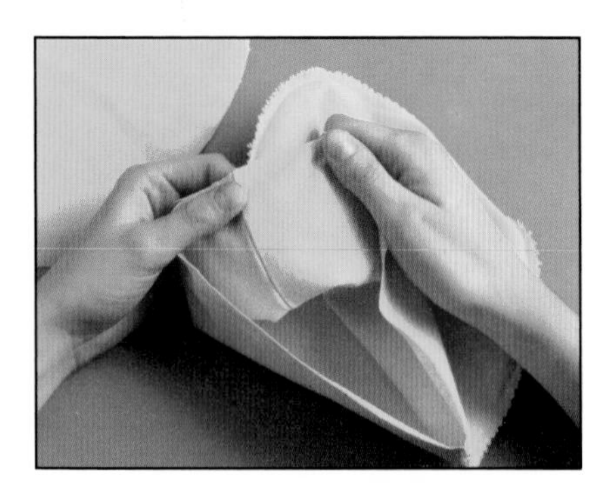

2 Cut out the fabric pieces for the pocket. Join the 2 pieces together by sewing around the curved edge, and turn right side out. Sew up the gap at the top.

3 Sew the pocket onto the apron. Cut out flower shapes, stalks and leaves from the felt and sew them onto the apron.

Cylindrical Bag

THE PERFECT CONTAINER FOR ABSORBENT COTTON BALLS

YOU WILL NEED ■ *Tape measure* ■ *Pinking shears* ■ *2 pieces of 15 × 38 cm (6 × 15 in) patterned fabric* ■ *2 pieces of 15 × 38 cm (6 × 15 in) plain fabric* ■ *Scissors* ■ *2 pieces of 15 × 38 cm (6 × 15 in) wadding (batting)* ■ *Needle and thread* ■ *6 metal eyelets* ■ *Hammer* ■ *35 cm (13½ in) cord*

1 Cut out the 4 fabric pieces using pinking shears and the 2 wadding (batting) pieces using scissors. For each bag side, trap one piece of wadding (batting) between 2 contrasting pieces of fabric and sew along one edge.

2 Position the 2 sides so that a patterned side is facing a plain one. Sew through all the layers around 3 sides, leaving an opening. Stitch around the open edges to sew down.

3 Turn right side out. Attach the metal eyelets along the open edge of the bag using a hammer and a firm work surface. Thread the cord through the eyelets and tie a knot.

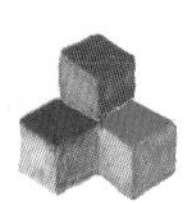

Bathroom **P**ockets

PRACTICAL WALL STORAGE FOR BATHROOM ITEMS

YOU WILL NEED ■ Scissors ■ 90 m (1 yd) fabric binding or ribbon ■ Needle and thread ■ Clear PVC (vinyl) plastic: 1 piece 42 × 55 cm (16½ × 21½ in); 2 pieces 14 × 14 cm (5½ × 5½ in); 1 piece 13 × 21 cm (5¼ × 8½ in) ■ Pieces of brightly coloured felt ■ Rubber-based glue ■ Fabric for pockets: 2 pieces 14 × 14 cm (5½ × 5½ in); 1 piece 13 × 21 cm (5¼ × 8½ in) ■ Coloured PVC (vinyl) plastic for the backing of each pocket: 2 pieces 14 × 16 cm (5½ × 6½ in); 1 piece 14 × 21 cm (5½ × 8½ in) ■ Pinking shears

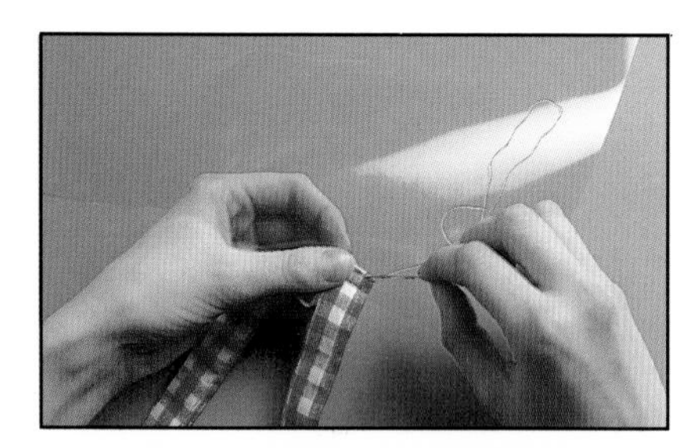

1 Cut the fabric binding or ribbon into 2 pieces of equal length and sew the centre of each onto the top edge of the largest piece of clear PVC (vinyl) plastic. You may find a thimble helpful for pushing the needle through the plastic more easily.

2 For the pockets, cut out 16 felt spots and glue them to the 3 fabric pieces. Sandwich between clear and coloured PVC (vinyl) plastic with the clear plastic on top. Sew the 3 sides, leaving the extra coloured plastic overlapping at the top.

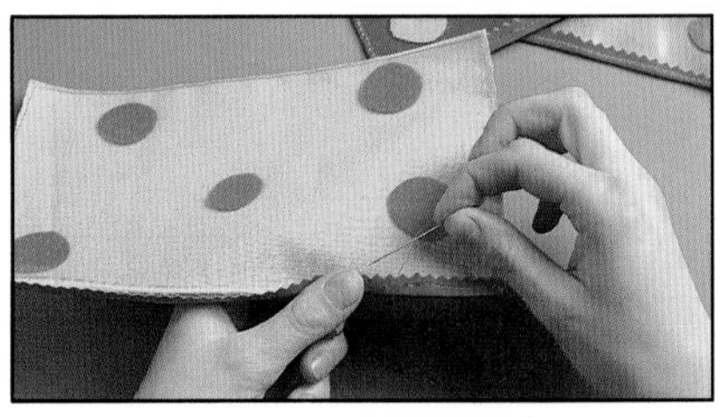

3 Trim the top coloured edge with pinking shears. Fold it over the front and sew down.

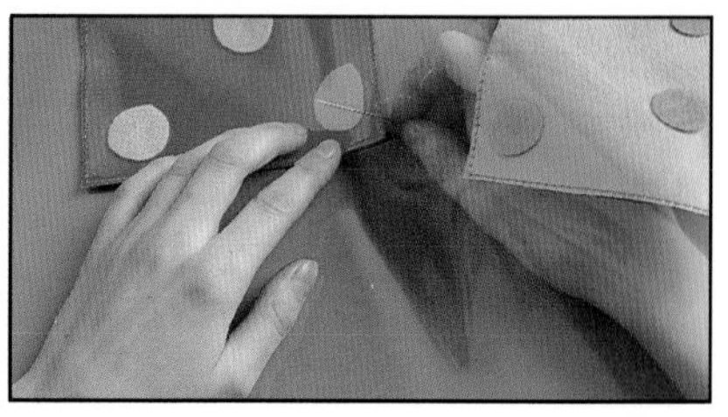

4 Place the pockets on the clear plastic base and sew.

Washbag

A PRACTICAL BAG FOR STORING AWAY THE BATHROOM ESSENTIALS

YOU WILL NEED ■ Scissors ■ Red PVC (vinyl-coated) fabric ■ Needle and thread ■ 2 pieces of 28 × 30 cm (11 × 12 in) polkadot plastic fabric ■ 8 metal eyelets ■ Hammer ■ 60 cm (24 in) ribbon or fabric binding

1 Cut out 2 red hearts from the PVC (vinyl-coated) fabric and sew 1 heart onto each piece of polkadot plastic fabric.

2 Fold over the top edge of both pieces of polkadot plastic fabric and sew.

3 Lay the 2 sides with the right sides together and sew around 3 edges.

4 Attach the metal eyelets evenly along the top edge, using a hammer and working on a firm surface.

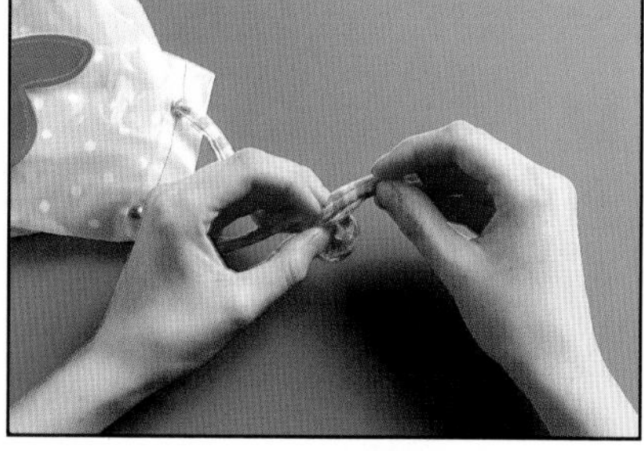

5 Thread the ribbon or fabric binding through the eyelets and tie a knot.

Decorated Towel

ADD A LIVELY TRIMMING TO A PLAIN TOWEL

YOU WILL NEED ■ *Pins* ■ *Length of blue cording or piping* ■ *Towel* ■ *Embroidery thread* ■ *Needle and thread* ■ *Scissors* ■ *Length of ric-rac braid*

1 Pin blue cording along one end of the towel in a wiggly line. Oversew down its length to secure it, using embroidery thread in a contrasting colour.

2 Using a different colour of embroidery thread, embroider cross-stitches along each side of the blue cording at regular intervals.

3 Cut 2 equal lengths of ric-rac braid in contrasting colours and then sew them neatly in place above the blue cording using a needle and thread.

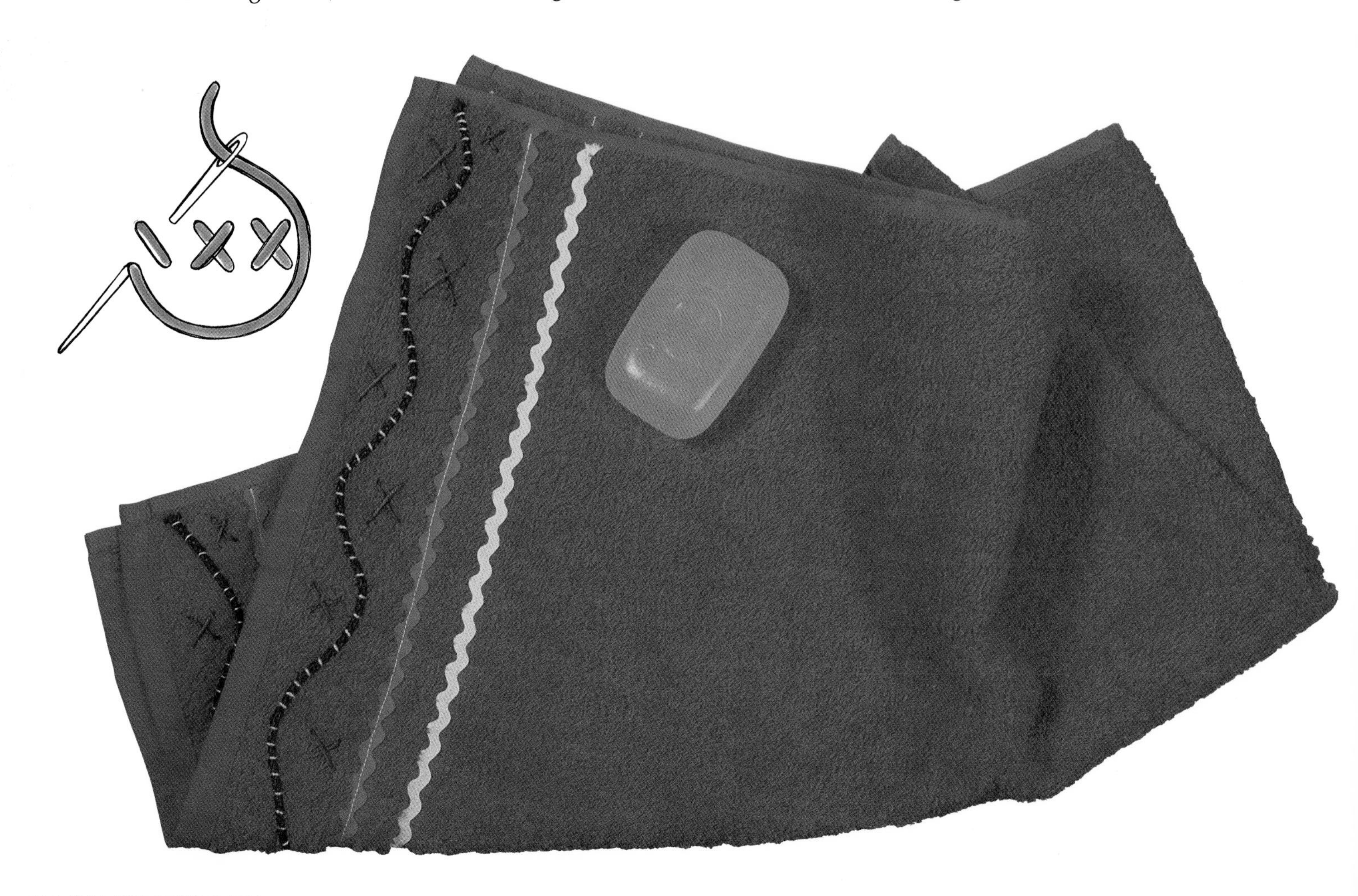

Lined Basket

THE LINER IN THE BASKET CAN EASILY BE REMOVED FOR WASHING

YOU WILL NEED ■ *Scissors* ■ *4 m (4½ yd) bias binding* ■ *Needle and thread* ■ *2 pieces of fabric large enough to cover the inside of the basket* ■ *Iron* ■ *Wicker basket with handles*

1 Cut 12 ties from the length of bias binding. Fold each length over and then sew down along the edge.

2 Trap one end of each tie between the 2 fabric pieces (right sides together) in convenient places for them to fasten to the basket. Sew round all the edges of the 2 pieces, leaving a gap at one edge.

3 Turn the fabric right side out, using a pin to 'pull out' the corners if necessary to make good right angles. Press the fabric firmly with an iron on a medium to hot setting, depending on the type of fabric you have used. Oversew the gap to complete the stitching. Place the fabric in the basket and fasten the ties to edges.

Spiky **F**abric **B**ib

MAKE MEALTIMES MORE FUN WITH THIS UNUSUAL BIB

YOU WILL NEED ■ *White paper* ■ *Pencil* ■ *Ruler* ■ *Scissors* ■ *Pins* ■ *2 pieces of contrasting fabric, 20 × 24 cm (8 × 9½ in)* ■ *Scraps of fabric for spikes* ■ *Needle and thread* ■ *Pinking shears* ■ *48 cm (19 in) ribbon or fabric binding*

1 Scale up the template onto white paper and cut it out. Pin onto the pieces of contrasting fabric and then cut out 2 bib shapes and 6 spikes.

2 To make the spikes, join the triangular pieces in pairs and sew along 2 edges. Trim the edges with pinking shears and turn right side out.

3 Cut the ribbon in half and sandwich the 2 lengths between the 2 bib pieces along with the 3 spikes, securing them with a pin.

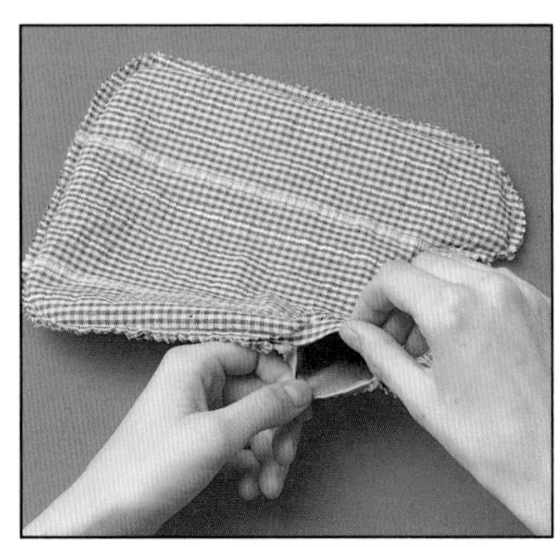

4 Sew around the edge of the bib, leaving a gap in order to turn the whole bib right side out. Once you have done this, sew up the gap and remove all the pins.

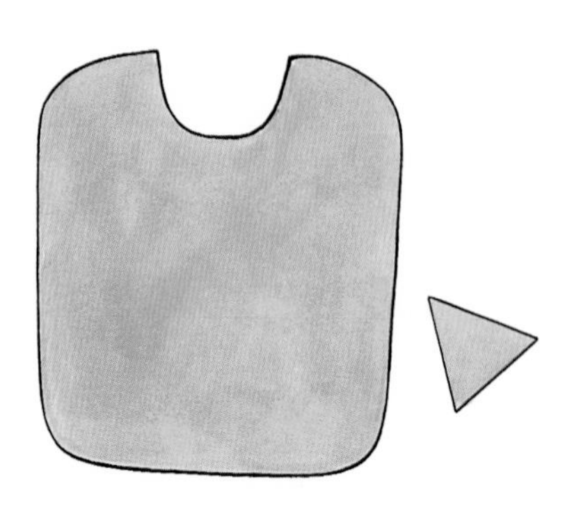

Toy Bag

AN ATTRACTIVE BAG THAT IS PERFECT FOR STORING TOYS

YOU WILL NEED ■ *Scissors* ■ *2 fabric squares 55 × 55 cm (21½ × 21½ in)* ■ *Pins* ■ *Needle and thread* ■ *120 cm (47 in) cord*

1 Cut out the 2 square pieces of fabric. Fold over all the edges and pin down, leaving a slightly larger hem at the top. Sew along the top edge where the cord will pass through.

2 Sew the other 3 sides together, leaving a gap at the top edges to allow the cord to pass through.

3 Thread the cord through and tie a knot at the end.

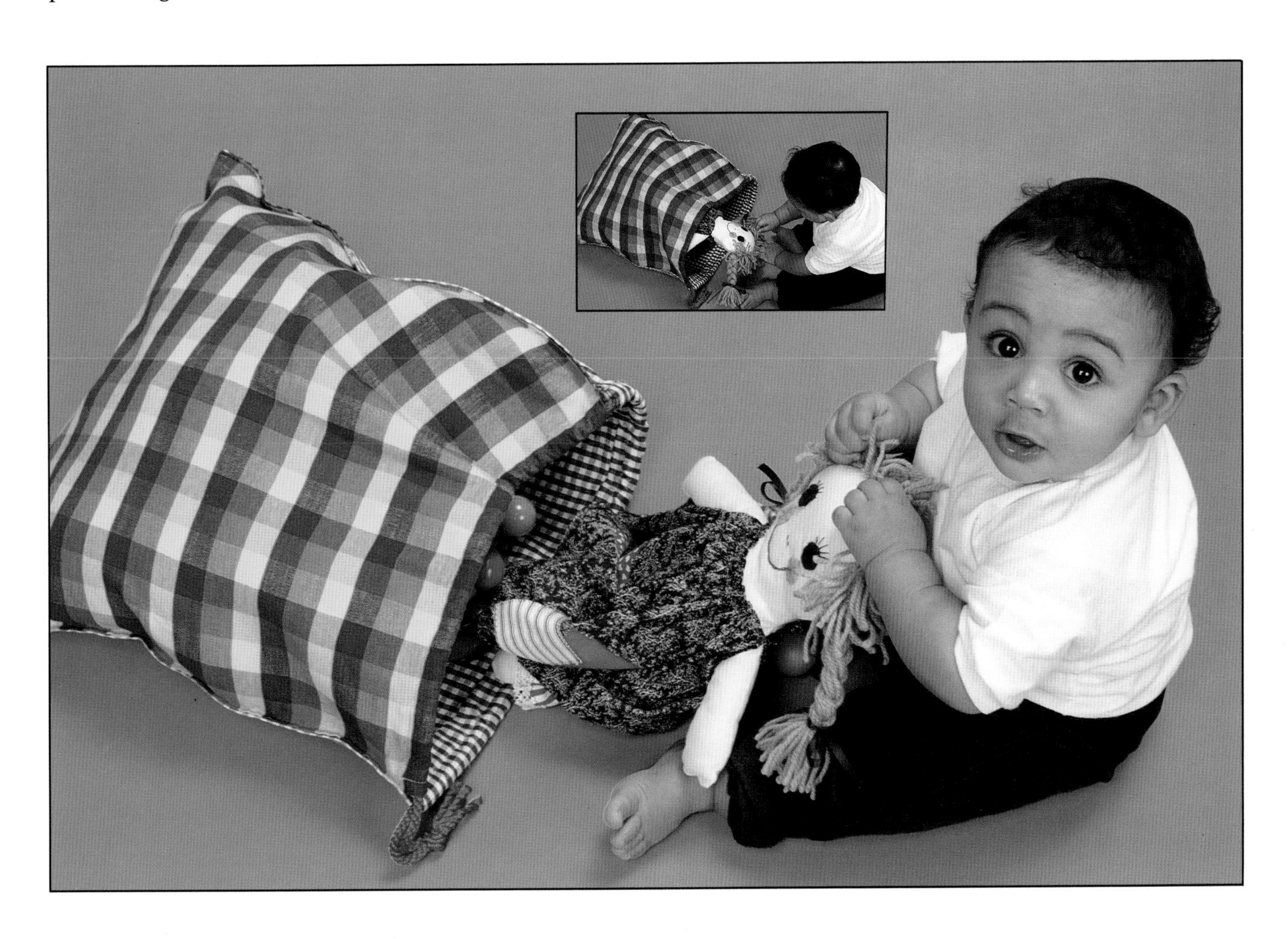

Beetle Drawer Freshener

AN UNUSUAL DESIGN FOR A SCENTED SACHET

YOU WILL NEED ■ Paper ■ Pen ■ Pins ■ Scissors ■ 15 × 23 cm (6 × 9 in) black felt ■ 12.5 × 12.5 cm (5 × 5 in) red felt ■ Non-toxic, flame retardant polyester filling (batting) ■ Hole punch ■ Rubber-based glue ■ Needle and thread ■ Chamomile and lavender pot pourri

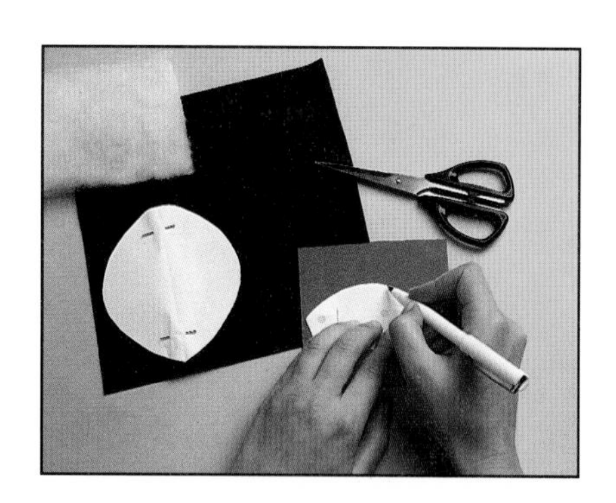

1 Scale up the templates and make paper patterns. Pin the patterns to the felt and draw round. Cut two body shapes from the black felt, and two wing shapes from the red felt. Cut out a body shape to match from the filling (batting). Remove the paper pattern and mark the arrangement of holes on the wing shapes with a pen. Punch the holes using the hole punch.

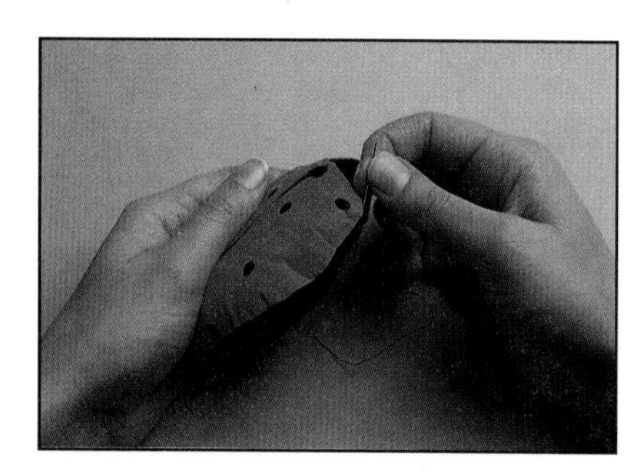

2 Using rubber-based glue, stick the wing shapes onto one of the body shapes, leaving a small gap in between for a strip of black felt to show through. Leave to dry then turn over and pin the filling (batting) to the upper body piece. Slip stitch the two body pieces together, wrong sides together, leaving the head open for stuffing.

3 Stuff the beetle's body with chamomile and lavender pot pourri and then oversew the opening to close.

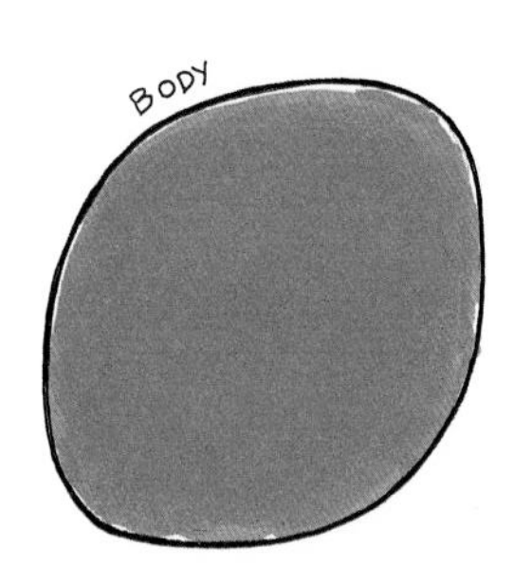

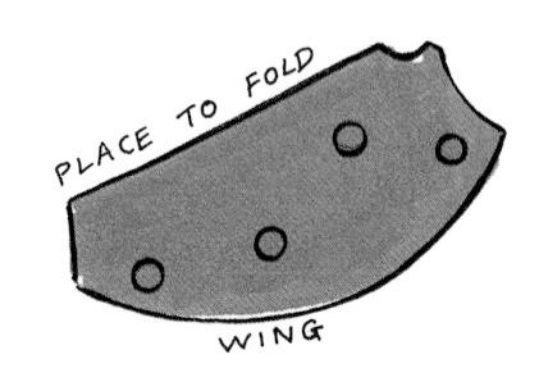

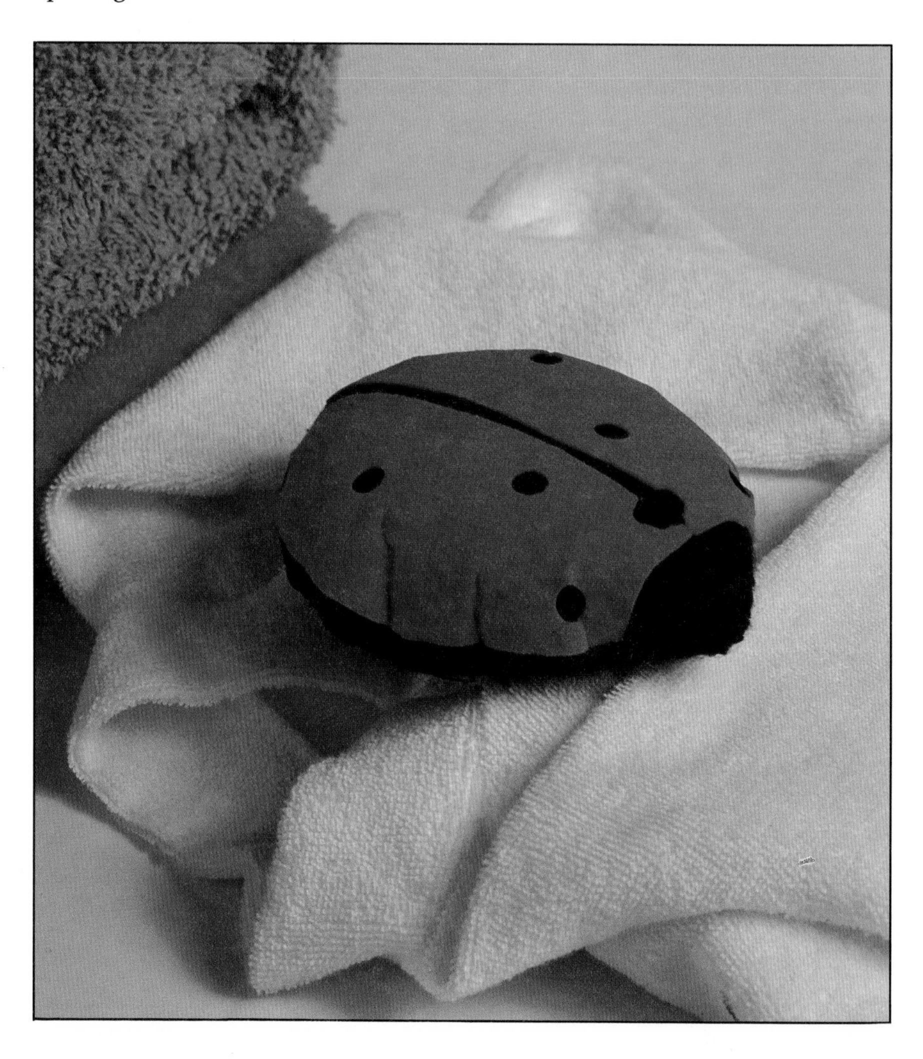

Candy Cushion

LET THE BABY ROLL AROUND THE NURSERY WITH THIS SOFT CUSHION

YOU WILL NEED ■ *Pencil* ■ *White paper* ■ *Ruler* ■ *Scissors* ■ *Oddments of fabric for spikes* ■ *Needle and thread* ■ *Pinking shears* ■ *65 × 92 cm (26 × 37 in) fabric for the main cushion* ■ *65 × 17 cm (26 × 6¾ in) fabric for inner flaps* ■ *14 metal eyelets* ■ *Hammer* ■ *92 cm (37 in) bias binding* ■ *58 × 47 cm (23 × 18½ in) cushion* ■ *120 cm (47 in) cord*

1 Draw a large triangle onto white paper. Cut it out and use it as a template for 16 fabric triangles. Cut out all the triangles and sew them together in pairs, then trim the seams and turn right side out. You should have 4 finished triangles for each end of the cushion.

2 Trim the cushion fabric with pinking shears to make a neat edge. Pin the triangles between the main piece of fabric and the flap, so that they are pointing inwards. Sew along each end to secure.

3 Attach 7 metal eyelets to each end of the fabric using a hammer and positioning the fabric over a hard surface.

4 Fold the fabric over lengthwise, right sides together, and then sew the bias binding along the seam to give a neat finish.

5 Turn the cushion cover right side out and insert the cushion. Cut the cord in half and thread through the eyelets at each end, then pull tight and fasten.

Ribbon Motif Frame

BRIGHTEN UP A SIMPLE WOODEN FRAME WITH THIS PRETTY RIBBON DESIGN

YOU WILL NEED ■ *Wooden picture frame* ■ *Masking tape* ■ *Non-toxic acrylic paints* ■ *Small paintbrush* ■ *Pencil* ■ *White paper* ■ *Ruler* ■ *Chalk* ■ *Non-toxic clear acrylic varnish*

1 Undo the frame carefully and stick masking tape around the edges of the glass to keep it clean while you are working. Put the glass back in and paint the frame with your base colour of acrylic paint.

2 Measure the width of the frame and then, using the template as a guide, draw the ribbon design onto the paper. Chalk the opposite side of the design and transfer to the frame by drawing over the outline.

3 Using the small brush, paint in the line of the design with a contrasting colour.

4 Add highlights by painting in touches of a slightly lighter hue and leave to dry. Varnish the frame with a coat of clear acrylic varnish and finally remove the masking tape.

Patchwork Frame

THIS PRETTY PATCHWORK FRAME IS IDEAL FOR A CHILD'S PHOTOGRAPH

YOU WILL NEED ■ Natural sponge ■ Blue, yellow and white fabric paints ■ 70 cm (3/4 yd) white cotton fabric ■ Iron ■ Craft knife ■ Ruler ■ Thin card ■ Mounting board ■ Scissors ■ Pencil ■ Paper ■ Pins ■ Needle and thread ■ Thin wadding (batting) ■ Brown parcel tape ■ Strong clear glue

1 Sponge the fabric using the fabric paints and a natural sponge in pastel shades of blue, yellow and green. Leave to dry before pressing firmly with an iron to fix the dye, following the manufacturer's instructions.

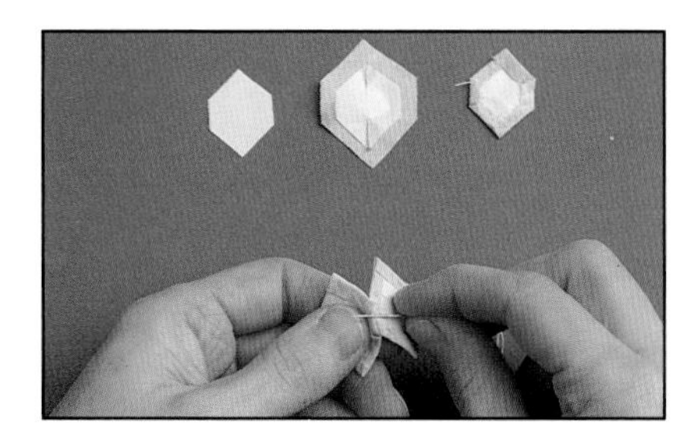

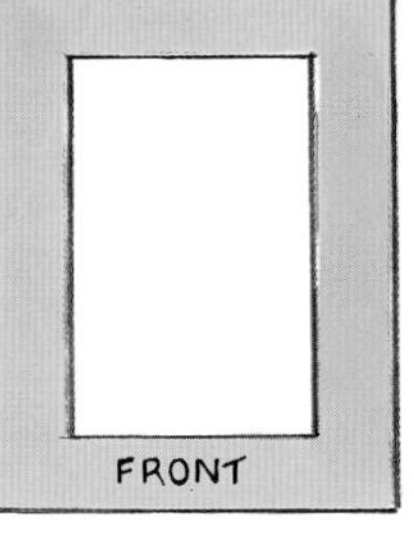

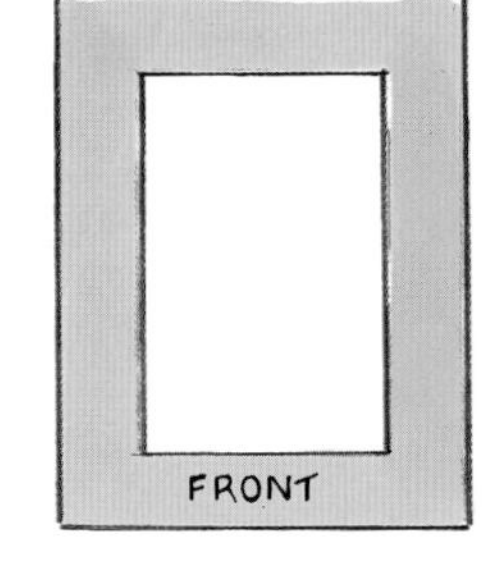

2 Using the template as a guide, cut out all the frame pieces in card and mounting board. Cut out paper hexagonal shapes for the individual patches, being as accurate as possible. Pin the paper shapes to the sponged fabric, with a grain line on one edge.

Cut out the hexagons, leaving a 0.5 cm (3/16 in) seam allowance. Turn the edges over and tack (baste). Sew the hexagons together using tiny oversewing stitches until the patchwork fits over the frame. Remove the tacking (basting) and press. Remove the papers.

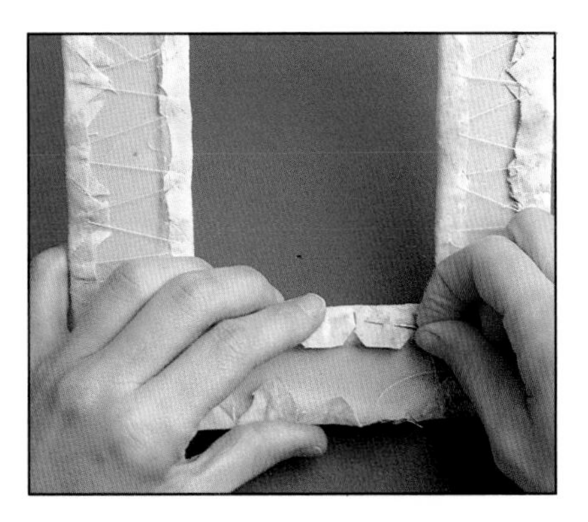

3 Cut a piece of wadding (batting) slightly larger than the frame, and then sew this and the patchwork to the frame, using herringbone stitch as shown to secure at the back.

4 Make the hinge of the stand with brown parcel tape and cover this and the remaining frame pieces with sponged fabric. Glue the frame together and press it under a heavy weight till dry.

Tapestry Cushion

A DECORATIVE AND SIMPLY MADE CUSHION FOR THE NURSERY

YOU WILL NEED ■ *Marker pen* ■ *Square of tapestry canvas* ■ *Tapestry needle* ■ *Tapestry yarns in various bright colours* ■ *Pinking shears* ■ *Square of fabric* ■ *Needle and thread* ■ *Non-toxic, flame retardant polyester filling (batting)*

1 Draw out the outlines of your design on the canvas.

2 Using tent stitch and one strand of yarn, begin stitching, using different colours for the different motif sections.

3 When the stitching is complete, cut out a fabric square with pinking shears to fit the canvas. Sew all round the 2 squares, right sides together, leaving a gap for turning.

4 After turning the cover the right way out, stuff the cushion with filling (batting) and sew up the gap to complete.

Spiky **C**ushion **C**over

A BRIGHT, FUN CUSHION FOR THE BEDROOM AND PLAYROOM

YOU WILL NEED ■ Black pen ■ Paper ■ Tape measure ■ Scissors ■ 2 pieces of 45 × 45 cm (18 × 18 cm) fabric for the main cushion ■ 2 pieces of 16 × 45 cm (6¼ × 18 in) fabric for the inner flaps ■ 12 pieces of 4.5 × 26 cm (1¾ × 10¼ in) fabric for the ties ■ 6 fabric triangles ■ Pinking shears ■ Pins ■ Needle and thread ■ 24 cm (9½ in) cotton fringing ■ Cushion pad

1 Using the templates, cut out paper patterns for all the pieces, and cut them out of contrasting fabrics with a pair of pinking shears.

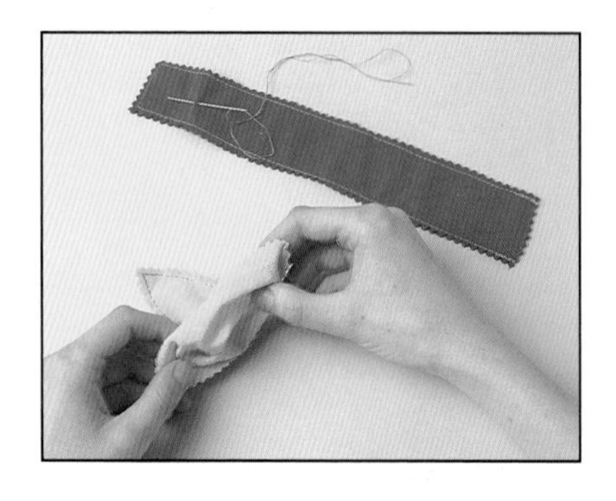

2 Make 6 ties and 3 spikes by pinning together the fabric pieces in pairs, right sides together. Sew along the edges leaving a gap at one side, and turn right sides out.

3 Place one flap piece along the edge of one main cushion piece of fabric, right sides together. Trap the ends of the 3 ties between the 2 pieces of fabric and sew along the edges. Turn right side out. Repeat with the other flap, cushion piece and ties.

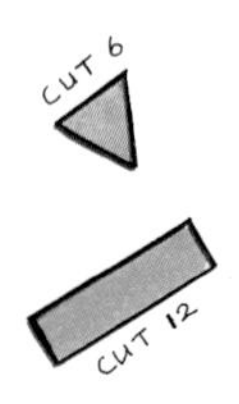

4 Join the 2 main pieces, right sides together, trapping the piece of fringing and the 3 spikes in between the layers and sew around the edge. Turn inside out and place the cushion pad inside.

Index

A

Appliquéd
  sleepsuit, 30
  toys, 70
Apron
  bathtime, 108
  practical, 112

B

Baby announcement card, 6
Baby changing bag, 106
Baby's gift box, 25
Bags
  baby changing, 106
  changing bag, 102
  cylindrical bag, 113
  toy bag, 119
  waist hold-all, 91
  washbag, 115
Bathroom pockets, 114
Bathtime apron, 107
Bear, denim, 65
Bedroom tidy, 100
Bedtime friends, 72
Beetle drawer freshener, 120
Beetle hat, 58
Bib, spiky fabric, 118
Blanket, crocheted, 14
Bonnets
  crocheted, 18
  knitted, 21
Bootees
  crocheted, 17
  cutie, 38
  fringed, 62
  knitted cuff bootees, 23
  sweetheart shoes, 42
  tall bootees, 33
Bow-tie T-shirt, 46
Bright-finned fish, 68
Bumper, reversible, 104
Busy bee slippers, 36

C

Candy cushion, 121
Cardigan, crocheted, 19
Cards
  baby announcement, 6
  pop-up card, 8
  quilted, 9
  rocking cradle, 10
  teddy bear, 7
Carousel, clown, 82
Changing bag, 102
Child's jacket, 44
Christening robe, 12
Christening shoes, 11
Clown carousel, 88
Clutch ball, 66
Collar, knitted, 22
Crochet
  beetle hat, 58
  blanket, 14
  bonnet, 18
  bootees, 17
  busy bee slippers, 36
  cardigan, 19
  dolls, 82
  matinée jacket, 16
  mittens, 15
Cuddly duck, 80
Cushion cover, spiky, 126
Cushions
  bright-finned fish, 62
  candy, 121
  hoppy, 78
  tapestry, 124
Cutie bootees, 38
Cylindrical bag, 113

D

Decorated baby shoes, 31
Decorated hair band, 49
Decorated towel, 116
Denim bear, 71
Dolls, *see* Toys
Drawer freshener, beetle, 120
Dresses
  fairy, 56
  reversible, 50
  smocked, 52

F

Fairy dress and wand, 56
Feely play mat, 64
Fish, bright-finned, 62
Fringed bootees, 62

G

Geometric mobile, 93
Gift box, 25

H

Hair band, decorated, 49
Hand painted stretchsuit, 41
Hat
  beetle, 58
  imp, 61
  poppy, 47
Height chart, 96
Hold-all, folded, 110
Holding ring, 67
Hooded jacket, 28
Hooded sweater, 20
Hooded towel, 109
Hoppy cushion, 84

I

Imp hat, 61

J

Jigsaw, turtle, 80

K

Keepsake pin cushion, 26
Knitting
  bedtime friends, 66
  christening shoes, 11
  hooded sweater, 20
  imp hat, 61
  knitted bonnet, 21
  knitted collar, 22
  knitted cuff bootees, 23
  knitted mittens, 24
  leg warmers, 35
  tall bootees, 33

L

Leg warmers, 35
Lined basket, 117

M

Matinée jacket, 16
Mat, feely play, 58
Mittens
  crocheted, 15
  knitted, 24
  ric-rac mitts, 34
Mobiles
  geometric, 87
  pompon, 79
  snake, 86

N

Nursery basket, 105

O

Overall, toddler's, 54

P

Padders, 40
Painted shoes, 63
Parrot, rocking, 85
Party pinafore, 48
Patchwork
  frame, 123
  quilt, 98
Photo frames
  patchwork, 123
  ribbon motif, 122
Pin cushion, keepsake, 26
Pinafore, party, 48
Play cube, 78
Pocketed quilt, 95
Pompon decorations, 43
Pompon mobile, 85
Pop-up card, 8
Poppy hat, 47
Practical apron, 112

Q

Quilt
  patchwork, 90
  pocketed, 127
Quilted card, 9

R

Rattle, cuddly duck, 74
Reversible bumper, 104
Reversible dress, 50
Ribbon motif frame, 122
Ribbons and bells, 87
Ric-rac mitts, 34
Robe, christening, 12
Rocking cradle card, 10
Rocking parrot, 91

S

Sachets
  beetle drawer freshener, 120
  scented, 27
Sarah sock doll, 76
Scented sachets, 27
Shadow quilting, appliquéd, 9
Shoes
  christening, 11
  decorated baby, 31
  painted, 63
  sweetheart, 42
  T-bar, 60
Slippers, busy bee, 36
Smiley toys, 81
Smocked dress, 52
Snake mobile, 92
Spiky cushion cover, 126
Spiky fabric bib, 118
Stretchsuits
  hand painted, 41
  tie-dye, 32
Stripy toy sack, 97
Sun toy, 74
Surprise play cube, 75
Sweater, hooded, 20
Sweetheart shoes, 42

T

T-Bar shoes, 60
T-shirt, bow-tie, 46
Tall bootees, 33
Tapestry cushion, 124
Teddy bear card, 7
Tie-dye, stretchsuit, 32
Tiger stripes, 94
Tissue box cover, 107
Toddler's overall, 54
Towels
  decorated, 116
  hooded, 109
Toy bag, 119
Toy sack, stripy, 89
Tugboat, 90
Turtle jigsaw, 86
Twirly fish, 79

W

Waist hold-all, 99
Washbag, 115